MW00587721

GOD *with* US

GOD *with* US

Exploring God's Personal
Interactions with His People
throughout the Bible

GLENN R. KREIDER

P.O. BOX 817 • PHILLIPSBURG • NEW JERSEY 08865-0817

© 2014 by Glenn R. Kreider

All rights reserved. No part of this book may be reproduced, stored in a retrieval system, or transmitted in any form or by any means—electronic, mechanical, photocopy, recording, or otherwise—except for brief quotations for the purpose of review or comment, without the prior permission of the publisher, P&R Publishing Company, P.O. Box 817, Phillipsburg, New Jersey 08865-0817.

Unless otherwise indicated, all Scripture quotations are from the HOLY BIBLE, NEW INTERNATIONAL VERSION®. NIV®. Copyright © 1973, 1978, 1984 by International Bible Society. Used by permission of Zondervan Publishing House. All rights reserved.

Scripture quotations marked (ESV) are from the ESV® Bible (*The Holy Bible, English Standard Version®*), copyright © 2001 by Crossway. 2011 Text Edition. Used by permission. All rights reserved.

To the group of men and women
who made Sunday evening from 5:00 to 6:00 my favorite hour
of the week
as we met to discuss "Theology for the Rest of Us."

I learned how to read the Bible better by doing it together with you.

I miss our time together.

CONTENTS

Acknowledgments   9

1. Introduction   11

2. Theological Foundations   19

3. God's Condescension in the Old Testament Stories,
   Part 1: From Creation to Abraham   47

4. God's Condescension in the Old Testament Stories,
   Part 2: From Isaac to the Conquest   75

5. God's Condescension in the Monarchy, Psalms,
   and Prophets   93

6. The Everlasting Incarnation of the Eternal Son   113

7. Jesus' Teaching on Greatness   133

8. Condescension in the Teaching of the Apostles   159

9. The New Creation: The Final Chapter in the
   Biblical Story   181

10. Conclusion   205

Questions for Study and Reflection   213

Select Resources   221

Index of Scripture   225

Index of Subjects and Names   235

ACKNOWLEDGMENTS

The Son of God just does what he sees his Father doing. He empties himself and takes the form of a servant because that's the way they do it in his family. And God exalts Jesus Christ and gives him the name above every name because that too is the Godly way—to exalt the humble, to get very enthusiastic about those who spend themselves for others.[1]

IT WAS THIS PARAGRAPH from a sermon of Cornelius Plantinga that gave birth to the idea for this book. I am grateful to the publisher for patience and for the prodding and the encouragement of Robert Peterson. He was gracious to me throughout the long process of bringing this work to completion. His feedback improved my work, and his friendship improved my walk with Jesus. Several other readers of the manuscript gave excellent and helpful feedback that improved the work, for which readers will be grateful.

The members of the "Theology for the Rest of Us" class at First Baptist Church of Duncanville, Texas, interacted with much of the content of this project long before it made it into print, and many of them will recognize their influence on my thinking. I am indebted to this group of Bible students, especially Phil Augsburger, Jerry and Joyce Beasley, Geraldine Beavers, Bobbye Hill, Marolyn and Vern Johnson, Richard and Kay Mabry, Stephen McConnel, Charles Pipes, Rupert Robbins, Dub Southers, Kurt

1. Cornelius Plantinga, "A Sermon for Advent: I Believe in Jesus Christ, God's Only Son, Our Lord," in *Exploring and Proclaiming the Apostles' Creed*, ed. Roger E. Van Harn (Grand Rapids: Eerdmans, 2004), 77.

Smith, and Kent Spielmann. In addition, the Adult 2 Sunday School class at this church, and especially the director, Barbara Miller Cox, granted me the privilege of being their teacher the past five years. I will always appreciate the way these saints accepted, loved, encouraged, and supported Janice and me.

Over the past decade, many students at Dallas Theological Seminary have been discussion partners and have encouraged me to pursue this project. In classes, in small groups, and through conversations in my office or over lunch or coffee, my ideas have been tested and my thinking has been shaped (and refined) by so many of them. Space and memory do not allow me to name each of them. Among others are John Adair, Kat Armstrong, Carisa Ash, Marnie Blackstone, Josh Bleeker, Benji Bruneel, Abraham Joseph, Jim Larson, Micki Maris, Tim Owens, Lisa Robinson, Deacon Smith, Armida Stephens, Sam Tyson, and Peter Vik.

Most importantly, I know what humility, forgiveness, and love look and feel like because I have experienced them from my wife, Janice, every day for nearly four decades. No one has been a better model for me of Christ's condescension than she. "Thank you" seems so inadequate to express my gratitude.

I

INTRODUCTION

BETWEEN APRIL AND JULY 1994, approximately one million people were killed in Rwanda as tribal conflict in that central African country escalated into genocide.[1] The conflict transcended religious and social boundaries. Nearly every family was touched by the tragedy. The Christian church in Rwanda was deeply impacted as well. During those one hundred days, approximately 70 percent of the pastors in the country were murdered, sometimes at the hands of other Christians. Hutu Christians killed Tutsi Christians, and Tutsi Christians killed Hutu Christians. Tribal loyalty had become more important than Christian identity. Brothers and sisters in Christ had become enemies of one another.

As this period of violence and bloodshed came to an end and relative calm returned, the church faced the overwhelming task of ministering to the survivors. Most had lost family members.

1. The information that follows is from Celestin Musekura, "Celestin Offers Forgiveness to Rwanda," DTS Stories, December 11, 2007, http:// http://www.dts .edu/media/play/celestin-offers-forgiveness-to-rwanda-celestin-musekura/, and "The History of ALARM," ALARM, October 5, 2012, https://www.youtube.com /watch?v=xcHyxqtWXFc&feature=youtu.be, as well as personal conversations with Célestin and Bernadette Musekura.

Some had been responsible for the deaths of others. Everyone was touched in one way or another. Survivors were asking deep and troubling theological questions. Where was God in such tragedy? How could God have allowed such evil? Why had God not intervened to protect his followers, especially the innocent? Others faced "survival guilt," asking why they had been spared while so many had been killed. Within the country as a whole— and the church in particular—feelings of guilt, shame, sorrow, grief, fear, and anger were rampant.

A Rwandan pastor, Célestin Musekura, was a student at Nairobi Evangelical Graduate School of Theology (NEGST) in Nairobi, Kenya, during the genocide. When he was able, he returned to Rwanda to minister to his family and church. Recognizing the need for a ministry of repentance and forgiveness, and desiring to raise up Christian leaders to lead the struggling churches, he founded ALARM, African Leadership and Reconciliation Ministries, in 1994.[2] The mission of ALARM is "to empower the African church to impact the African continent by developing and equipping leaders with skills and tools to nurture and deepen the Christian faith for the transformation and reconciliation of the African communities."[3] Through conferences and seminars, by starting schools and training programs, and through its Youth Advocacy Program and African Women's Initiative, ALARM serves the African church with a transformative ministry of reconciliation.[4]

This ministry of reconciliation and forgiveness soon became intensely personal for Célestin. Several years after

2. For a brief history of ALARM, see "ALARM's History," ALARM, accessed July 3, 2012, http://alarm-inc.org/who_we_are/our_history.

3. "Who is ALARM?," ALARM, accessed July 3, 2012, http://alarm-inc.org/who_we_are.

4. See ibid. See also Célestin Musekura, "An Assessment of Contemporary Models of Forgiveness" (Ph.D. diss., Dallas Theological Seminary, 2007), as well as L. Gregory Jones and Célestin Musekura, *Forgiving As We've Been Forgiven: Community Practices for Making Peace* (Downers Grove, IL: InterVarsity Press, 2010).

the founding of ALARM, in December 1997, five members of his family were murdered in a revenge killing connected to the genocide. Although such a response could hardly have been more difficult, Célestin chose to react to this horrific incident by forgiving the murderers of his family. In God's providence, one year later, he came face to face with several members of the families who had been responsible for the murders. In a Christlike expression of love, he personally extended forgiveness to them. Believing that love and forgiveness can break the cycle of vengeance and violence, Célestin and his family incarnated this message in their interaction with the very face of evil.

Forgiveness

Forgiveness and reconciliation are powerfully transformative forces. Forgiveness breaks the cycle of retribution that ultimately leads to more violence. Forgiveness breaks the cycle of death and destruction and leads to peace. Forgiveness of those who commit horrible atrocities is made possible through the humble and gracious heart of one who has been forgiven, who recognizes a responsibility to forgive as God has forgiven him.[5] Because of his understanding of God's character and what is expected of his followers, Célestin was able to grant the gift of forgiveness instead of pursuing vengeance.[6]

Forgiveness is a gift of grace. Because grace is unmerited favor, it cannot be earned or deserved. Thus, forgiveness can never be forced or mandated. Yet the Scriptures teach that the recipients of grace should be good stewards of it. Having received

5. Even those without the Spirit sometimes manifest grace. For several stories of grace experienced outside the church, see Philip Yancey, *What's So Amazing about Grace?* (Grand Rapids: Zondervan, 1997). Especially poignant is the story told in the film *Babette's Feast* (see ibid., 19-23).

6. See also Miroslav Volf, *The End of Memory: Remembering Rightly in a Violent World* (Grand Rapids: Eerdmans, 2006).

grace from God, we have the privilege and the responsibility to extend that grace to others.[7]

Jesus teaches his followers to pray, "Forgive us our debts as we also have forgiven our debtors" (Matt. 6:12). He continues, "For if you forgive men when they sin against you, your heavenly Father will also forgive you" (v. 14). He says elsewhere, "Forgive, and you will be forgiven" (Luke 6:37). Jesus does not mean that forgiveness is conditional, as if it needs to be earned. Rather, since "right thinking shapes right living," those who have experienced forgiveness will extend that forgiveness to others.[8] Elsewhere, Jesus teaches his disciples that they should forgive up to seventy times seven times (Matt. 18:22). Having been forgiven, they must forgive others.

Forgiveness is extravagant. In fact, the more one has been forgiven, Jesus teaches, the more one will love. In defending the excessive gift of a forgiven woman, Jesus says, "Therefore, I tell you, her many sins have been forgiven—for she loved much. But he who has been forgiven little loves little" (Luke 7:47). The extravagance of grace grows exponentially as it transforms the lives of those it touches and as they extend the grace of forgiveness to others.

Forgiveness is rooted in the character of God. Jesus' opponents correctly noted that no one can forgive sins except God (Mark 2:7). At the heart of the character of God is love for sinners, mercy and compassion that is manifested in forgiveness (Ex. 34:6–7). God condescends toward rebellious humans when he forgives them.

Humility

God's humility, expressed in sacrifice, submission, forgiveness, and condescension toward his creation, is a major biblical

7. The purpose of extending grace to others is not to pay God back for the grace he extended, but to demonstrate a forward-looking faith in God's future grace. See John Piper, *The Purifying Power of Living by Faith in Future Grace* (Sisters, OR: Multnomah, 1995).

8. Piper, *Living by Faith in Future Grace*, 12.

theme. His humility is displayed in his creation, his response to the fall, and the promise of a new creation. This is the biblical story in microcosm. In short, the self-sufficient, wholly other, transcendent, and holy God condescended to create a world and creatures, knowing that they would reject him and rebel against him and that he would, because of his love, condescend to provide for their redemption. Story after story in the biblical narrative manifests this attribute of God. Then, in the incarnation, we see the ultimate example of condescension. In Jesus, God became human while remaining fully God. The Creator became a creature without ceasing to be the one through whom all things come into existence and continue to exist. The infinite One became finite, retaining his infinitude.

Although he was eternally self-sufficient, God created the universe and entrusted its care to humans. His decision to create evidences his condescension. He did not create anything out of need. Then, when the first humans rebelled against him, God began a plan of redemption that culminated in the death, resurrection, and return of his Son. In order to redeem humanity and to bring to completion the regeneration of all things, God himself came to earth, became a creature, and submitted to the created order—even to the power of sin and death—to defeat evil and subdue it. The redemptive work of God culminates in a new heaven and a new earth, the eternal home of the redeemed and the Redeemer, under the reign of the King of Kings.

Condescension

The term *condescension* is used in two significantly different ways in contemporary discourse. It evokes negative emotions when it is used in the sense of "a patronizing attitude or behavior," but the connotation is much different when it indicates "voluntary descent from one's rank or dignity in relations with an inferior."[9] In the latter sense, condescension is intertwined with humility, grace, submission, forgiveness, compassion, looking out for the interests of others, and love. The greatest of all, the transcendent God, cares for his creatures by coming into their world. And he serves them, cares for them, provides for them, obligates himself to them, and loves them.

From the beginning of the biblical story, God's humility is on display in his activity in the created order. Since what he does reveals who he is, God is revealed as a transcendent being who condescends to care for his creation. The ultimate example of condescension is in the incarnation, but this is not the first time in the biblical story that God humbles himself for the sake of his creation. Rather, the incarnation of the eternal Son of God was prefigured or foreshadowed in God's appearances on earth, his active involvement in the created order from the beginning, and his engagement with his creatures in their world. God's way of relating to his creatures is by condescending to come to where they are. In the incarnation, the eternal Son of God became the eternal God-man, permanently condescending to be one of us.

If the condescension of God is central to the biblical story, then why has this theme not received the attention within theological and biblical literature that it deserves?[10] I suspect there may be a number of reasons for the lack of extensive treatment of the subject of God's humility. I will propose two. First, it may be because there is something counterintuitive about the idea that God is humble and condescends toward his creatures. God is sovereign; he is transcendent and wholly other. He is great in power and position. How then could he be humble? Isn't humility a form of weakness? This would seem to be a misunderstanding of humility, but such thinking is widespread.

9. "Condescension," Merriam-Webster Online, accessed March 12, 2013, http://www.merriam-webster.com/dictionary/condescension.

10. See K. Scott Oliphint, *God with Us: Divine Condescension and the Attributes of God* (Wheaton: Crossway, 2011).

Second, I suspect that the humility of God is difficult to accept because of the implications that such a doctrine would have for us. If God is humble, then his people ought to be humble. If God submits himself, by giving up the rights and prerogatives of his transcendence, then his people ought to submit to one another. If God condescends to look out for the interests of his creatures, then his people ought to care for one another. If God is merciful and compassionate, then his people ought to treat one another with mercy and compassion. In short, if God is most clearly revealed in his Son, and if this revelation is humble and sacrificial, and if God wants his followers to be like him, then surely understanding God in this way compels his followers to give up their rights, privileges, and prerogatives for the sake of others.

As the Rwandan genocide illustrates, selfishness, tribalism, arrogance, fear, revenge, and anger lead to violence, destruction, and death. But repentance and forgiveness can produce reconciliation and peace. Had Célestin waited for the murderers of his family to ask for forgiveness, he would likely still be waiting. Both his family and the families of the murderers would have continued living in fear or plotting revenge. Instead, Célestin forgave them and, having granted the gift of forgiveness, replaced fear and anger with love and peace. This is, after all, what Micah says that God requires: "to act justly and to love mercy and to walk humbly with your God" (Micah 6:8).

The rest of this book will explore God's condescension in the biblical story. Chapter 2 provides biblical and theological foundations for our study. Chapters 3 through 5 read through the Old Testament stories to see God's condescension to his creation, particularly to the people of faith. Chapters 6 and 7 explore the incarnation as condescension. Then chapter 8 continues through the book of Acts and the Epistles. The new creation, as the permanent home of the Creator, is the focus of chapter 9. Chapter 10 concludes our study with a call to live as people of love.

2

THEOLOGICAL FOUNDATIONS

GONXHA AGNES BOJAXHIU was born in Skopje, Macedonia, on August 26, 1910, into a devout Catholic family. As a preteen, she believed that God had called her to be a missionary. At eighteen, she joined the Sisters of Loreto, an Irish order of nuns that ran missions in India. She was given the name Sister Mary Teresa, after Thérèse of Lisieux. After receiving training in Dublin, she was sent to India, where she took her vows on May 24, 1931. Six years later, upon completion of her final vows, she became known as Mother Teresa. From 1931 to 1948, she taught at St. Mary's High School in Calcutta.[1]

During a train ride from Calcutta to Darjeeling on September 10, 1946, Mother Teresa had a vision in which she sensed a call from Jesus to minister to the poor. In response to this vision, the details of which she seldom discussed, she began to serve with the Little Sisters of the Poor among the poorest of the poor in the slums of Calcutta. She was soon joined by a growing number of

1. "Mother Teresa—Biographical," in *Nobel Lectures, Peace 1971–1980*, ed. Tore Frängsmyr and Irwin Abrams (Singapore: World Scientific Publishing Co.), 1997, available online at http://nobelprize.org/nobel_prizes/peace/laureates/1979/teresa-bio.html.

volunteers, including several of her former students. On October 7, 1950, Missionaries of Charity was established in the archdiocese of Calcutta. Since then, her charity has sent missionaries throughout the world to minister to the needs of those in extreme poverty. She received many awards for her humanitarian work, including the Nobel Peace Prize in 1979. By 1997, the year of her death, her order included nearly four thousand sisters serving in 123 countries.[2]

In his homily on World Mission Sunday, October 19, 2003, on the occasion of the beatification of Mother Teresa, Pope John Paul II said,

> *"Whoever wants to be great among you must be your servant"* (Mk 10:43). With particular emotion we remember today Mother Teresa, a great servant of the poor, of the Church and of the whole world. Her life is a testimony to the dignity and the privilege of humble service. She had chosen to be not just *the least* but to be *the servant of the least*. As a real mother to the poor, she bent down to those suffering various forms of poverty. Her greatness lies in her ability to give without counting the cost, to give "until it hurts."[3]

Mother Teresa's works of charity earned her worldwide respect.[4] Her humble self-sacrifice and service to those in extreme poverty touched the lives of many people. Whether or not one agrees with her theological reasons for doing so, or with the Roman Catholic theology that she embraced and

2. "Short Biography," Mother Teresa of Calcutta Center, accessed February 16, 2012, http://www.motherteresa.org/layout.html.

3. John Paul II, "Beatification of Mother Teresa of Calcutta" (homily, Rome, October 19, 2003), available online at http://www.motherteresacause.info/omelia.htm.

4. Of course, there are always exceptions. See the sarcastic comments of "new atheist" Christopher Hitchens, "Mommie Dearest: The Pope Beatifies Mother Teresa, a Fanatic, a Fundamentalist, and a Fraud," Slate, posted October 20, 2003, http://www.slate.com/articles/news_and_politics/fighting_words/2003/10/mommie_dearest.html.

affirmed, her example of selflessness surely served as a model of the gospel.

The Attractiveness of Humility

Models of self-sacrifice, of humility and condescension, are almost universally respected and honored, even by those who are unfamiliar with the gospel. Why would people without a Christian commitment respect these embodiments of the gospel? What is it about selfless service that elicits a sympathetic reaction from most people? Why do stories and sights of needy people, particularly children, bring forth such emotions? It could be simply that people admire humility when seen in others because it is so foreign to their own experience. We do seem to admire in others what we do not find in ourselves. It might be that something deep inside of us understands our own vulnerability, that "but for the grace of God" all of us could experience such poverty, in which case we would want someone to care about us. In short, it might be one indication of our common humanity, our common vulnerability and dependence on something or someone bigger than ourselves.

A more theologically nuanced answer is found in the doctrines of common grace. Extending mercy and compassion to the needy is a godly act, an evidence of God's grace. It is, further, a form of God's revelation of himself in creation. Having been created in God's image, people have something in their hearts that resonates with God's character. Thus, God's concern for the "least of these," his compassion for the helpless, the poor, the disenfranchised, the oppressed, and the needy, is recognized, perhaps unconsciously, by those created in his image. There is nearly universal recognition that there is something wrong with the world, that it is not the way it is supposed to be.[5] Beyond that,

5. Cornelius Plantinga Jr., *Not the Way It's Supposed to Be: A Breviary of Sin* (Grand Rapids: Eerdmans, 1995).

there is embedded in the world the hope that one day things will be made right.[6]

We live in a fallen world. Death is just around the corner for every living thing. Whether animal or human, living things are born to die. Death is inevitable. The presence of death is unambiguous evidence of the presence of sin, since the wages of sin is death (Rom. 6:23). Evil in a variety of forms is experienced in a world that longs for redemption. Whether it is the extreme poverty of the slums of Calcutta or the inhumane cruelty of genocide and tribal warfare, evidence of sin is easily seen in a fallen world. But in the midst of such horrific and horrifying circumstances, grace is also clearly seen. In this world, seldom are the circumstances so dire and the devastation so total as to obscure the flickers of grace.

Mother Teresa devoted her life to ministry among the poorest of the poor in Calcutta. An intelligent and gifted woman, she forsook the potential of a comfortable life in a convent or service to the church in a more prominent position or place of ministry. Why? Her testimony was that this is what Jesus had called her to do in her "call within a call."[7] Her life was poured out serving humans in extreme poverty. These were people who were unable to repay her monetarily, but they were creatures who bore God's image and thus, for that reason, were worthy of respect and honor. In her ministry of mercy, she embodied the heart of the Savior.

The Good Samaritan

Jesus' concern for people was obvious to those who came in contact with him. People were attracted to him, especially those in need. Out of a heart of compassion, he responded to the needs

6. Philip Yancey, *Rumors of Another World: What on Earth Are We Missing?* (Grand Rapids: Zondervan, 2003).
7. "Short Biography," http://www.motherteresa.org/layout.html.

of those he met. He taught his followers to follow his example. One of the clearest examples of his teaching about compassion for others is found in Luke 10, the parable of the good Samaritan. When a teacher of the law of Moses came to test him, Jesus asked the teacher to sum up the teaching of the law. The expert on the law quoted two of its requirements: "'Love the Lord your God with all your heart and with all your soul and with all your strength and with all your mind'; and, 'Love your neighbor as yourself'" (v. 27).[8] Jesus responded that this was correct (v. 28). In an attempt to justify himself, Jesus' questioner asked a follow-up question: "Who is my neighbor?" (v. 29). Jesus' parable of the good Samaritan was his response to this question.

The hero of this story was a despised Samaritan who, in the course of traveling between Jerusalem and Jericho, came across a man who was suffering. This unnamed, presumably Jewish, traveler had been beaten, robbed, and left for dead along the road.[9] A priest and a Levite had passed without stopping. But the unnamed Samaritan, at great personal cost to himself, came to the aid of this stranger. The Samaritan humbled himself to serve a Jew. At the conclusion of the story, Jesus asked the questioner to identify the one who had acted in love, who had treated this suffering man as a neighbor.[10] The answer is obvious, and the expert in the law answered correctly: "The one who had mercy

8. The expert in the law brought together Deuteronomy 6:5 and Leviticus 19:18. Later in his ministry, Jesus answered a test question by another teacher of the law, "Teacher, which is the greatest commandment in the Law?" (Matt. 22:36), with the same two summary commandments. Further, he affirmed, "all the Law and the Prophets hang on these two commandments" (v. 40).

9. Luke does not explicitly mention the ethnicity of the traveler, but it seems fairly obvious that he was Jewish. In the background of this story is the conflict between Jews and Samaritans (see John 4:9).

10. The question Jesus asked was not, "Which of these men is your neighbor?" but "Which of these three do you think was a neighbor to the man who fell into the hands of robbers?" In short, the issue Jesus raises is not which man was a neighbor, not which man should be loved, but which man had behaved like a neighbor. The neighbor is the one who acts in a godly way.

on him" (v. 37). Jesus' application is pointed and direct: "Go and do likewise" (v. 37).

Thus, the followers of Jesus, those who keep the law of God, those who are like God, will help those who are in need, whether those needs are due to wounds inflicted by robbers or to some other cause. In a fallen world, where bad things happen to good and bad people, to both the rich and the poor, there are many opportunities for Christians to minister to needy people. To do so, as both Mother Theresa and the Good Samaritan did, is to act in a godly way. There is something particularly Christlike in bending down to serve the hopeless and helpless.

The Incarnation

The incarnation is the ultimate example of condescension. Although the word *condescension* in contemporary usage often implies a superior's viewing of an inferior in some negative way, the word itself need not imply that. To *condescend* means to "descend to a less formal or dignified level" or "to waive the privileges of rank."[11] To condescend, thus, would be to humble oneself, to give up the privileges that are one's prerogative for the sake of others. Andy Crouch explains, "In an earlier day, condescension meant the powerful treating everyone they met with dignity and respect."[12] This is an apt description of divine condescension, especially in the life of Jesus.

But it is not just the incarnation that reveals God by means of condescension. Any involvement of God in his world is an act of condescension. Further, that God humbles himself and interacts with his creation is the major plotline of the Bible and of each of the biblical stories.

11. "Condescend," Merriam-Webster Online, accessed May 11, 2012, http://www.merriam-webster.com/dictionary/condescend.
12. Andy Crouch, *Culture Making: Recovering Our Creative Calling* (Downers Grove, IL: InterVarsity Press, 2008), 229.

The Biblical Story

The Scriptures are the inspired, or God-breathed, Word of God (2 Tim. 3:16). Although the Bible contains a variety of books written over a long period of time by a number of different human authors in many different genres, it tells one coherent story. It is the story of God's plan for his creation.[13]

The biblical story is divided into three main sections—it is a three-act drama of creation, fall, and redemption (or re-creation).[14] These three sections are not equal, either in terms of attention in the story or in terms of length. The first and third sections are relatively brief. Only the first two chapters of Genesis are devoted to the story of creation, although the significance of creation for the biblical story is addressed in numerous other places, and only the last two chapters of Revelation are devoted to the new creation, although it is the goal toward which the biblical story is moving, and it is the implicit focus of every word of the biblical text. The trajectory of the biblical story is toward the new creation.

Creation

The biblical story begins at creation. Prior to creation, there was nothing except God; likewise, there is nothing except by God.

13. For an excellent introduction to this concept, see Richard Bauckham, "Reading Scripture as a Coherent Story," in *The Art of Reading Scripture*, ed. Ellen F. Davis and Richard B. Hays (Grand Rapids: Eerdmans, 2003), 38–53.

14. This description of three stages of the biblical story is not original to me. For one example, see Cornelius Plantinga Jr., *Engaging God's World: A Christian Vision of Faith, Learning, and Living* (Grand Rapids: Eerdmans, 2002). Plantinga uses the terms *creation, fall,* and *redemption*. I prefer to describe the final stage of the story as *re-creation*. This designation connects the final act of the story to the first, while also emphasizing that the end is better than the beginning. God does not simply restore the world to its pre-fall state; he makes all things new. All things will be better in the re-created world than they ever could have been if there had been no fall. This does not make sin and the fall good, but it does mean that God's redemptive grace transforms everything that is broken into something much better.

Although it is not possible for any creature to know why God decided to create, we can know that it was not due to any lack in him or any necessity outside of himself. His decision to create was a free and sovereign decision of his will. God condescended to bring into existence that which remains dependent upon him. In so doing, he voluntarily obligated himself to what he made.

God created the heavens and the earth and all the inhabitants of each (Gen. 1–2). He created a man and a woman in his image and likeness to be the caretakers of his creation. He gave them a pristine environment and all the provisions to enjoy life in fellowship with him. But something happened to this good creation. Rather than serving God and caring for the creation, Adam and Eve listened to the voice of the Serpent and chose to believe him rather than God. This rebellion introduced sin into the created order. Everything in this creation is now "not the way it's supposed to be."

The Fall and Redemption

The second act of the biblical story is the account of the fall and its effects. The bulk of the biblical story is devoted to the world in its fallen state (Gen. 3–Rev. 20). But this second act is not just a tragic tale of decay and death; it is the story of redemption. When the first humans, Adam and Eve, rebelled against God in the garden and introduced sin and death into creation, God's plan of redemption was set in motion. The fall did not catch the Creator by surprise; it was part of his plan. Since he knew from the beginning that this rebellion would occur, redemption must have been at the heart of God's plan prior to the creation.

Having allowed sin into his world, God began to act redemptively in this world, moving toward the culmination of that plan in the work of his Son. The incarnation of the Son of God is the means by which he decreed that sin and its effects would be destroyed. Until that time, God was present and active in the fallen world, imparting redemptive grace in anticipation of the culmination of the story in its third act.

Re-creation

The third act of the biblical story is the completion of God's work of redemption, the culmination of his plan for his creation in the re-creation of all things in a new heaven and a new earth. Rather than destroying the earth and replacing it with a new earth, God plans to re-create the earth he had cursed.[15] In the culmination of his plan of redemption in the eschatological state, God does not take his creatures to be with him; rather, he moves into their world. Rather than taking us to be with him in heaven, God will bring heaven to earth. The Creator will move into our neighborhood forever (Rev. 21–22).

The good news of the redemption story is that rebellious creatures and the fallen world were not rejected by God. He did not forsake the rebels. Rather, in his grace, God condescended to care for his creation. He has taken the initiative to bring healing. He entered into the world and brought redemption to it. God's work of redemption required the incarnation of God the Son. The eternal second person of the Trinity came to earth as Jesus of Nazareth and assumed full humanity. As the God-man, he submitted to the limitations of the created order, yet without ceasing to be fully divine. As a substitute for the sin of the creatures, he submitted to death in order to defeat death through the resurrection of the dead. This act of condescension was not a temporary one; having become incarnate, Jesus will remain human forever.

---

15. For an excellent discussion of this theme, see Herman Bavinck, *Reformed Dogmatics*, ed. John Bolt, trans. John Vriend, vol. 4, *Holy Spirit, Church, and New Creation* (Grand Rapids: Baker, 2008), 715–30.

Condescension in Divine Revelation

God's creatures are dependent upon God for any knowledge of him. Gerald Bray expresses it well: "God makes himself known to us by *revelation*. This means that unless he tells us about himself, we cannot know him."[16] Apart from his condescension, God could not be known. Wayne Grudem agrees: "If we are to know God at all, it is necessary that he reveal himself to us."[17]

Revelation in the Scriptures

God has revealed himself in the Scriptures using human language. In so doing, he has condescended to come to us in order to be known by us. Grudem explains,

> All that Scripture says about God uses anthropomorphic language—that is, language that speaks of God in human terms. . . . If God is going to teach us about things we do not know by direct experience (such as his attributes), he has to teach us in terms of what we do know. This is why all that Scripture says about God is "anthropomorphic" in a broad sense (speaking of God either in human terms or in terms of the creation we know).[18]

John Calvin wrote,

> For who even of slight intelligence does not understand that, as nurses commonly do with infants, God is wont in a measure to "lisp" in speaking to us? Thus such forms of speaking do not so much express clearly what God is like as accommodate the

16. Gerald Bray, *The Doctrine of God* (Downers Grove, IL: InterVarsity Press, 1993), 15.

17. Wayne Grudem, *Systematic Theology: An Introduction to Biblical Doctrine* (Grand Rapids: Zondervan, 1994), 149.

18. Ibid., 159 (emphasis original).

knowledge of him to our slight capacity. To do this he must descend far beneath his loftiness.[19]

Creation is dependent upon God. Only if God condescends to make himself known, only if he takes the initiative to provide redemption, only if he accommodates himself to his fallen and rebellious creation—only then is there any hope for his creatures. And that is exactly what the Scriptures teach that God has done. Because God is revealed to be what he is by what he has done, the Scriptures teach that condescension to his creation is an attribute of deity.

God is the Creator and also the Preserver of his creation. He did not abandon the project when his creatures rebelled, but instead began a work of redemption that will culminate in a new creation, where sin and all its effects will be removed forever. God has condescended to us to be known by us. Herman Bavinck summarizes,

> Inasmuch as the revelation of God in nature and in Scripture is specifically addressed to humanity, it is a human language in which God speaks to us of himself. For that reason the words he employs are human words; for the same reason he manifests himself in human forms. From this it follows that Scripture does not just contain a few scattered anthropomorphisms but is anthropomorphic through and through. From the first page to the last it witnesses to God's coming to, and searching for, humanity. The whole revelation of God is concentrated in the Logos, who became "flesh" and is, as it were, one single act of self-humanization, the incarnation of God. If God were to speak to us in a divine language, not a creature would understand him. But what spells out his grace is the fact that from the moment of creation God stoops

19. John Calvin, *Institutes of the Christian Religion*, ed. John T. McNeill, trans. Ford Lewis Battles (Philadelphia: Westminster, 1960), 1.13.1.

down to his creatures, speaking and appearing to them in human fashion.[20]

Revelation in Creation and Providence

God has revealed himself in his works of creation and providence. Such revelation is an act of condescension, since God was under no obligation to create and, when his creatures rebelled, he was under no obligation to continue to sustain them. His creatures continue to rebel against him; his preservation of them is surely due only to his grace. Even though God's revelation of his eternal power and divine nature in creation is plain, clear, seen, and understood by his creatures (Rom. 1:18–20), they continue to rebel. Yet God provides salvation through his Son as known through the Scriptures. The Westminster Confession explains,

> Although the light of nature, and the works of creation and providence, do so far manifest the goodness, wisdom, and power of God, as to leave men inexcusable; yet are they not sufficient to give that knowledge of God, and of his will, which is necessary unto salvation; therefore it pleased the Lord, at sundry times, and in divers manners, to reveal himself, and to declare that his will unto his Church; and afterwards for the better preserving and propagating of the truth, and for the more sure establishment and comfort of the Church against the corruption of the flesh, and the malice of Satan and of the world, to commit the same wholly unto writing; which maketh the holy Scripture to be most necessary; those former ways of God's revealing his will unto his people being now ceased. (1.1)[21]

20. Herman Bavinck, *Reformed Dogmatics*, ed. John Bolt, trans. John Vriend, vol. 2, *God and Creation* (Grand Rapids: Baker, 2004), 99–100.
21. "Westminster Confession of Faith," in *Creeds of the Churches: A Reader in Christian Doctrine from the Bible to the Present*, ed. John H. Leith, 3rd ed. (Louisville: John Knox, 1982), 193.

Revelation in Salvation

God's provision of salvation is a further act of condescension. A good and obedient creature could never obligate the Creator to act, much less a fallen and rebellious one. Only if the Creator, the offended one, takes the initiative could the creature have any hope. Again, as the Westminster Confession explains,

> The distance between God and the creature is so great, that although reasonable creatures do owe obedience unto him as their Creator, yet they could never have any fruition of him as their blessedness and reward, but by some voluntary condescension on God's part, which he had been pleased to express by way of covenant. (7.1)[22]

When humanity by virtue of disobedience failed to keep the covenant of works, God condescended to "make a second, commonly called the covenant of grace; wherein he offered unto sinners life and salvation by Jesus Christ, requiring of them faith in him, that they may be saved, and promising to give unto all those that are ordained unto life his Holy Spirit, to make them willing, and able to believe" (7.3).[23] Thus, God's condescending grace is a necessary prerequisite if any human is to have life. Only those chosen by God, those whom he has granted the Holy Spirit, have the ability and the desire to believe.

From the beginning of the biblical story, God is revealed in his activity of condescending to his creation. Beginning at creation, through his response to the fall in providing atonement for sin, and culminating in his work of redemption in the new creation, God takes the initiative to accommodate himself to his creation. Later chapters in this work will validate that claim by examining the unfolding of the narrative canonically.

22. Ibid., 202.
23. Ibid.

But first, we will briefly look at the argument from the apostle Paul's well-known christological passage in Philippians 2. In this passage, the apostle draws ethical implications for the church based upon the condescension of God as expressed in the incarnation of his Son.

The Condescension of God the Son

In his epistle to the Philippians, the apostle Paul encourages Christians to pursue unity in the church and to love one another. Specifically, he asks them to "do nothing out of selfish ambition or vain conceit, but in humility consider others better than yourselves" (Phil. 2:3). This lifestyle of humility evidences itself in self-sacrifice, in submission for the sake of others. The admonition to consider others better does not necessarily mean that others are better. In fact, his illustration of Christ would make little sense in that case.

Paul also does not encourage Christians to ignore or discount their own interests, their own needs. Instead, "Each of you should look not only to your own interests, but also to the interests of others" (v. 4). Paul is not describing a lifestyle that rejects taking care of one's needs; rather, it is a way of living marked by an appropriate and proper care of one's own interests while also looking out for the interests of others.

To drive this point home to his audience, Paul uses an illustration. And when he does, he is reminding this church of something they already know by using a christological confession that was almost certainly already familiar to them. Gerald Hawthorne concludes, "Here is at least one thing that calls forth almost universal agreement. It is that vv. 6–11 constitute a beautiful example of a very early hymn of the Christian church."[24]

24. Gerald F. Hawthorne, *Philippians*, Word Biblical Commentary 43 (Waco, TX: Word, 1983), 76.

In this passage, Paul does not set out to write a high Christology, to defend the doctrine of Christ apologetically, or to engage in academic theologizing. His focus, rather, is ethical, practical, and liturgical.[25] His audience is already grounded in the faith. They already know who Christ is. In order to drive home his instruction about humility, love, unity, and similar Christian virtues, Paul uses Christ as an example: "Your attitude should be the same as that of Christ Jesus" (v. 5).

In what way should Christians be like Christ? Paul's answer here is simple yet profound. Christians should emulate his humility. Christ is the perfect example of one who did nothing out of selfish ambition or vain conceit; rather, he demonstrated his humility by considering others better than himself.[26] He was (and is) God "in very nature" (v. 6). He who is fully God "did not consider equality with God something to be grasped, but made himself nothing" (vv. 6–7).[27] Jesus humbled himself, sacrificed himself, gave himself, poured himself out, submitted his own desires and interests to the well-being of others, and condescended to become something he was not. To his divine nature he added a human nature. God himself became human; he who was "in very nature God" took "the very nature of a servant, being made in human likeness" (v. 7). The Creator of the universe became a creature without ceasing to be the Creator. This is the wonder and mystery of the incarnation—not simply

25. All good theology is intensely practical.

26. Of course, no one is greater than Christ, and no one knows that better than Christ. For him to treat those who are inferior to him as greater, to submit himself to them for their sakes, is the height of, and perhaps even the definition of, humility.

27. In the incarnation, Jesus remained fully and completely divine; he gave up nothing of his deity. Instead, he gave himself. Hawthorne concludes, "The Philippian text does not say that Christ gave up anything. Rather it says that he added to himself that which he did not have before—'the form of a servant,' 'the likeness of a man.' Thus the implication is that at the incarnation Christ became more than God, if this is conceivable, not less than God" (Hawthorne, *Philippians*, 85).

that the second person of the triune God became fully human, but that in doing so he remained fully God.[28]

Paul's encouragement to the Philippians, and to all Christians, is to be like Christ. Consider others better than yourselves, humble yourselves (see James 4:10), and serve others, he says. Christians should follow the example of the One whose name they claim.[29]

This is one of the major ethical implications of the incarnation. The Scriptures teach that Jesus Christ shows his followers how to live, how to treat others. Paul puts it this way in his letter to the Romans: "God demonstrates his own love for us in this: While we were still sinners, Christ died for us" (5:8). The apostle John explains that sacrifice is the essence of love: "This is how we know what love is: Jesus Christ laid down his life for us" (1 John 3:16; see also 4:9); "God is love" (4:8, 16); and "we love because he first loved us" (v. 19). John also emphasizes the ethical impact of this truth: "We ought to lay down our lives for our brothers" (3:16).[30]

Hawthorne explains that Paul is not only using Jesus as the prime example of humility for humans; he also links Jesus' condescension in the incarnation to the character of God.

28. "Here are two mysteries for the price of one—the plurality of persons within the unity of God, and the union of Godhead and manhood in the person of Jesus. It is here, in the thing that happened at the first Christmas, that the profoundest and most unfathomable depths of the Christian revelation lie. 'The Word became flesh' (Jn 1:14): God became man; the divine Son became a Jew; the Almighty appeared on earth as a helpless human baby, unable to do more than lie and stare and wriggle and make noises; needing to be fed and changed and taught to talk like any other child. And there was no illusion or deception in this: the babyhood of the Son of God was a reality. The more you think about it, the more staggering it gets. Nothing in fiction is so fantastic as this truth of the Incarnation" (J. I. Packer, *Knowing God* [Downers Grove, IL: InterVarsity Press, 1977], 53).

29. This use of Christ as an example is not to propose an example model of the atonement. Rather, in his atoning work, Christ died as a substitute for sinners, the righteous for the unrighteous (2 Cor. 5:21). The substitutionary atonement of Christ is an example of humility, self-sacrifice, and condescension for the sake of the hopeless and helpless.

30. Similarly, James rebukes those who show favoritism (2:1–4) and insists that faith without works is dead, worthless, and useless (vv. 14–26). Many other biblical examples could be cited.

Hence, in this connection the participial phrase that begins v 6—ὅς ἐν μορφῃ̄ θεοῦ ὑπάρχων ("who *being* in the form of God"), often wrongly translated as a concessive participle—"who *though* he was in the form of God" (RSV, NASB, Beck, Confraternity, Goodspeed, Williams), is more correctly translated as a causative: "precisely *because* he was in the form of God he reckoned equality with God not as a matter of getting but of giving" (Moule, "Manhood," 97). This then makes clear that contrary to whatever anyone may think about God, his true nature is characterized not by selfish grabbing, but by an open-handed giving.[31]

Cornelius Plantinga draws a similar conclusion.

> The Greek text doesn't say that *although* he was in the form of God he emptied himself. What it says is, "*Being* in the form of God he emptied himself." You might almost read, *because* he was in the form of God he emptied himself. Because he was in the form of God he took the form of a servant, washing the feet of disciples who would never dream of doing the same thing for each other.[32]

Thus, Paul is arguing that the character of God as humble condescension is the reason for the incarnation. God became human because that is the kind of thing God does.

It is not my claim that this is the only way to read this hymn. Many interpreters argue for a concessive force of the participial phrase.[33] Nor do I claim to defend the humility of God from the exegesis of this one text. Rather, whether the

---

31. Hawthorne, *Philippians*, 85 (emphasis original).

32. Cornelius Plantinga Jr., "A Sermon for Advent: I Believe in Jesus Christ, God's Only Son, Our Lord," in *Exploring and Proclaiming the Apostles' Creed*, ed. Roger E. Van Harn (Grand Rapids: Eerdmans, 2004), 76 (emphasis original).

33. See, for example, Daniel B. Wallace, *Greek Grammar beyond the Basics: An Exegetical Syntax of the New Testament* (Grand Rapids: Zondervan, 1996), 634–35.

participle has a concessive or a causative force is a decision made on theological grounds.[34] The remainder of this book provides biblical support for this claim that condescension is a divine attribute.

Divine Humility

Only the second person of the Trinity condescended to become human, but divine humility is not limited to the incarnation. Plantinga proposes that it is a family tradition within the Trinity to behave in such a way.

> The Son of God just does what he sees his Father doing. He empties himself and takes the form of a servant because that's the way they do it in his family. And God exalts Jesus Christ and gives him the name above every name because that too is the Godly way—to exalt the humble, to get very enthusiastic about those who spend themselves for others.[35]

Thus, according to Plantinga, the incarnation is a manifestation in history of the divine family's long-standing tradition of condescension for the sake of creation. When the Son of God humbled himself and became human, he was demonstrating his divinity. He was behaving like his Father.

The Purpose of the Incarnation

Christ's coming to earth achieved several purposes. The incarnation was the means by which redemption would be accomplished. Christ came to die in order to be raised from the dead and thereby bring eternal life to those who trust in him. Further, by his resurrection he also achieved the basis for

34. All exegetical decisions are informed by theology. It could hardly be otherwise.
35. Plantinga, "A Sermon for Advent," 77.

the hope of all creation, liberation from sin and its effects (see Rom. 8:18–34).

Another purpose of the incarnation was to reveal God in the created order. Although God has been present in the created world from the beginning, and the heavens declare his glory (Ps. 19:1), and his eternal power and divine nature are clearly seen through what he has made (Rom. 1:18–20), the ultimate revelation of God to and in the created order is in the person of his Son. Jesus is the image of the invisible God, the creator of everything that is, the preeminent one, the one in whom all the fullness of deity dwells (Col. 1:15–20). He is the radiance of God's glory and the exact representation of his being, the final word of God, who is inferior to no one and no thing (Heb. 1:1–4).

In John 1, the apostle makes this point clear. Jesus is the Word, the one through whom God created the world (v. 3). He is life and light, and this light shines in the darkness. He brought life into the deadness of a fallen world. "The Word became flesh and made his dwelling among us" (v. 14). The Word added to his deity full and complete humanity; he became flesh and lived among us on the earth he had created. He came to bring life and light to a world cursed by sin. Further, John says, "No one has ever seen God, but God the One and Only, who is at the Father's side, has made him known" (v. 18; see also 1 John 4:12). The Son came to reveal the Father.

A third purpose seems to follow from the first two. Jesus also came to earth to demonstrate God's love for his creation (Rom. 5:8). In his first epistle, John asserts that apart from this act of condescension, love is unknowable (1 John 3:16; 4:9–10; see also John 3:16). "We love," John says, "because he first loved us" (1 John 4:19). In his life and work, Christ revealed the love of God. This demonstration of love was a means to an end, that followers of Jesus would be like him, that his followers would love one another and be actively engaged in redemptive works in the world (1 John 2:6; 3:7, 16, 23–24; 4:7, 16, 19; 5:2–3, 16). John puts it this way: "The reason the Son of God appeared was to destroy the devil's work" (3:8). Those who are in Christ do his work, while the children of the Devil do his work. "This is how we know who the children of God are and who the children of the devil are: Anyone who does not do what is right is not a child of God; nor is anyone who does not love his brother" (v. 10).

The Scriptures Speak of Jesus

God has spoken and continues to speak through the Scriptures. When we read the Bible, we read the story of God's interaction with the world he created. The Bible is the story of God's plan for the world he created.[36]

Since there is only one God, there is only one story. The God revealed in the Hebrew Scriptures is the same God revealed in Jesus of Nazareth. The Old Testament stories point toward and are fulfilled in the incarnate Son of God. Thus, all the biblical stories, not simply those in the New Testament, should be read through Christ.

In the gospel of John, Jesus defends himself against his critics and gives them instructions on how to read the Bible. He rebukes their hermeneutical approach, pointing out their failure to read the Bible with the correct theological perspective. Further, he asserts that his works emulate those of his Father. He claims that he does only what he sees his Father do. His works reveal the Father since Jesus is only doing the works of the Father. Since Jesus' works evidence his condescension to his creation, the Father is also a God of condescension.

---

36. God is the major character in the biblical narrative, but the story of God's work takes place in the created order. What happened before God's work of creation and what happens elsewhere than on the earth are not told in Scripture. In fact, only a portion of what could be told has been told (see Deut. 29:29).

The Son's Works Emulate the Father's Works

In the fifth chapter of his gospel, John records a healing miracle of Jesus. Like many of his miracles, this healing occurred on the Sabbath; as regularly happened when Jesus healed on the Sabbath, he faced opposition from the Jewish leaders.[37] "Because Jesus was doing these things on the Sabbath," John says, "the Jews persecuted him" (John 5:16). In this case, Jesus' response to his critics was direct and clear: "My Father is always at his work to this very day, and I, too, am working" (v. 17). In this statement, Jesus affirms several things. He claims that the Father's work is constant. Thus, it would seem, the Father is working even on the Sabbath. Jesus also affirms a consistency between his work and the work of the Father. In short, Jesus seems to link his work, even on the Sabbath, with the work of the Father.

The Son Calls God His Father

His answer infuriates his hearers: "For this reason the Jews tried all the harder to kill him; not only was he breaking the Sabbath, but he was even calling God his own Father, making himself equal with God" (v. 18). They clearly recognize the implications of what he said. Jesus is not claiming to be the Father.[38] He is, rather, linking his work to the work of the Father, making himself equal to the Father. Jesus is claiming that the legal prohibition of work on the Sabbath does not apply to him because it does not apply to God.[39]

37. John refers to the opposition as "the Jews" (5:10, 15, 16, 18). It would seem that the opposition was coming particularly from the Jewish leaders. It would be inappropriate to see here evidence of anti-Semitism. Rather, the leaders of the Jews opposed Jesus, and it is they who received his rebuke.

38. This text, then, would seem to provide evidence of a Trinitarian view of God. It is hard to imagine why there would have been opposition to a unitarian or modalistic statement.

39. Whether Jesus was breaking the Mosaic Sabbath laws or only the traditions of the rabbis makes little difference. The critics recognized that he was claiming a

The Son Explains How to Read the Scriptures

Jesus' answer to this objection is an extended teaching on how to read the Bible. First, he gives a lesson on eschatology, reminding his hearers of the coming resurrection of the dead and the day of judgment (vv. 24–30). The life-giving voice, the one who calls the dead to life, is God himself, for only God can grant life. This voice that gives life, Jesus says, is his (v. 21; see also 11:25; 14:6). Further, the voice they will hear on the day of judgment is his, for the Father has granted the Son of Man authority to judge (5:27). He rebukes their unbelief, their refusal to accept him, when he says that his words are God's words, his voice is God's voice, and his works are God's works. Their rejection of him is a rejection of the Father (v. 23).

He then gives his audience a lesson in hermeneutics. The Scriptures, Jesus says, testify about him (v. 39). If they will read the Scriptures properly, they will see him there and come to him for life (v. 40). He reminds them of the testimony of John the Baptist, who proclaimed Christ (vv. 31–36). He reminds them of Moses, who wrote about Christ (vv. 45–47). "If you believed Moses," Jesus says, "you would believe me, for he wrote about me. But since you do not believe what he wrote, how are you going to believe what I say?" (vv. 46–47). To those who respected Moses and thought themselves to be the authoritative interpreters of Moses, these were harsh words of rebuke. But it is not just John and Moses who testify about Christ; all the Scriptures point to him, Jesus says (v. 39).

Jesus claims that his critics are blind and deaf, have rebelled against God and the prophets he sent, and have even rebelled against God's Son. They have been unable to hear God and see him, even though he has been speaking plainly and has been present in their midst. Jesus says,

---

unique relationship with the Father ("making himself equal with God") and that this was the basis of his Sabbath work.

You have neither heard his voice nor seen his form, nor does his word dwell in you, for you do not believe the one he sent. You diligently study the Scriptures because you think that by them you possess eternal life. These are the Scriptures that testify about me, yet you refuse to come to me to have life. (vv. 37–40)

This is a strong rebuke of the way in which these Jewish scholars were reading the Scriptures. They considered themselves to be experts in the law, but Jesus points out that their approach was wrong; their readings of the Scriptures were in error. They mistakenly thought that studying the Scriptures was the way to have eternal life, that the study of the Scriptures was the end in itself. The flaw in their approach is that the Scriptures are not the means of life—Jesus is. The Scriptures testify about him. Those who read the Scriptures correctly recognize this and come to him for life. To study the Scriptures without recognizing their proper aim is to misread them.[40]

Jesus' point is that the study of the Scriptures is not enough; they must be studied correctly. It is not enough to read the Word of God; it must be read properly. Every reading is an interpretation—the Scriptures do not simply speak for themselves. Since the Scriptures testify about Jesus, any reading that fails to hear Jesus, any interpretation that fails to elevate Jesus, and any Bible study that fails to focus on Jesus is incorrect and worthy of judgment. These Jewish leaders were failing to read the Scriptures correctly. Thus, Jesus says that Moses himself would be called to accuse these rebels before the Father (v. 45). They had elevated Moses and his law, thinking that in doing so they were honoring God. Instead, they were missing the whole point of the Scriptures, since Moses wrote about Jesus

40. See 2 Timothy 3:15, where Paul reminds Timothy of what he had learned from infancy, that the Scriptures "are able to make you wise for salvation through faith in Christ Jesus."

(v. 46).[41] When God himself, in the incarnate Son, came to them and spoke to them, they failed to hear his voice. When God himself came and appeared before them in Jesus of Nazareth, they failed to see him. When God himself came and did the works of the Father in their midst, they failed to perceive him.

The Son Explains His Works

In John 5:19, Jesus claims that "the Son can do nothing by himself; he can do only what he sees his Father doing, because whatever the Father does the Son also does." Jesus is affirming not only that his actions are consistent with the works of his Father, but also that he learned what to do by watching his Father work. The eternal Son had been watching the Father work prior to the incarnation. In fact, the Father and the Son had been working together in perfect harmony. But when the Son humbled himself and took on humanity, he had a new perspective on his Father. As he grew in wisdom (Luke 2:40, 52), as he studied the Scriptures, he watched his Father work.[42] As Jesus read the Scriptures, he learned to recognize and to tell the story of God's work of creation and redemption.[43] As he read the Old Testament stories, he recognized the hope of the culmination of

41. It is unlikely that Moses understood that he was speaking of Christ. But Moses, rightly interpreted, wrote of the Son. The divine author intended more than the human author did.

42. As he learned to read the Scriptures, Jesus learned to see his Father at work in them and in his world.

43. One of the many mysteries of the incarnation is the relationship between the divine and the human attributes. Omniscience is an attribute of deity, while humans come to learn and develop in their understanding. That Jesus grew and learned is clearly taught in Scripture (Luke 2:40, 52; Heb. 5:8). On the temptations of Jesus, Grudem concludes, "As difficult as it may be for us to understand, Scripture affirms that in these temptations Jesus gained an ability to understand and to help us in our temptations. *'Because he himself has suffered and been tempted,* he is able to help those who are tempted' (Heb. 2:18)" (Grudem, *Systematic Theology,* 537 [emphasis original]). Jesus learned how to read and specifically how to read the Bible in the same way that other humans learn.

redemption. Jesus read the Scriptures as God's testimony about himself and, it would seem, patterned his life after the example of his Father.[44] In short, Jesus read the Scriptures as the story of God's work in the created order and learned to emulate his Father in what he did.

The Son is not the Father, but in his works he reveals the Father to be his Father. His critics got it right. They understood Jesus to be claiming to be in a unique relationship with the Father (John 5:18). He was. They should have believed him—not simply because he said it, but because the Scriptures testify about him. Their attention to the Scriptures was a good thing, but because they were not reading them properly, their study of the Scriptures brought them condemnation, not life.

The Scriptures Concern Jesus (Luke 24)

In his gospel, Luke tells us that after his resurrection, Jesus met two of his disciples on the road to Emmaus. He walked with them for some time, although they were not aware that it was he. They related to him the events of the past couple of days— how Jesus of Nazareth had been executed, how disappointed they were since they thought he was the one who was going to redeem Israel, and how they had heard the claim that the tomb was empty (Luke 24:19–24). Jesus' response to them was a stern rebuke: "How foolish you are, and how slow of heart to believe all that the prophets have spoken! Did not the Christ have to suffer these things and then enter his glory?" (vv. 25–26). These disciples would have known this, had they been reading the Old Testament correctly. Jesus then began with "Moses and all

44. Article 1 of the Dallas Theological Seminary Doctrinal Statement states, "We believe that all the Scriptures center about the Lord Jesus Christ in His person and work in His first and second coming, and hence that no portion, even of the Old Testament, is properly read, or understood, until it leads to Him" ("DTS Doctrinal Statement," DTS, accessed July 21, 2014, http://www.dts.edu/about/doctrinalstatement/). John 5:39 is included in the list of biblical support.

the Prophets" and "explained to them what was said in all the Scriptures concerning himself" (v. 27). Even with this instruction, they still did not know the identity of their teacher. Only when "he took bread, gave thanks, broke it and began to give it to them" were they able to recognize him (vv. 30–31).

These two disciples returned to Jerusalem, where they found the Eleven and the others assembled with them and gave them the news that Jesus was alive (vv. 33–34). Jesus himself appeared in their midst, and they were all startled and frightened (v. 37). Again, it was only when he had something to eat that they were able to recognize him (vv. 40–43). Then he repeated himself to this larger group of disciples.

> "This is what I told you while I was still with you: Everything must be fulfilled that is written about me in the Law of Moses, the Prophets and the Psalms." Then he opened their minds so they could understand the Scriptures. He told them, "This is what is written: The Christ will suffer and rise from the dead on the third day, and repentance and forgiveness of sins will be preached in his name to all nations, beginning at Jerusalem." (vv. 44–47)

All of the Old Testament—the Law, the Prophets, and the Psalms—testifies to Christ and his works. In short, all Scripture is to be read christologically.

Does this mean that every word on every page is explicitly about Christ? That could hardly be the case. Rather, it seems that a christological reading of the Scriptures recognizes that Jesus is the fulfillment or culmination of the biblical story. Everything prior to Christ anticipated his person and work. Everything prior to Christ culminated in him. As Phillips Brooks expressed it in the Christmas carol "O Little Town of Bethlehem," "The hopes and fears of all the years are met in thee tonight."[45] Everything in Scripture prior to Jesus points forward to his person and work in his first and second coming, and everything after his first coming continues to point forward to the culmination of the work of redemption.

Conclusion

Jesus asserts that his works reveal who he is. If he did only the works of his Father, and if he learned to work by watching his Father work, then it follows that we could learn who God is and what he is like by watching Jesus work. There is continuity between the God revealed in the Old Testament stories and the God revealed in Jesus of Nazareth. The Son of God is true God from true God, begotten not made, the eternal Son of the eternal Father. God is revealed by what he does, and the works of the Father reveal the character and essence of the Son. In the same way, the works of Jesus reveal the essence of the Father and the Spirit.[46]

Although God is eternally triune, he has always been one God in three persons; the tri-unity of God was revealed in history in the incarnation of God the Son. The hints of plurality are clearly revealed to be true in the revelation of the Trinity in Jesus. Although we can know that the triune God was active in the stories told in the Old Testament, trying to discover which person of the Godhead was active in each account seems unprofitable. It was God at work. At the same time, if all the Old Testament testifies to Christ, then it all points toward the coming to earth of God the Son to complete the work of redemption.

---

45. Phillips Brooks, "O Little Town of Bethlehem," 1868.

46. Of course, there are some works that are uniquely limited to one person of the Godhead. The Father sent the Son. The Son did not send the Father. The Son alone became incarnate, died, and was resurrected. Neither the Spirit nor the Father became human. These functional distinctions must be maintained. The essence of deity is, however, possessed and revealed by the works of each person in the Godhead.

In short, the behavior of the incarnate Son is consistent with the behavior of the God who is revealed prior to the incarnation. We see continuity between the two testaments in the character and practice of God. If the incarnation of the Son of God is a demonstration of humility and condescension, and if he did only what he saw his Father do, then reading the Old Testament should provide numerous examples of God's condescension. That is exactly what we shall see in the upcoming chapters of this work.

3

God's Condescension in the Old Testament Stories, Part 1: From Creation to Abraham

SHE IS A SERVANT in the household of a religious patriarch. An Egyptian, Hagar probably joined the family of Abram during their brief sojourn in the land of Egypt because of the great famine in the land of Canaan (Gen. 12:16). As a household slave, her life is in the hands of her mistress and the patriarch (16:1).

Although Abram's God has promised him many descendants, Abram and Sarai have no children. Sarai is aging, her biological clock is ticking, and time is running out. Perhaps out of desperation, one day Sarai proposes a plan. Recognizing her inability to provide Abram with an heir, she offers her servant Hagar to her husband. He agrees, takes her as his second wife, and sleeps with her. Hagar conceives a child (16:3–4). Almost immediately, there is conflict in the household. Hagar despises Sarai (v. 4), and in response Sarai mistreats Hagar with Abram's permission, and eventually Hagar flees from her.

To this point in the story, the plot follows a predictable trajectory. Jealousy and envy lead to conflict and abuse, and one party, the less empowered one, ends up fleeing to preserve her health and perhaps even her life. But then something amazing happens. The God of Abram, the God who promised to bless all peoples on earth through Abram (12:3), intervenes to bless this woman, the rejected wife of the patriarch.

When the pregnant Hagar flees from the home of her mistress, the reader of this story knows what none of the characters in the narrative yet knows. The reader knows that Hagar is not merely pregnant, but bearing a son, the heir of the patriarch. Abram, the husband and father, appears not to be concerned with the health of his wife and their unborn child.[1]

Abram's God, on the other hand, cares a great deal. In the person of the angel of the Lord, Yahweh finds Hagar near a spring in the desert.[2] The angel inquires about her identity and destination. When Hagar identifies herself as the mistress of Sarai, the angel instructs Hagar to return and submit to her (16:9) and promises Hagar many descendants (v. 10), thus promising her protection and the preservation of her life and the life of her unborn child.[3] The reader hears in these words the echoes of God's promise of many descendants to Abram (see 12:2; 15:4–5). The angel also says to her,

> You are now with child
> and you will have a son.

1. Although the ancients did not view children as sentimentally as moderns do, especially in the Western world, it is still jarring to see Abram, the father of the faithful, treat his unborn child and its mother this callously.

2. Identified as an "angel of the LORD," it is possible that this character is a messenger or an angelic being, but Hagar seems to understand him to be Yahweh. See the narrator's identification of the one who spoke to her as the Lord in Gen. 16:13. See M. F. Rooker, "Theophany," in *Dictionary of the Old Testament: Pentateuch*, ed. T. Desmond Alexander and David W. Baker (Downers Grove, IL: InterVarsity Press, 2003), 863–64.

3. This story should not be used to establish biblical support for the view that an abused spouse or child should remain in an abusive environment. In cases of abuse, Christians should provide protection for the abused. Usually this means that the abused should leave the abuser and seek refuge somewhere, and the police should be called. In this case, Hagar's return is mandated by the God who also promises to protect and care for her and her child.

You shall name him Ishmael,
    for the LORD has heard of your misery.
He will be a wild donkey of a man;
    his hand will be against everyone
    and everyone's hand against him,
and he will live in hostility
    toward all his brothers. (16:11–12)

The angel promises Hagar's son the same blessings previously promised to Abram, for he is Abram's seed.[4] God has condescended to care for this Egyptian slave woman, doing so when no one else did, even her husband or her mistress.

Then the story takes an even more surprising twist. Abram's God now condescends to grant her a gift that no other human has ever received.[5] Hagar, the Egyptian slave woman, is given the privilege of naming the God of Abram: "She gave this name to the LORD who spoke to her: 'You are the God who sees me,' for she said, 'I have now seen the One who sees me'" (v. 13). Hagar saw God; thus, the invisible God condescended to make himself visible to her. Hagar heard God; thus, God condescended to speak to this covenant outsider. Hagar named God; thus, God condescended to allow a creature to define and describe him. No one else in Scripture is granted such privilege—not Adam or Enoch or Abram or Moses or David or Solomon or Isaiah or even the apostle Paul. That she named God is more important than what she named him, but the name is not insignificant. She calls him "El Roi," or "The God Who Sees Me." The God of Abram sees Hagar and cares for her; he provides for her and blesses her.

The God of Abram has promised to bless Abram and through him all peoples on earth. Hagar will be the mother of one of those peoples. Hagar also names the place in honor of this God: "The

4. In a later conversation, God specifically calls Ishmael Abraham's "offspring" (Gen. 21:13).
5. At least there are no other examples recorded in Scripture.

well was called Beer Lahai Roi; it is still there, between Kadesh and Bered" (v. 14).[6] Both the name of God and the name of the place have a long tradition among the people of faith, and both were given by Hagar.

When Hagar returns to the household of the patriarch, she relates this conversation with "The God Who Sees Me" to Abram. The narrator does not tell us much about that exchange with her husband or how her circumstances changed, although it does appear that the abuse stopped, at least for a time. He does, however, relate that when Hagar bore a son, "Abram gave the name Ishmael to the son she had borne" (v. 15). This is the name given to the boy by the angel of the Lord, and only Hagar was present during that conversation. That Abram believed her and obeyed the word of his God indicates his faith in the God who appeared to Hagar and his trust in her testimony.

For the reader of the biblical narrative of creation and redemption, this story is unusual only in degree, not in kind. The transcendent and eternal God is revealed consistently in Scripture as the God who condescends to care for his creatures, for his creation. He regularly provides for his people and for the rest of creation what they could never provide for themselves. And he seems to take particular delight in choosing the outcasts and marginalized to be recipients of his help.

Creation: The Beginning of the Biblical Story

The biblical story begins, "In the beginning God created the heavens and the earth" (Gen. 1:1). There is no extended introduction to this God, no apologetic for his existence, and no descrip-

6. At the time of the exodus, this place apparently still had this name, given to it by Hagar. Ironically, when Abraham's servant brought Rebekah to Isaac to be his wife, Isaac was living at this place (see Gen. 24:62). Rather than dwelling in the same vicinity as his father, Isaac apparently settled in the region where God had appeared to his half-brother's mother.

tion of his attributes or character. The story merely begins with the declaration of the God who speaks and causes something good, or redemptive, to happen. Into an earth that was "formless and empty," with darkness "over the surface of the deep" (v. 2), God spoke, and light appeared. God spoke; dry ground appeared. God spoke; vegetation was produced on the earth. God spoke; living creatures filled the water and sky. God spoke again, and land animals filled the earth. Then God spoke one more time, and humans, male and female, created in his image and likeness, appeared on the earth. This preexistent, powerful God speaks things into existence. He is before all things, the cause of all things, and the sustainer of all things.[7]

There is, of course, much more to this story than is told here. What was God doing before he created? How did the earth become formless and empty? How long was it in this condition? Why did God create what he did, when he did? These and many other questions cannot be answered because the narrator does not tell us.[8] What is clear from this creation account is that there is a God who preexisted his creation, who created through his powerful word, and whose creation is dependent upon him.

Why did God create? Surely not out of necessity or out of some lack, for God needs nothing, nor is there any deficiency in him. Rather, creation was his sovereign choice within the mystery of his inscrutable will. He chose to bring into existence an earth and its inhabitants that will forever be dependent upon him. And he did so, knowing that the creation would quickly

---

7. The creation account in Genesis 1 does not state these conclusions explicitly, although other passages of Scripture do. But God must exist prior to his creation if he is its cause (see Ps. 90:2). He is the cause of everything that is not him, or else there would be some other cause (see John 1:3). He is the one who holds all things together (see Col. 1:17).

8. "The secret things belong to the LORD our God, but the things revealed belong to us and to our children forever, that we may follow all the words of this law" (Deut. 29:29).

be thrown into chaos because of the rebellion of those bearing his image, Adam and Eve, and knowing what he would do to redeem them.

The Naming of Creation

In the poetic description of each day of creation, several phrases are repeated: "And God said," "Let there be . . . and there was," and "it was good," among others.[9] Other phrases are repeated several times, but then the repetition stops. One of these is the pattern of God's naming what he has made. On the first day of creation, God names day and night (Gen. 1:4). On the second day, he names the sky (v. 8). On the third day, he names the land and the seas (v. 10). But when he creates vegetation, trees, and creatures that live on the land, he does not name them. The silence might be merely coincidental, were it not for the emphasis on naming that is found in Genesis 2.[10] There, when the Lord God creates animals, he brings them to the man "to see what he would name them; and whatever the man called each living creature, that was its name" (v. 19).

To name is to exercise authority and dominion over the thing named. This is true not just in the ancient world, for even today the one who names is functioning in a position of authority over the one named.[11] The one who makes something has the

9. That Genesis 1 is poetic does not mean that it is not historical. Rather, the story of creation is told in this chapter in the genre of poetry. See Tim Keller, *The Reason for God: Belief in an Age of Skepticism* (New York: Riverhead Books, 2009), 96–98. Keller writes, "I think Genesis 1 has the earmarks of poetry and is therefore a 'song' about the wonder and meaning of God's creation. Genesis 2 is an account of how it happened" (p. 97). How these two accounts of creation fit together is the subject of extended discussion among biblical scholars and theologians.

10. On the function and significance of naming, see the discussion in Thomas R. Schreiner, "Women in Ministry," in *Two Views on Women in Ministry*, ed. James R. Beck and Craig L. Blomberg (Grand Rapids: Zondervan, 2001), 206–7.

11. "As is well known, in the ancient Near East to name would be tantamount to exercising dominion. When Yahweh brought the animals to Adam 'to see what he would name them,' he was in effect transferring from Himself to Adam the domin-

prerogative to give it a name. So the Creator of the heavens and the earth names what he has made—that is, until he creates the creatures that live on his earth. God does not name the plants, shrubs, trees, or living creatures. He turns the naming of those things over to Adam. God does, however, name Adam (5:2; "male and female"), created in his image and likeness (1:26–28).

In the story that begins our chapter, God condescends to allow Hagar to name him and the place where they meet. In so doing, he humbles himself, placing himself in the role of a servant and allowing this creature to exercise authority over him. Of course, in doing so, God does not cease to be God or elevate the creature to the status of God. Instead, he looks out for the interests of this woman and condescends to improve her position.

The Blessing of Creation

Another phrase that is repeated in Genesis 1 appears, for the first time, after God creates the creatures that live in the sea and in the sky. He "blessed them and said [to them], 'Be fruitful and increase in number'" (v. 22). This is the first mention of blessing in the biblical story. It is not humans who are blessed here, nor even mammals, but creatures that live in the water and in the air. When God creates man and woman at the end of the next day, he also "blessed them and said to them, 'Be fruitful and increase in number; fill the earth'" (v. 28). The narrator's introductory phrase and the command of God are nearly identical in these two instances of divine blessing. God blesses his creatures—those that live on the earth, those in the sea and sky, and those created in his image and likeness. But then humanity is commanded to

---

ion for which man was created. This of course is perfectly in line with the objects of human dominion listed in the pivotal text of Genesis 1:26: fish, birds, livestock, and 'all the creatures that move along the ground'" (Eugene H. Merrill, "A Theology of the Pentateuch," in *A Biblical Theology of the Old Testament*, ed. Roy B. Zuck [Chicago: Moody, 1991], 15).

"subdue it. Rule over the fish of the sea and the birds of the air and over every living creature that moves on the ground" (v. 28).

Created to rule over the earth, the man and woman were intended to be mediators of blessing to the creatures that live there, as well as to those that live in the sea and sky. To subdue and rule means to care for, to provide for, and to look out for the interests of another. In short, these creatures are loved and blessed by their Creator. Their care has been entrusted by God to Adam (humanity), created in his image.

The Creation of Adam

The description of the creation of humanity in Genesis 1 is significantly different from that of the rest of God's creative work in this chapter. The means of creation remain the same: God speaks; the man and woman are created.[12] But Moses explains that prior to speaking Adam into existence, God engages in some self-reflection: "Let us make man in our image, in our likeness, and let them rule over" everything else that has been created (v. 26). This deliberative reflection within the Godhead seems to anticipate what later is made explicit in the coming of Jesus: the God who creates is triune.

To be created in the image and likeness of God surely does not mean that humanity looks like God, for God is not material. Rather, it means that humanity represents and reveals the Creator.[13] In a similar way that, in the ancient world, a statue or image represented the king and an image stamped on a coin indicated sovereignty over the money (see Matt. 22:19–21), humans represent

12. In chapter 2, the man and the woman are created not by divine speech, but through another means of condescension.

13. "Imaging God thus involves representing and perhaps extending in some way God's rule on earth through the ordinary communal practices of human sociocultural life" (J. Richard Middleton, *The Liberating Image: The* Imago Dei *in Genesis 1* [Grand Rapids: Brazos, 2005], 60). Of course, there is much more that could be said about the image of God, but included in it are the functions of representation, revelation, and rule.

the invisible God. In short, as humans created in his image, we are the visible representation of the invisible God. We are physically and materially present in this world; God is not materially present. We reveal him to the creation. When the creatures see us, they see God. We are God's representatives and rule for him.

God has condescended to give the care and control of his world to these creatures created in his image—to humans. Surely God is capable of taking care of his creation all by himself, and he would do the job better than an infinite number of human caretakers. But God has chosen this way. He has turned his world over to us. In delegating his creation to those who bear his image, God retains ownership of his creation. We are stewards, accountable to him for our faithfulness to care for his earth and the creatures that inhabit it.

Creation in Genesis 2

In the second account of creation, found in Genesis 2, the creation of humanity is related differently.[14] In this story, there is a time gap between the creation of male and female. The male is created first: "The LORD God formed the man from the dust of the ground and breathed into his nostrils the breath of life, and the man became a living being" (v. 7). In this story, a master craftsman, an artist, forms the man out of material at hand, the dust of the ground, and implants life by breathing into his nostrils. This description discloses an imminent, intimate, relational, personal Creator who condescends to come to the earth to create the man from dust. Then he comes even nearer to this creature to breathe the breath of life into him. Finally, he puts the man in the garden he has made and brings animals

---

14. Unlike the poetic structure of Genesis 1, this account is narrative. These two stories are complementary, not contradictory. They are not the same, however. Numerous differences are found in the two stories, yet they both recount the creation of the heavens and the earth by God.

to him to see what he will name them. To name the animals is to function in the place of God to them.[15]

"It is not good for the man to be alone" (v. 18), declares the Lord God. In the context of the first creation account, with the constant refrain that "God saw that it was good" (1:4, 9, 12, 18, 21, 25, 31), these words are jarring to the reader. How is it possible that in a perfect, sin-free world, something is not good? Goodness is clearly not a moral quality here, for everything a good God does is morally good. Rather, "It is not good for the man to be alone" is a declaration that God's work is not yet complete. The man was never intended to exist in isolation from other humans. Of course, the male cannot obey the command to "be fruitful and increase in number" (1:28) by himself, but the need for other humans extends beyond the need for a partner in procreation. God creates a woman out of one of the man's ribs, and the man declares of her, "This is now bone of my bones and flesh of my flesh; she shall be called 'woman,' for she was taken out of man" (2:23). She is fully as human as he is, but she is different from him. He is masculine; she is feminine.

God's creativity is displayed in the diversity of his creation. Every human being is unique, but we share a common humanity. God loves unity and diversity. In redemption, God re-creates unity in diversity. People of every language, nation, and tribe assemble to worship God (Rev. 7:9). The body of Christ is made up of many members, but there is one body (1 Cor. 12). The members are not the same; they are different and have diverse functions, but together they form one body. Unity in the midst of diversity is necessary for life.

Significantly, in the story of creation in Genesis 2, the man does not name his helper. Rather, he calls her what she is (v. 22).[16]

---

15. Genesis 1 explicitly states that humanity is created in the image and likeness of God. In Genesis 2, the function of naming makes the same point, albeit implicitly. Adam's actions reveal who he is.

16. The passive construction ("she shall be called woman") argues against the view that Adam is exercising authority over her here. He does not name her; he confesses

He is man; she is woman. Neither one of them has a personal and individual name. But that is about to change. When the Serpent enters the garden, when sin becomes the major plotline of the story, diversity becomes a threat. In the original creation, there was unity and diversity, but no conflict. The fall will change everything, and none of the change is good.

Imagers as Caretakers

Why did God create the heavens and the earth? The Scriptures do not answer that question. We can, however, know why God created humans, for the Scriptures explain that humanity, male and female, was created in his image and given the responsibility to fill the earth, subdue it, and rule over the creatures that God had created (1:28).[17] In short, humans were created to serve God and creation. God gave humanity this task not because he needed help. Not only is God capable of taking care of his earth by himself, but he would surely do a more efficient and effective job than humans have done.

God condescended to turn over the care of his creation to creatures, to humans created in his image. He did so knowing they would rebel against him. The fall was not a surprise to God. When God created, he did so with the plan of redemption already in place. Herman Bavinck puts it well.

> For God the fall was neither a surprise nor a disappointment. He anticipated it, incorporated it into his counsel, and already took account of it in creating the world. Creation, therefore, took place in such a way that, in case Adam as its head fell, the whole world could become as it is now. Prior to the fall, the

---

that "woman" is what she will be called.

17. The commandment to work the garden of Eden and take care of it (2:15) seems to parallel the commandment to subdue and rule over the earth (1:28). It is not merely the garden alone, but the whole earth, that is under the care of those bearing the divine image.

state of humanity and of the earth as a whole was a provisional one that could not remain as it was. It was such that it could be raised to a higher glory but in the event of human transgression could also be subjected to futility and decay.[18]

The first act of the biblical story, creation, is covered in two chapters in the book of Genesis. Most of Scripture (Gen. 3–Rev. 20) deals with the second act of the story, the effects of sin on the good creation and how God acts redemptively in the fallen world. As a transition to the second major act of the biblical story, the narrator asserts, "The man and his wife were both naked, and they felt no shame" (Gen. 2:25)—a statement of ominous foreshadowing. For what is about to happen in the story is that the humans' nakedness will need to be covered because of their shame.[19]

The Fall: Everything Changes

The third chapter of Genesis begins abruptly, with the introduction of the Serpent, a creature who is "more crafty than any of the wild animals the LORD God had made" (3:1). In a brief conversation, the Serpent suggests that God has forbidden Adam and Eve to eat from any tree in the garden (v. 1), has not told them the truth (v. 4), and is not good (v. 5). The man and woman together choose to submit to the creature and eat fruit of the tree from which God had forbidden them to eat (v. 6). They are willing coconspirators in this act of rebellion against God.

The tragic story unfolds quickly. Immediately upon eating the forbidden fruit, their eyes are opened, they realize they are naked, and they attempt to cover their nakedness with fig leaves

18. Herman Bavinck, *Reformed Dogmatics*, ed. John Bolt, trans. John Vriend, vol. 3, *Sin and Salvation in Christ* (Grand Rapids: Baker, 2006), 182.

19. In addition to their literal nakedness, Adam and Eve were figuratively naked—open, honest, vulnerable, and shameless. After the fall, they not only tried to cover their physical nakedness, but also attempted to hide from their Creator.

(v. 7). When God appears in the garden, they attempt to hide from him (v. 8).

The garden was the dwelling of the man and woman, and God came to visit them there. But the garden was never intended to be the final home for humanity or for God. Rather, God's plan of redemption will culminate in a new creation, as the triune God makes his dwelling on the earth with redeemed humanity in the new Jerusalem (Rev. 21:1–3), thus completing the transition from garden to city.[20] The final act of the story is a significant improvement over the original creation. The garden was good; the eternal city will be much better.

Mercy in Judgment

God's appearance in the garden after the fall brings judgment to the rebels, but it is judgment full of mercy and compassion. God appears, not as a confrontational despot, but as a searching friend. "Where are you?" he calls out to Adam. That they are still alive means that the promised threat—"When you eat of it you will surely die" (Gen. 2:17)—was not enforced immediately.[21] Instead, God comes to visit them in their home, the garden, and when he does, he gives them the opportunity to own up to their sin, acknowledge the error of their ways, confess their rebellion, and repent. They do none of those things, choosing instead to blame others for their sin. The man blames the woman; the woman blames the Serpent. Even then God remains merciful. He curses the Serpent and the ground, but he does not curse the man or the woman. He promises increased pain in childbearing and painful toil in getting food from the ground, as well as

---

20. Many have observed this trajectory in the biblical story. For one example, see John Dyer, *From the Garden to the City: The Redeeming and Corrupting Power of Technology* (Grand Rapids: Kregel, 2011).

21. Surely they died in the sense that their relationship with God was ruptured, but they were still alive.

conflict between men and women, but he delays death by nearly a millennium (5:5).[22]

But even that is not the end of God's mercy to them. He makes clothes for them out of animal skins (3:21). Thus, the first recorded death was not the death of the guilty man or woman, but of an animal sacrificed to cover their sin, introducing substitutionary atonement to the biblical story.[23] Finally, he banishes them from the garden to ensure that they (and we) would not return to the garden, eat from the Tree of Life, and live forever (v. 22). God protects them from themselves.

But they do not die—yet. Their relationship with God experiences a kind of death, as does their relationship with each other and all creation. But they are still alive, still breathing, still enjoying the gift of life. Eventually the wages of sin will be paid to them and they will die, but in God's grace they will experience a long life on the earth (see 5:5). God grants them a gracious gift; he extends their lives well beyond what they deserve.

Cain and Abel

When one of Adam's sons kills his brother, God is again gracious to the guilty and his descendants. This condescending graciousness of God to sinners is a major theme in the biblical story (see Rom. 5:8; Eph. 2:4–5).

Cain and Abel both offer sacrifices. For reasons that are not clearly stated, "the LORD looked with favor on Abel and his offering, but on Cain and his offering he did not look with favor"

22. Increased pain in childbearing does not mean that there would have been pain in childbirth prior to the fall. Rather, it emphasizes the intensity of pain in childbirth as a result of the fall. See Bavinck, *Sin and Salvation in Christ*, 176–82. Bavinck is correct: "Without sin there would be no suffering" (p. 176).

23. From the garden, through the patriarchal sacrifices, through the Mosaic system, to the cross, substitutionary atonement—the death of the innocent instead of the guilty—is the means by which God provides redemption. John Murray, *Redemption Accomplished and Applied* (Grand Rapids: Eerdmans, 1955), 5, correctly describes atonement as "central in our Christian faith."

(Gen. 4:4–5).[24] That makes Cain angry. Prior to Cain's doing anything with his anger, God condescends to come to earth to meet with Cain, to warn him of the danger of being controlled by his anger. Yet, when God leaves, Cain kills his innocent, righteous brother.

After the murder, God again comes to earth to speak to Cain. He tells Cain that he will be under a curse and be a restless wanderer on the earth, for the cursed ground will no longer yield crops for him (vv. 10–12). When Cain objects that this "punishment is more than I can bear" (v. 14), God promises to preserve his life.[25] Cain takes a wife, has a son, settles down, builds a city, and produces a line of artists, craftsmen, and entrepreneurs. Cities, music, animal husbandry, metalworking, and other cultural gifts come to humanity through this line of the cursed. Abel, the righteous man, is dead, and Cain, his guilty brother, is still alive. Cain, the cursed (v. 11), is blessed by God with a long life and, through him, all humanity is blessed with these gifts of culture.[26]

Judgment by Water

That Cain's rebellion is not an anomaly for humanity is clear as we continue to turn the pages of Scripture. Generation after generation of humans sin and disobey the commandments of the Creator. The wickedness becomes so great that God is grieved that he has created humanity (Gen. 6:6). The corruption and violence escalate to the point where God says to Noah, "I am

24. "By faith Abel offered God a better sacrifice than Cain did" (Heb. 11:4).

25. God's promise to preserve the life of the unrighteous Cain, when he had not preserved the life of the righteous Abel, is a stunning act of grace. The righteous man suffers and dies because he is righteous; the unrighteous man thrives even under divine judgment. This is not unusual in the fallen world. In fact, it seems to be the general pattern. The wicked face eternal punishment in hell, yet they still experience grace in this life.

26. Dyer, *From the Garden to the City*, 79, observes that "these three areas—agriculture, art, and technology—broadly summarize human culture."

going to put an end to all people. . . . I am surely going to destroy them and the earth" (v. 13).[27]

Again, as with Cain, God condescends to reveal his plans for the future to a man and, also as with Cain, calls this one man to be a mediator of blessing to all creation; God does not put an end to "all" people—he preserves the life of Noah and his family. He does not put an end to "all" living creatures—he preserves the lives of two of every unclean animal and seven (or seven pairs) of every clean animal (7:2). He does not destroy the earth—when the flood is finished, the earth remains and the remnant of preserved animals and humans repopulates the earth.

Human beings and all living creatures were created to inhabit the earth. In the judgment at the time of the flood, the righteous are not taken from the earth; rather, they are preserved. The wicked are taken. This event establishes a pattern seen again and again in the biblical story. Since the earth is the dwelling place of humanity, wicked people are taken in judgment while long life on the earth is a sign of divine blessing (see Ex. 20:12; Eph. 6:1–3). In the final judgment, the wicked will be removed from the earth and thrown into the lake of fire (Rev. 20:15). The righteous will experience eternal life with the Creator in the new heaven and the new earth (21:1–5).

Through the gracious provision of God, Noah is preserved, along with his family and the animals that are with them, through the flood in an ark. When the water recedes, Noah and his family are left behind; they come off the ark onto dry ground. Noah builds an altar and sacrifices animals to the Lord, and the aroma of the sacrifices pleases the Lord (Gen. 8:21).[28]

27. Violence is the specific cause of God's pain and the reason for sending the flood in judgment (Gen. 6:13).

28. There were seven pairs of clean animals, instead of two, so that Noah and his family would have animals to sacrifice to God to atone for their sins and to worship him after the flood. During the flood, God overlooked their sin (see Rom. 3:25). God condescended to provide for them what they were not even aware they needed.

So the Lord says, "Never again will I curse the ground because of man, even though every inclination of his heart is evil from childhood. And never again will I destroy all living creatures, as I have done" (v. 21). The ground has been cursed twice; it will never be cursed again. All living creatures, except those on the ark, died in the flood; that will never happen again. Although sin and rebellion will continue, God promises never to respond as harshly as he did in the flood.

The Covenant with Creation

God makes a covenant in which he promises never again to send a flood upon the earth. It is a covenant made not only with humanity, but also with all living creatures and with the earth itself. The covenant includes a sign, the rainbow. The appearance of the rainbow after the rain will forever be a sign that God's mercy is constant and that never again will he curse the ground because of human sin. As God puts it,

> This is the sign of the covenant I am making between me and you and every living creature with you, a covenant for all generations to come: I have set my rainbow in the clouds, and it will be the sign of the covenant between me and the earth. Whenever I bring clouds over the earth and the rainbow appears in the clouds, I will remember my covenant between me and you and all living creatures of every kind. Never again will the waters become a flood to destroy all life. (Gen. 9:12–15)

Even though humans remain sinful, even though judgment will be deserved, God promises to be gracious.

This promise assures the earth and her inhabitants that they will never be destroyed. As the covenant promise continues, God says, "Whenever the rainbow appears in the clouds, I will see it and remember the everlasting covenant between God and all living creatures of every kind on the earth" (9:16). An everlasting covenant implies the promise of an everlasting earth. God also promises, "Never again will I destroy all living creatures, as I have done" (8:21).

When the apostle Peter describes the judgment at the end of the age, he parallels the coming cataclysmic destruction to the deluge and devastation at the time of the flood (2 Peter 3:5–7). The flood did not annihilate the earth. Rather, the waters covered the earth, resulting in the death of all living things, but when the waters receded, the earth remained. Thus, if the judgment by fire will be similar, the earth presumably will remain.

Similarly, Paul describes the hope of creation as waiting "in eager expectation" that it "will be liberated from its bondage to decay and brought into the glorious freedom of the children of God . . . groaning as in the pains of childbirth right up to the present time" (Rom. 8:19, 21–22). The hope of creation is compared to the hope of "the sons of God," "the children of God," and those who have "the firstfruits of the Spirit" (vv. 19, 21, 23). Since our hope is resurrection and re-creation (1 Cor. 15; 2 Cor. 5), not annihilation, creation's hope also is re-creation. The figures of speech that Paul uses are not consistent with annihilation or destruction. In short, it would make little sense for Paul to express creation's hope as "liberation from bondage to decay" if what he means is that creation will be annihilated.

Finally, Jesus uses the term "renewal" to describe the eschatological age (Matt. 19:28). It would be odd to describe annihilation as renewal. Rather, as Bavinck concludes, "Only such a renewal of the world, for that matter, accords with what the Scripture teaches about redemption. For the latter is never a second, brand-new creation but a re-creation of the existing world."[29]

29. Herman Bavinck, *Reformed Dogmatics*, ed. John Bolt, trans. John Vriend, vol. 4, *Holy Spirit, Church, and New Creation* (Grand Rapids: Baker, 2008), 717.

That the Creator of the universe intends to make the earth his eternal home is an extreme act of condescension. Rather than taking the righteous to heaven to be with him, he will bring heaven to earth. But, more than that, even though "every inclination of [the human] heart is evil from childhood" (Gen. 8:21), the Creator promises that he will never again judge their evil as he did in the flood. God is consistently merciful and compassionate, as manifested in his continuing graciousness toward rebels.

The Call of Abram: The Announcement of the Gospel

In his letter to the Galatians, Paul proclaims that the gospel was announced in advance to Abraham when God declared, "All nations will be blessed through you" (3:8). This is the promise God made to Abram when he called him (Gen. 12:1–3).[30] The selection of Abraham is the means by which God will bless all nations. Abraham, the patriarch of Israel, is the father of all people of faith (Rom. 4:11; Gal. 3:9).

God chose Abraham to be the mediator of blessing not because he was the most righteous man on the planet, because there was no one else whom God could use, because there were no worshippers of the Lord in the land of Canaan, or because he was a perfect man. He came, rather, from a family of idolaters (Josh. 24:2). Further, as the biblical account of the life of Abraham makes clear, he was a man whose life was marked by doubt, unbelief, rebellion, disobedience, and missteps. But God condescended to choose and bless him. In God's economy, Abraham is characteristic of the kind of people God uses (see 1 Cor. 1:26–31).

Although there are moments of faithfulness and commendable behavior in the stories of Abraham, the patriarch's life is more often marked by incomplete faithfulness. From his repeated

30. Abram's name was later changed to Abraham (Gen. 17:5).

attempts to save himself and his property by asking his wife to claim to be his sister (Gen. 12:11–13; 20:11–13), to his inability to get along with Lot and his servants (ch. 13), to his sleeping with Hagar the Egyptian (16:3–4), to his willingness to have pregnant Hagar mistreated (v. 6), his walk of faith was far from perfect. The good news of the stories about Abraham is the incredible faithfulness of his God. The descendants of Abraham, thus, have hope because God is faithful (Gal. 3:29).

Abraham and Melchizedek. Abraham often interacts with people who do not share his faith. He is a stranger and an alien in the land of promise. This makes one interaction particularly surprising. When he returns to the land of Canaan after rescuing Lot from his kidnappers, he meets Melchizedek at the city of Salem. Melchizedek was "king of Salem" and "priest of God Most High" (Gen. 14:18). When these two meet, it is Melchizedek who blesses Abraham; it is the patriarch who pays tithes to the king of Salem (vv. 19–20). This demonstrates that Melchizedek was greater than Abraham: "Just think how great he [Melchizedek] was: Even the patriarch Abraham gave him a tenth of the plunder!" writes the author to the Hebrews. "He collected a tenth from Abraham and blessed him who had the promises. And without doubt the lesser person is blessed by the greater" (Heb. 7:4, 6–7). Melchizedek was a king and a priest, mediating in Salem (later called Jerusalem) between Abraham's God and the people of faith in that God. There was a vibrant, faithful, powerful, worshiping community of people in the land of Canaan long before Abraham got there, led by a man greater than Abraham. So why did God bring Abraham from Ur to Canaan instead of establishing Melchizedek as the head of the people through whom all nations on earth would be blessed? Although that question cannot be answered, the selection of Abraham further illustrates God's condescension in the kind of person he chose. God seems to take pleasure in selecting unlikely candidates while passing over those who might appear more suitable.

Finally, we should note that God chose Melchizedek not only to be a recipient of divine blessing, but also to play a major role in the biblical story as head of a priestly line that would ultimately be filled by the Messiah (Ps. 110:4; Heb. 5:4–6). The priesthood of the Messiah has its roots in a Canaanite king and priest, a further revelation of gracious condescension.

The Covenant Promises Made to Abraham. God's condescension to Abraham is also seen in the story of the covenant that God makes with him. In Genesis 12, God makes a series of promises to the patriarch, promises that culminate in blessing for all peoples. In short, the Creator of the universe chose to mediate his blessing to his creation through a particular man and his descendants. These blessings would come through the Chaldean Abraham and his seed. The ultimate fulfillment of this promise is found in Jesus, the seed of Abraham (see Gal. 3:16–29).

Some time passes after the Lord appears to Abram in Ur of the Chaldeans (Gen. 12:1; see also Acts 7:2–4). Abram arrives in the land of Canaan, goes down to Egypt, returns to Canaan, separates from Lot, rescues Lot from his kidnappers, and meets with Melchizedek while returning to his family.[31] Then, in Genesis 15, the Lord again appears to Abram. He reminds the patriarch that he, the Lord, is his "very great reward" (v. 1). Abram's lack of understanding, or perhaps his limited faith in God, is expressed by his question, "What can you give me since I remain childless?" (v. 2), and his lament, "You have given me no children" (v. 3). The Lord responds with a promise of many descendants that is

31. I am assuming that the stories told in Genesis 12–14 are arranged in chronological order. Since 15:1 begins with "after this," I am further assuming that the covenant-cutting ceremony happened after the events in chapter 14. This order in the narrative's structure seems important for the story Moses is telling.

confirmed by a sign, the comparison to the innumerable stars of the heavens (v. 5).

Although Abram is a man of faith, he still struggles to grasp the promise of God.[32] To the reminder from the Lord that Abram is being led by God to the land that he will possess, Abram responds, "O Sovereign LORD, how can I know that I will gain possession of it?" (v. 8). If God were to respond in anger and judgment, no one could blame him. But God's response is compassionate, gracious, and kind. He cuts a covenant with Abram (v. 18).[33]

The covenant does not make the promises of God more secure, but it does give Abram something he knows and understands. By this covenant, God stoops into Abram's world to contextualize his relationship with the patriarch. In Abram's day, one means by which a master would enter into a relationship with a servant was through a covenant. Such relationships were regularly covenantal. God did not invent the covenant, nor did he reinvent its form. Rather, he used a covenantal treaty form common to Abram's world to contextualize this relationship.

In coming into Abram's world, God continues the pattern begun in creation and culminating in a new heaven and a new earth. God's method is one of redemption and re-creation, not annihilation and replacement. The trajectory of the biblical story is one of improvement. As God enters into the world he created,

32. "Abram believed the LORD, and he credited it to him as righteousness" (15:6). This surely does not mean that this is the point in time when Abram becomes a man of faith. Abram left Ur of the Chaldeans by faith (Heb. 11:8–10). Rather, this is a declaration of the means by which Abram and his descendants are justified (see Rom. 4:1–4). Further, that Abraham is the "father of all who believe" (v. 11) does not mean that he is the first man to be justified, since Enoch (Gen. 5:21–24) and Noah (6:9) were righteous men. Justification is always and only by grace through faith. Abram was a righteous man. He was righteous because of the imputation of divine righteousness by grace through faith. The significance of Genesis 15:6 is that Abraham is an example of how one who is unrighteous can become righteous: it is only by grace through faith (see Rom. 4:1–5; Gal. 3:6–14).

33. On the cutting of this covenant, see Michael Horton, *Introducing Covenant Theology* (Grand Rapids: Baker, 2009), 40–45.

he acts redemptively, so that the results are even better than what was there before he arrived. God uses what is already there and redeems it. He does not usually invent something new; he takes what is already there and uses it for his purposes. In so doing, he provides a model for his people to follow. The presence of God's people should make the world better than it was prior to their appearance.

The Covenant Sign for Abraham. When, sometime later, Abram continues to struggle with faith in God, God adds to the covenant the sign of circumcision.[34] God appears to Abram again. By this time, the patriarch is ninety-nine years old and still has no son with Sarai. When God reminds him of the promise of many descendants, Abram falls facedown and laughs (17:3, 17).[35] Two signs follow; in both, God uses the culture of Abram's day to confirm his promises to the patriarch. First, God changes Abram's name to Abraham, saying, "For I have made you a father of many nations" (v. 5).[36] From this day forward, Abraham will be reminded of God's promise whenever he uses or hears his name. Abraham is already familiar with the God who names. For the past thirteen years, he has been the father of a son whose name was given to him by "the God who sees me," as related to

34. How much later? We cannot know for sure, for there is no time indicator in Genesis 15 as there is in 17:1 ("Abram was ninety-nine years old"). Abram was at least seventy-five years old when he arrived in the land of Canaan (12:4). Thus, nearly a quarter century has passed since God first appeared to him.

35. It appears that Abram's laughter in verses 3 and 17 are for similar reasons: "Will a son be born to a man a hundred years old? Will Sarah bear a child at the age of ninety?" (v. 17). The implied negative answer explains the laughter.

36. Since the name change is a reminder of the promise to Abram, and the change occurs after Abram's first fit of laughter, I take the new name to be a sign to Abram. Of course, Abram is not yet the father of many nations. He is the father of only one son, Ishmael. But since the God who has promised is faithful, he can describe a promise not yet realized as if it already has been fulfilled. In Romans 4:17, Paul describes Abraham's God as "the God who gives life to the dead and calls things that are not as though they were." In short, God's word creates.

Abram by Hagar (see ch. 16). God also changes Sarai's name to Sarah (17:15–16). Second, God institutes the sign of circumcision. From this day forward, every male of the covenant people will bear in his flesh the sign of the covenant, a graphic (and painful, especially for adult converts) and concrete cultural icon for the people of faith. Since Abram was circumcised after he became a man of faith, Paul explains, he is the father of both circumcised and uncircumcised believers (Rom. 4:11–12).[37]

The Covenantal Blessings for All People. It is as the mediator of blessing to all people that Abraham is most significant. This, after all, is the content of the gospel (see Gal. 3:8). Two stories stand out in particular. In the first, Abraham mediates blessing for the people of the cities of the plain. In the second, he mediates blessing for all the redeemed as he sacrifices his son as a foreshadowing of the atonement of Christ.

As a foretaste of what is to come when God will come to earth and make his dwelling with us forever (Rev. 21:3), and as a foretaste of the incarnation (John 1:14), the Creator comes to where Abraham lives (Gen. 18:1). Abraham sees three men (v. 2). Because he is a gracious host, he prepares a meal for his guests.[38] When the time comes to leave, the Lord comments, "Shall I hide from Abraham what I am about to do? Abraham will surely become a great and powerful nation, and all nations on earth will be blessed through him. For I have chosen him" (vv. 17–18). Having chosen him as a mediator of blessing, God by his self-deliberation appears to imply some sense of responsibility on his

37. To use language that is admittedly anachronistic, Abraham is a Gentile. Abraham is not a Jew; he dies long before his grandson Jacob's name is changed to Israel. He is thus the father of both Gentile and Jewish believers (see Gal. 3).

38. The description of "three men standing nearby" (v. 2) has led to speculation that they were the three persons of the Trinity. But since "the LORD" visited Abraham (v. 1), and "two angels" went on to Sodom (19:1), it is probably best not to speculate about which person or persons of the Godhead appeared to Abraham. The sovereign Lord of the universe condescended to appear to him.

part to reveal to Abraham what he intends to do.[39] So the Lord explains to Abraham that he is on the way to see if the conditions in Sodom and Gomorrah are "as bad as the outcry that has reached" heaven (v. 21).

Abraham replies that the righteous Lord should not treat the godly and the wicked the same. He argues that the Judge of all the earth should spare the wicked for the sake of the righteous (vv. 24–25), and God agrees to deliver the city for the sake of fifty righteous people.[40] From fifty to forty-five, forty, thirty, twenty, and finally to ten, at Abraham's request, God agrees to preserve the city for the sake of the righteous. Throughout this conversation, Abraham is pleading for God to deliver the wicked because of the righteous; he is mediating blessing to the citizens of Sodom. In so doing, he is, perhaps unknowingly, serving as a means of blessing to the nations, the purpose for which he was called.

Inexplicably, Abraham stops at ten. There were not ten righteous people in the city—only a few (Lot and his family; see 2 Peter 2:6–9). We do not know why Abraham stopped at ten; perhaps he thought there were ten there, or perhaps he was afraid to continue further. Nor can we know for sure how God would have responded, had Abraham continued. But since God was willing to be gracious to the citizens of Sodom and Gomorrah, it does seem plausible that he would have delivered the city simply at Abraham's request.

God chose Abraham and promised to bless all peoples through the patriarch. Further, God allowed him to influence

---

39. Of course, any responsibility would be due to divine grace and condescension, not because of anything in Abraham. God appears to condescend to Abraham when he notes that he is under a divinely mandated responsibility to engage with the patriarch.

40. It is not the lives of the righteous that are the focus of Abraham's plea, but the lives of the wicked. He asks God to "spare the place for the sake of the fifty righteous people in it" (v. 24; see also v. 28). In each stage of the negotiation, God promises not to destroy the city for the sake of the righteous (vv. 26, 28, 30, 31, 32).

God's work in this world.[41] Abraham foreshadowed another mediator between God and his people, Moses. And both of them foreshadowed the ultimate mediator between God and man, the man Christ Jesus (1 Tim. 2:5).

Then, several years later, Abraham again became the mediator of blessing through his obedience. In a story that foreshadows the Father's sacrifice of his Son for the sin of the world, God asks Abraham to sacrifice his son, his only son, the son he loves, Isaac. Abraham promptly obeys (Gen. 22:2–3). He takes Isaac to Mount Moriah, places him on the altar, and prepares to sacrifice him to God. Out of his great mercy, God, in the person of the angel of the Lord, intervenes and provides a ram for the sacrifice. Once again an animal dies so that humanity might live. Because of Abraham's action, his God declares,

> I swear by myself . . . that because you have done this and have not withheld your son, your only son, I will surely bless you and make your descendants as numerous as the stars in the sky and as the sand on the seashore. Your descendants will take possession of the cities of their enemies, and through your offspring all nations on earth will be blessed, because you have obeyed me. (vv. 15–18)

Abraham's faith was demonstrated to be genuine by his obedience to the God who called him (James 2:21–24).

Conclusion

The eternal God is the source of everything that is. His creation is dependent upon him. He creates man, male and female,

41. That God allowed Abraham to interact with him in this way does not mean that God's plan was dependent upon Abraham. Rather, in some mysterious way, God ordained not only the end, but also the means to accomplish his plan. Abraham's negotiation was a means by which God's plan was carried out. This is also the great mystery of prayer. See my "Jonathan Edwards's Theology of Prayer" in *Bibliotheca Sacra* 160 (October–December 2003): 434–56.

to care for his creation—not because he needs help, but as an act of condescension. When Adam rebels against God and introduces sin and death into the created order, God responds with mercy and compassion. He condescends to redeem his rebellious creatures. Then he selects one man, Abraham, to be the means by which all peoples will be blessed. This story of redemption continues in the generations of Abraham's descendants, to which we now turn.

4

God's Condescension in the Old Testament Stories, Part 2: From Isaac to the Conquest

IN THE PREVIOUS CHAPTER, we traced the story of God's relationship with humanity from creation through the life of Abraham. The covenant that God graciously made with Abraham promises to bless him and his descendants and, through them, all peoples. The blessings will come not through his first son, Ishmael, but rather through Isaac. Yet Ishmael also receives the promise of blessings.

> And as for Ishmael, I have heard you: I will surely bless him; I will make him fruitful and will greatly increase his numbers. He will be the father of twelve rulers, and I will make him into a great nation. But my covenant I will establish with Isaac, whom Sarah will bear to you by this time next year. (Gen. 17:20–21)

The Blessing of Isaac

Isaac is born—just as God promised—and grows to maturity. When a severe famine strikes the land, God appears to the patriarch Isaac, warns him not to go to Egypt, and repeats the promises of many descendants, land, and blessing for all nations through him (Gen. 26:2–4).[1] Later God appears to Isaac again, promising him his presence and many descendants. In what will become a consistent pattern, God identifies himself in relationship to the patriarchs. To Isaac, he is "the God of your father Abraham" (26:24). Having chosen Abraham to be the means by which he will bless all nations, God chooses to identify himself by the name of this one he has chosen. In a cultural context where names matter a great deal, where names indicate the character of the person, and where giving names indicates authority or sovereignty, God condescends to take Abraham's name as his. In short, God identifies himself as the God of Abraham, and later as the God of Abraham, Isaac, and Jacob (Ex. 3:6). He is not just the God who has chosen Abraham—he is Abraham's God.

The Blessing of Jacob

The patriarch Isaac and his wife, Rebekah, have two sons, the twins Jacob and Esau. Even before they are born, the Lord predicts conflict between them (Gen. 25:23). Their sibling relationship is marked by conflict, particularly in the two incidents in which Jacob steals his brother's birthright (vv. 27–34) and his father's blessing (ch. 27). After the latter, Jacob flees from his father's house in fear of his brother. God appears to Jacob in a dream and reminds him of the promises of many descendants and the blessing of all nations through him. Jacob is fleeing the land in fear of his life, but God gives him this assurance: "I will bring you back to this land. I will not leave you until I have done what I have promised you" (28:15).

After several decades serving his uncle Laban, Jacob sets out to return to the land of promise. He receives word that Esau is

---

1. God also tells Isaac that the reason for the blessing was Abraham's obedience (26:5), echoing the language of 22:16–18.

heading toward him. Fearing retribution for his deception, fearing that Esau is on his way to carry out the threat of murder, Jacob cries out to the God of Abraham and Isaac (32:9–12). God meets Jacob at the Jabbok River and, incredibly, condescends to take the form of a man and wrestle with him.[2] The match extends until daybreak, and the man is unable to defeat Jacob (v. 25). Jacob refuses to let him go without a blessing.[3] In addition to the blessing, Jacob receives a "wrenched" hip (v. 25) and a new name: "Your name will no longer be Jacob, but Israel, because you have struggled with God and with men and have overcome" (v. 28).

The sign of a name change is a constant reminder of the incident, since *Israel* means "he struggles with God." Jacob, or Israel, could have overcome God only if God had condescended to allow it to occur. The omnipotent Creator could never be matched by a creature without condescension on the part of God. And that is what God did; he came down to the level of this fearful, doubting, and deceitful patriarch.

Israel in Egypt

God promised Abraham that his descendants would spend four hundred years being mistreated in another land, but would then return to the land of promise in the fourth generation (Gen. 15:13–16). Through betrayal and kidnapping, through famine and deception, the entire family of Jacob eventually migrates to Egypt, where Joseph, one of Jacob's sons, becomes

2. The wrestling partner is called "a man" (32:24). Yet when Jacob receives a blessing from him, Jacob names the place "Peniel, saying, 'It is because I saw God face to face, and yet my life was spared'" (v. 30). Thus, it appears that the man who wrestled with Jacob was God himself in human form. Robert L. Reymond, *A New Systematic Theology of the Christian Faith* (Nashville: Thomas Nelson, 1998), 208, places this man in the same category as the angel of the Lord: "both *identified* as God and yet *differentiated* from God" (emphasis original).

3. Jacob recognizes this man to be superior to him. Surely Jacob is not stronger than God unless God condescends to take on weakness. This condescension foreshadows the incarnation.

their savior. As a type of Christ, Joseph embodies in advance the salvation that God will provide in his Son, who, because of his great love (see Eph. 2:4), gives himself for the sake of others.[4]

When God delivers his people out of slavery in Egypt, he does so through a "mighty hand" and powerful wonders (Ex. 3:19–20). He chooses Moses, a murderer, who, like Jacob before him, has run away from his family because of fear (2:14–15). Moses is tending his father-in-law's sheep in the desert when God appears to him in a burning bush to commission him to be the deliverer of the Israelites from slavery in Egypt. The Creator of the universe deigns to choose a disgraced murderer to be the liberator of his people and deigns to speak to him out of a bush, a bush that burns but is not consumed.

When God speaks to Moses, he identifies himself in terms of his relationship with the patriarchs: "I am the God of your father, the God of Abraham, the God of Isaac and the God of Jacob" (3:6). When Moses requests that God tell him his name, God declares his existence: "I AM WHO I AM" (v. 14), and then says, "The LORD, the God of your fathers—the God of Abraham, the God of Isaac and the God of Jacob . . . is my name forever, the name by which I am to be remembered" (v. 15). The God who is, who created by his powerful word, has again condescended to enter into the experience of his people, the descendants of the patriarchs, and he has taken their name as his own; he is the God of Abraham, Isaac, and Jacob.

Moses objects to God's call several times. God responds to each one calmly and compassionately. God, who already knows how this conversation will end, treats Moses as if he has something to contribute to the project. In short, God condescends to enter into

4. Jonathan Edwards observes, "The remarkable similitude there is between very many things in the history of Joseph and the Old Testament prophecies of the Messiah argue the former to be a type of the latter" ("Types of the Messiah," in *The Works of Jonathan Edwards*, ed. Mason I. Lowance Jr. with David H. Watters, vol. 11, *Typological Writings* [New Haven: Yale University Press, 1993], 228).

a "job interview" with this reluctant deliverer. The final protest, however—"O Lord, please send someone else" (4:13)—results in the Lord's anger against Moses. But as evidence that even Moses' objections were known to God beforehand, he has already planned for this event: "Your brother, Aaron the Levite . . . is already on his way to meet you" (v. 14). Aaron began the journey well in advance of this moment. To the objections of the unwilling Moses, God provides a colleague and helper, his own brother.

The Exodus

Before Moses returns to Egypt, the Lord explains to him that Pharaoh will not let the Israelites go "unless a mighty hand compels him" (Ex. 3:19). After a series of ten plagues, during the latter seven of which God preserves his people from harm, God delivers his people out of slavery in Egypt. When Pharaoh changes his mind and sends his army to force the Israelites to return to Egypt, God drowns them in the waters of the Red Sea after dividing the water for his people to cross on dry land (14:21–31). The God who is at work in this great act of deliverance is a God of great power, demonstrating through these great signs that no Egyptian king or god can oppose his plan. He delivers the people through a mighty hand, as he promised.

God accomplishes the deliverance through a series of plagues, a series of horrible events that culminates in the destruction of the Egyptian army in the Red Sea. Rather than putting on a single cataclysmic display of power, God acts progressively over a period of weeks or months.[5]

After the exodus and the deliverance at the Red Sea, Moses leads the people to Mount Sinai as a sign that God is with him: "When you have brought the people out of Egypt, you will worship

5. The exact length of time is not stated in the text, but it must have taken more than a few weeks for these plagues to be poured out on Egypt.

God on this mountain" (3:12). God appears to his people on the mountain in a display of smoke and fire, with a loud trumpet blast and an earthquake (19:16–19). The people are, understandably, afraid of God and request, instead of an unmediated interaction between the Lord and his people, that Moses function as a mediator between them. God pronounces this a good plan, declaring, "Everything they said was good" (Deut. 5:28). So, in response to the request of the people, God institutes the office of mediator. From this time on, God will speak to the people through a human mediator, and the people will speak to God in the same way. In an intimate and condescending way, "The LORD would speak to Moses face to face, as a man speaks with his friend" (Ex. 33:11). The use of a mediator was part of his eternal plan, but it was put into effect in time and space at the request of the people of Israel.

The Covenant at Sinai

God makes a covenant with his people at Sinai. Just as in the covenant with Abram, God uses a covenant form that was familiar to the culture of that day—the suzerain/vassal treaty used by the Hittites in Canaan.[6] Rather than creating something new as a means of mediating his relationship with his people, the Lord goes into the culture of that day and uses a treaty form found there. This is consistently the way the God of Abraham, Isaac, and Jacob operates. His acts of redemption occur through condescension into the culture of the day.

Moses spends forty days with God on the mountain to receive the law and instructions for the building of the tabernacle and its furnishings. During his absence, the people approach Aaron with the request that he make them a god to go before them (32:1). Apparently without hesitation or objection, Aaron com-

6. On the ancient Hittite treaty form, see W. J. Dumbrell, *Covenant and Creation: A Theology of Old Testament Covenants* (Nashville: Thomas Nelson, 1984), 94–99.

plies, using the gold earrings of the people. He forms an idol in the shape of a calf and declares a day of worship to "your god, O Israel, who brought you up out of Egypt" (v. 4, margin).[7] The people—whom God had delivered from slavery in a remarkable and miraculous way and had given a human mediator between himself and them, as they requested, and for whom he had provided food consistently and faithfully—were unable or unwilling to trust him during forty days of silence and absence.

The people's rebellion invokes God's fierce anger. Yet the story does not end with death and destruction. Rather, Moses pleads for God to fulfill the promise made to Abraham and to accompany this people to the land of promise. He argues that if God's presence is not with the people, then they are the same as all the other nations (33:15–16). What makes the Israelites unique among the nations is that their God actually exists and is present with his people. In short, the God of Abraham, Isaac, and Jacob is a real and living God and has condescended to live in the midst of his people. This is what will distinguish the Israelites "from all the other people on the face of the earth" (v. 16); they alone have a God who exists and is present with his people.

Moses is not naive. He knows these people are rebellious, or stiff-necked (vv. 3–5), and do not deserve to be in the presence of God. Yet, Moses argues, having chosen them as his people, and having chosen to redeem them out of slavery, God has an obligation to finish what he started. He pleads with God to fulfill his promises to them, to be gracious and merciful to them. Moses seems to understand that this is the character of the God of Abraham, Isaac, and Jacob, that God is merciful and forgiving.[8]

7. That Aaron was able to make an idol of gold, "fashioning it with a tool" (32:4), might indicate that he had been trained in metallurgy in Egypt. It is unlikely that he was telling the truth when he claimed a miraculous source for the calf: "They gave me the gold, and I threw it into the fire, and out came this calf!" (v. 24).

8. He will soon hear God proclaim that he is compassionate, gracious, and forgiving (34:6). But Moses has already seen God reveal his character by his behavior.

God agrees to Moses' request with these words: "I will do the very thing you have asked, because I am pleased with you and I know you by name" (v. 17). This is an amazing statement of condescension from the Creator of the universe! God will grant Moses' request because he is pleased with him. Moses is not perfect, but Moses brings God pleasure.

However, God's agreement to be present with the people is not enough for Moses. Moses makes an audacious request: "Now show me your glory" (v. 18). Much like the people who asked for an idol, Moses wants to see God; he asks to see his glory.[9] Like them, Moses wants a God he can see, one who makes his presence visible. Like so many of God's followers throughout history, Moses finds it difficult to believe in a God who cannot be seen. Thomas, one of Jesus' disciples, is a New Testament example. Thomas insists that he will not believe in Jesus unless he sees his wounds for himself (John 20:25). But when Jesus appears, Thomas calls to him, "My Lord and my God!" (v. 28). Jesus responds in words of blessing for all those who believe in him apart from sight: "Because you have seen me, you have believed; blessed are those who have not seen and yet have believed" (v. 29).

God's response to Moses is gracious in two ways. He does not give Moses what he requested—"for no one may see me and live" (Ex. 33:20). But what he does give Moses is even better—"I will cause all my goodness to pass in front of you, and I will . . . have mercy on whom I will have mercy, and I will have compassion on whom I will have compassion" (v. 19). God gives him the gracious gift of the verbal proclamation of his attributes.

The next day, God condescends to come to Moses one more time. Again, as when God cut the covenant, Moses is given explicit

9. The glory of God is his presence. See John Hannah, "To God Be the Glory: How Can That Be?" (chapel message, Dallas Theological Seminary, Dallas, TX, September 18, 2008), available online at http://www.dts.edu/media/play/to-god -be-the-glory-how-can-that-be-john-d-hannah.

instructions to meet God on top of the mountain (34:1–3). Moses cannot ascend to heaven; he cannot reach God. There is no mountain or anything else on earth high enough to reach up into God's heaven. So, in an act of condescension,

> the Lord came down in the cloud and stood there with him and proclaimed his name, the Lord. And he passed in front of Moses, proclaiming, "The Lord, the Lord, the compassionate and gracious God, slow to anger, abounding in love and faithfulness, maintaining love to thousands, and forgiving wickedness, rebellion and sin. Yet he does not leave the guilty unpunished; he punishes the children and their children for the sin of the fathers to the third and fourth generation." (vv. 5–7)

God's self-description begins with a repeated declaration of his name, followed by a pronouncement of his grace and compassion. It is not appropriate, in light of divine simplicity, to prioritize divine attributes in terms of importance, but any description of God must begin somewhere.[10] God starts with the declaration that he is gracious and compassionate (v. 6). God is also slow to anger (v. 6)—though he does get angry, as Moses knows well (see 32:9–10). God is not simply love (see 1 John 4:16)—he is abounding in love that is faithful (Ex. 34:6). It is to God's great love and mercy that Paul attributes the redemptive work of Christ: "God, who is rich in mercy, made us alive with Christ even when we were dead in transgressions" (Eph. 2:4–5). God maintains love to thousands (Ex. 34:7)—surely to thousands of people, but the reference here is probably to

10. Michael Horton explains that God's simplicity and unity mean that he "is not the sum total of his attributes but is simultaneously everything that all the attributes reveal, . . . [and] each of these attributes identifies a different aspect of God's existence and character that cannot be reduced to the others." Horton adds, "One implication is that we cannot rank God's attributes or make one more essential to God than another" (Michael Horton, *The Christian Faith: A Systematic Theology for Pilgrims on the Way* [Grand Rapids: Zondervan, 2011], 228).

thousands of generations. Yet God is also just. He punishes the guilty from generation to generation (v. 7).[11]

Jonah as a Case Study of God's Character

This description of God's character plays a pivotal role in the canon of Scripture. Phrases from the passage are commonly found in reflections upon the character of God (e.g., Neh. 9:17; Pss. 103:8; 111:4; Joel 2:13). But the clearest example of the significance of this divine disclosure is found in the story of Jonah. When God sent word to Jonah that he was to go to Nineveh and preach against its wickedness, Jonah ran away from the Lord and headed for Tarshish (Jonah 1:1–3). There is no reason to speculate about the reason Jonah fled, for he declares the motivation for his action.

> O LORD, is this not what I said when I was still at home? That is why I was so quick to flee from Tarshish. I knew that you are a gracious and compassionate God, slow to anger and abounding in love, a God who relents from sending calamity. Now, O LORD, take away my life, for it is better for me to die than to live. (4:2–3)

In short, Jonah declares, his rebellion against God was due to his awareness that God is gracious and compassionate. He believed that God would be gracious to the people in Nineveh. He preferred to die at God's hand, rather than see them receive mercy from Israel's God.

The God who is "slow to anger" then asks the quick-tempered prophet, "Have you any right to be angry?" (4:4). Surely Jonah believes that his anger is justified. He appears to miss the irony of contrast between the long-suffering and patient God and his quick-tempered prophet.

---

11. This is a difficult saying, that God punishes children for the sin of the fathers. Many biblical stories illustrate the truthfulness of this claim, as when God punishes the family of Achan for the sin of Achan (Josh. 7:24–25), or when the infant son of David and Bathsheba dies as a result of their sin (2 Sam. 12:18).

The God who has promised to bless all nations intends to do just that, but his own prophet attempts to stand in his way. However, God's blessing of the nations is not really dependent upon the action of his reluctant prophet. Ironically, as the story unfolds, Jonah himself is the recipient of God's grace and mercy, even in the midst of rebellion.

The condescension of God in this story is not limited to people. God also expresses his compassion for the animals in the city. The Creator of the heavens and earth, the one who blessed the creatures, continues to bless his creation. In a not-so-subtle rebuke of the prophet, Jonah's book concludes with God's words.

> You have been concerned about this vine, though you did not tend it or make it grow. It sprang up overnight and died overnight. But Nineveh has more than a hundred and twenty thousand people who cannot tell their right hand from their left, and many cattle as well. Should I not be concerned about that great city? (vv. 10–11)

Jonah's concern about a vine that had grown up apart from any effort on his part pales in comparison to God's concern for the people and animals in the city, created and sustained by him.

The Tabernacle

Mercy in the midst of judgment is seen in the incident of the golden calf. Many die at the hands of the Levites (Ex. 32:28, "about three thousand") and by a plague (v. 35), but the nation is not destroyed. God does not reject his people, but continues to fulfill his promises to them. God does not remove his presence from them.

Moses carries out the instructions for the building and furnishings of the tabernacle. Although the people have been unfaithful to God and have broken the covenant, God responds to them with compassion, mercy, grace, and forgiveness. Although they do not deserve it, God continues to dwell in their midst. Although they deserve to be condemned because of their sin, God provides atonement through the sacrificial system. Their faithlessness to God and rebellion in the golden calf incident do not result in God's casting them off, destroying them, or beginning anew with another people. He remains faithful to them.

When everything is completed and the tabernacle is set up as commanded by the Lord, "the glory of the LORD filled the tabernacle. Moses could not enter the Tent of Meeting because the cloud had settled upon it, and the glory of the LORD filled the tabernacle" (Ex. 40:34–35). This is not a temporary filling of the temple, but a permanent condescension of God to dwell in the midst of his people. Moses explains,

> In all the travels of the Israelites, whenever the cloud lifted from above the tabernacle, they would set out; but if the cloud did not lift, they did not set out—until the day it lifted. So the cloud of the LORD was over the tabernacle by day, and fire was in the cloud by night, in the sight of all the house of Israel during all their travels. (vv. 36–38)

God not only condescended to dwell in the midst of his people, but also made his presence visible in the cloud by day and in the fire by night.

The Journey toward Canaan

Throughout the story of the exodus, the wilderness wanderings, and the conquest of the land of Canaan, God demonstrates that he is compassionate, merciful, and slow to anger toward his people. Again and again they fail to remain faithful to him, yet he remains faithful to them. At Sinai, he says to them, "Now if you obey me fully and keep my covenant, then out of all nations you will be my treasured possession" (Ex. 19:5). Of course, the

Israelites fail to keep all God's decrees; they do not obey him fully. In fact, throughout the progression from Egypt to the Promised Land, they consistently and constantly whine, complain, and murmur. But God remains faithful, merciful, and long-suffering. He does judge them eventually, but only after years of disobedience and rebellion. Yet even in judgment there is mercy. A clear illustration of this is seen in the years following the judgment at Kadesh, where the people overwhelmingly side with the spies who have given a bad report about the Promised Land (Num. 13:31–33).

Because of their refusal to trust him, because of their lack of trust in his promises, and because they choose to believe the report of the majority of the spies, God again threatens to destroy them and make a new people through Moses (14:11–12). As at the rebellion of the golden calf, Moses pleads with God to consider his reputation with the Egyptians and the other nations. Moses even goes so far as to remind God of his own words.

> Now may the Lord's strength be displayed, just as you have declared: "The LORD is slow to anger, abounding in love and forgiving sin and rebellion. Yet he does not leave the guilty unpunished; he punishes the children for the sin of the parents to the third and fourth generation." In accordance with your great love, forgive the sin of these people, just as you have pardoned them from the time they left Egypt until now. (vv. 17–19)

The Lord agrees not to destroy the rebels, but declares that "not one of the men who saw my glory and the miraculous signs I performed in Egypt and in the desert but who disobeyed me and tested me . . . will ever see the land I promised" (vv. 22–23). Instead,

> In this desert your bodies will fall—every one of you twenty years old or more who was counted in the census and who grumbled against me. Not one of you will enter the land I swore with uplifted hand to make your home, except Caleb son of

Jephunneh and Joshua son of Nun. . . . For forty years—one
year for each of the forty days you explored the land—you will
suffer for your sins and know what it is like to have me against
you. (vv. 29–30, 34)

The judgment is strong, the rhetoric harsh, and the condemnation final. These people will wander around for forty years until
the entire generation has died. But even here, God remains gracious and merciful to them. He does not destroy them immediately; he gives these rebels years of life. He does not reject them;
he continues to lead and provide for them. While they wander in
the wilderness, he gives them manna to eat and water to drink.
Moses summarizes God's care this way:

> Remember how the LORD your God led you all the way in the
> desert these forty years, to humble you and to test you in order
> to know what was in your heart, whether or not you would
> keep his commands. He humbled you, causing you to hunger
> and then feeding you with manna, which neither you nor your
> fathers had known, to teach you that man does not live on
> bread alone but on every word that comes from the mouth of
> the LORD. Your clothes did not wear out and your feet did not
> swell during these forty years. (Deut. 8:2–4)

God continues to be merciful to them, even in the midst
of judgment—not because they deserve it, but because he is a
faithful and merciful God. As Moses explains,

> The LORD did not set his affection on you and choose you
> because you were more numerous than other peoples, for you
> were the fewest of all peoples. But it was because the LORD
> loved you and kept the oath he swore to your forefathers that
> he brought you out with a mighty hand and redeemed you from
> the land of slavery, from the power of Pharaoh king of Egypt.
> Know therefore that the LORD your God is God; he is the faithful

God, keeping his covenant of love to a thousand generations of those who love him and keep his commands. (7:7–9)

The Conquest: The Judgment on the Cursed (the Canaanites)

When the people of Israel enter the land promised to the patriarchs, God's instructions to them concerning the Canaanites are clear: "Do not leave alive anything that breathes. Completely destroy them" (Deut. 20:16–17).[12] God's gracious treatment of one Canaanite family thus stands out in strong contrast.

Blessing on the Canaanite Rahab

Prior to entering the land of Canaan, Joshua sends two spies into Jericho. The spies stay in the house of a prostitute named Rahab. When word reaches the king of Jericho that Israelites are in his city, he sends a message to Rahab: "Bring out the men who came to you and entered your house, because they have come to spy out the whole land" (Josh. 2:3). Rahab, however, hides the men and sends word to the king that although she has seen the two, they have already left her house. "I don't know which way they went," she says. "Go after them quickly. You may catch up with them" (v. 5). These statements are not true; she has hidden them on the roof of her house (v. 6). She knows exactly where they are, but sends away the king's men under false pretenses. After the king's men leave her house, she explains to the spies that the citizens of Jericho fear the Lord,

12. For an excellent discussion of God's judgment on the Canaanites, see Christopher J. H. Wright, *The God I Don't Understand: Reflections on Tough Questions of Faith* (Grand Rapids: Zondervan, 2008), 76–110. This point seems crucial: "The action of Israel against the Canaanites is never placed in the category of oppression but of divine punishment operating through human agency" (p. 90). The reason the Bible gives for the judgment of the Canaanites is that they were cursed (see Gen. 9:25).

for the LORD your God is God in heaven above and on the earth below. Now then, please swear to me by the LORD that you will show kindness to my family, because I have shown kindness to you. Give me a sure sign that you will spare the lives of my father and mother, my brothers and sisters, and all that belong to them, and that you will save us from death. (vv. 11–13)

The spies promise Rahab deliverance, confirming it with an oath. As a sign of the promise and a sign to the conquering people, a scarlet cord is hung in the window through which the spies escape.[13]

This Canaanite woman is aware of the condescension of the God of Israel. She declares him to be not only the God of heaven, but of earth as well (v. 10). Her faith in God is evident by what she does and is the means by which she, like Abraham, is justified (see James 2:25). In response, God, who has given explicit instructions that the Israelites must "completely destroy" the inhabitants of the cities in the land (Deut. 20:16–17), preserves the life of Rahab the Canaanite prostitute and her extended family (Josh. 6:17).[14]

The deliverance of this family in Canaan does not establish precedent. It does not mean that all the Canaanites will be saved. It does not even mean that Canaanites who ask for mercy will receive it. Rather, Rahab's life was preserved as an act of divine grace. She received unmerited favor, as did another woman a few generations later.

Ruth

During the days of the judges, a family from Bethlehem travels to Moab. Elimelech and Naomi settle in Moab, and their two

13. There are echoes of the Passover in this deliverance. In the same way that the firstborn of Israel were preserved by blood applied to the door (Ex. 12:21–30), Rahab's family is preserved from harm by the scarlet cord hung in the window.

14. On the contrast between the salvation of the outsider Rahab and her family and the judgment of Achan and his family, see Frank Anthony Spina, *The Faith of the Outsider: Exclusion and Inclusion in the Biblical Story* (Grand Rapids: Eerdmans, 2005), 52–71.

sons marry Moabite women. The Moabites are descendants of Lot, Abraham's nephew (see Gen. 19:37). This "righteous man" (2 Peter 2:7–8) had committed incest with each of his daughters. Moab and Ammon were the two sons born to Lot by his daughters.[15] Because of their mistreatment of Israel during its journey to the land of promise, the God of Israel had declared a curse on the descendants of Moab and Ammon.

> No Ammonite or Moabite or any of his descendants may enter the assembly of the LORD, even down to the tenth generation. For they did not come to meet you with bread and water on your way when you came out of Egypt, and they hired Balaam . . . to pronounce a curse on you. (Deut. 23:3–4)

All three men in Elimelech's family die, and eventually Naomi decides to return to Bethlehem. She sends her two daughters-in-law back to their families, but Ruth refuses to go. She promises in an emotional speech to be loyal to Naomi until death (Ruth 1:16–17), and so the two women set out for the land of Israel. When they settle in Bethlehem, Ruth goes to the fields to gather grain, where she meets Boaz. Boaz knows from his first meeting of Ruth that she is from Moab (2:6). Nonetheless, he immediately begins to provide for her. Eventually he marries her, functioning as the means by which God "raises the poor from the dust," "lifts the needy from the ash heap," and "settles the barren woman in her home as a happy mother of children" (Ps. 113:7–9). In a blessing pronounced at the wedding, the elders in Israel recognize some of the significance of Ruth's redemption through Boaz: "Through the offspring the LORD gives you by this young woman, may your family be like that of Perez, whom

---

15. Lot's behavior was despicable and evil. He was enticed by his daughter through the use of wine, but he was nonetheless culpable for this behavior. But thanks be to God that his grace is greater than all sin. Peter declares both Noah and Lot, each of whom sinned through drunkenness, to be righteous men (2 Peter 2:5, 7).

Tamar bore to Judah" (Ruth 4:12). Tamar, the Canaanite wife of Judah's son, had entrapped Judah by pretending to be a prostitute in order to get him to fulfill his promise to provide a son to her (Gen. 38). In a similar way, the elders express hope that Ruth, another Canaanite woman, will receive blessing from God and be the source of blessing to the nation of Israel through Boaz, a descendant of Perez, the son of Judah and Tamar.[16]

Ruth bears Boaz a son, Obed. He is the father of Jesse, the father of David (Ruth 4:17, 22). David, of course, is Israel's second king, the recipient of a divine covenant, the "father" of the Messiah (2 Sam. 7; Ps. 89). Thus, David is a descendant of a descendant of Moab, only three generations removed from the curse. According to Deuteronomy 23:3, David should be excluded from the assembly of the Israelites. He not only is not excluded, but becomes king of Israel and father of the king who builds the temple. God not only condescends to provide food for Ruth, but provides a family for her within the nation of Israel. And through her line comes the Messiah of Israel.[17]

Conclusion

The God of Abraham, Isaac, and Jacob is faithful to his people, even in the midst of their rebellion and sin. He demonstrates to them that he is gracious, forgiving, and merciful. He does judge them, but his judgment is tempered by mercy. He condescends to care for them, provide for them, do for them what they could never do for themselves, and remain consistently faithful to them, all for the sake of his covenant promises. He will bless all nations through them.

---

16. That Boaz was also descended from Rahab (Matt. 1:5) may help to explain his compassion and concern for a foreign woman.
17. See Glenn R. Kreider, "No Moabites Allowed," DTS, June 15, 2011, http://www.dts.edu/media/play/no-moabites-allowed-kreider-glenn-r/.

5

God's Condescension in the Monarchy, Psalms, and Prophets

COLLEGE STUDENT Jennifer Thompson, twenty-two years of age, was brutally raped at knifepoint one horrifying night in 1984. During the attack, she committed every detail of her attacker's face to memory, holding on to the hope that she would be able to identify him if she survived. She escaped from her rapist and sat with a police sketch artist the next day. Ronald Cotton was arrested after Thompson picked him out of a photo lineup and again in a police lineup. She was the only eyewitness and was absolutely convinced he was the rapist. The jury believed her, convicting Cotton after deliberating for less than an hour.

Cotton was later retried and again convicted of the crime. But, after serving eleven years of his life sentence, Cotton was exonerated by a DNA test. The rapist of Jennifer Thompson was Bobby Poole, who had served time with Cotton and admitted several years earlier to another inmate that Cotton was innocent. After DNA tests established his guilt, Poole confessed to the crime and died in prison.

During his years in prison, Cotton clung to the hope that one day he would be released. Rather than harbor hatred and anger toward his accuser, he forgave her. Cotton explains the power of forgiveness: he had been "an angry man and gotten real comfortable with it. But that kind of emotion was keeping me a prisoner in my own private jail. I had to let the hate go, and learn to live and forgive."[1]

Thompson felt intense shame and guilt for accusing an innocent man and being responsible for his incarceration for over a decade. She contacted Cotton and asked if they could meet. The two eventually became friends; the turning point came when Thompson looked into the eyes of the man she had accused of a brutal attack.

> I asked Ron if he could ever forgive me. And with all the mercy in the world he took my hands and with tears in his eyes, he told me he had forgiven me a long time ago. At that moment I began to heal. Ronald taught me how to let go of all that pain; his forgiveness set me free that night. Without Ronald, I would still be shackled to that moment in time, and it would own me forever. I soon discovered that I could even forgive the man who had raped me—not because he asked me to, nor because he deserved it—but because I did not want to be a prisoner of my own hatred.[2]

This remarkable story of hope, forgiveness, and redemption is told in the book *Picking Cotton: Our Memoir of Injustice and Redemption*.[3]

Both these people found forgiveness to be liberating. Both of them had experienced injustice. Both of them were victim-

---

1. Ronald Cotton and Jennifer Thompson-Cannino, "Finding Freedom in Forgiveness," NPR, March 5, 2009, http://www.npr.org/templates/story/story.php?storyId=101469307.

2. Ibid.

3. Jennifer Thompson-Cannino and Ronald Cotton with Erin Torneo, *Picking Cotton: Our Memoir of Injustice and Redemption* (New York: St. Martins Press, 2009). Readers should be aware that the description of the brutal attack and rape is graphic and difficult to read. It could hardly be told otherwise.

ized by the rapist, Bobby Poole. Both of them came to realize that a desire for vengeance was destroying them. Through the power of the gift of forgiveness, each was set free. In giving up the right to anger and revenge, and granting the humble gift of forgiveness, each one experienced the gift of life.

The God of Abraham, Isaac, and Jacob is a God of forgiveness, as he explains when he describes himself to Moses as "the compassionate and gracious God, slow to anger, abounding in love and faithfulness, maintaining love to thousands and forgiving wickedness, rebellion and sin" (Ex. 34:6–7). He is a God who demonstrates such character by what he does. Over and over again in the stories of his interaction with the nation of Israel, he forgives and continues to care for them. Even in the midst of Israel's rejection of his rule, when they ask for a king so they can be the same as all the nations, he condescends to grant them what they want and to deal patiently and mercifully with them.

The Monarchy in Israel

The Beginning of the Monarchy

After the years of the judges, as Samuel the prophet is advancing in age, the Israelites ask him for a king. Samuel is troubled by this request, but God reassures him that the people are rejecting not Samuel, but rather God's rule over them (1 Sam. 8:7). In fact, the Lord declares, they have rejected his rule "from the day I brought them up out of Egypt until this day, forsaking me and serving other gods" (v. 8). God, through Samuel, warns them that a king will take their sons and daughters, a tithe of their crops and possessions, and their freedom (vv. 10–18). But they persist in their request. Their desire to be "like all the other nations" (v. 20) makes them deaf and blind to the warnings of God.

God gives them what they want, even though it will not be good for them; condescension sometimes acts this way.[4] He gives them Saul, fills him with the Holy Spirit, and empowers him to lead the nation (10:9–10). Eventually God rejects Saul because of his disobedience (15:26–29) and chooses David, the youngest son of Jesse, as his replacement (16:1–13). After a period of transition, during which Saul repeatedly tries to kill David, Saul dies; David is anointed king at Hebron (2 Sam. 2:4).

The Kingdom under David

Having defeated his enemies, David conceives a plan to build a house for the ark of God (2 Sam. 7:2). He consults Nathan the prophet, who grants his permission. Within hours, the word of the Lord corrects Nathan, tells him that God rejects David's offer, and instead promises David an eternal kingdom. In short, God rejects the "house" that David wants to build for him, but grants David an eternal "house," putting the promise in the form of a covenant (Ps. 89:3).[5]

In making this covenant with David, God condescends to grant him a gracious gift and obligate himself to mediate his rule over his creation through a Davidic king. "I will establish a house for you," the Lord declares. "I will raise up your offspring to succeed you. . . . I will establish the throne of his kingdom forever" (2 Sam. 7:11–13). In contrast to the short-lived dynasty of Saul, David's dynasty will be eternal: "My love will never be taken away from [David's son], as I took it away from Saul, whom I removed from before you. Your house and your kingdom will endure forever before me; your throne will be

4. God had promised them a king (Gen. 49:10), but not now and not for the reason they give.
5. David offers to build a house for the Lord; the Lord instead builds a house for him. The former is a building, a temple. The latter is a monarchy, a kingdom that will endure forever (2 Sam. 7:16). This arrangement is not called a covenant in chapter 7, but it is in Psalm 89:3.

established forever" (vv. 15–16). This covenant has been established to last as long as the heavens endure (Ps. 89:29), like the sun and the moon (Ps. 89:36–37). Even though the Israelites reject God, fail to keep the covenant he made with them at Sinai, and even defile their king, God's promises to David will endure (Ps. 89:38–52). God has again linked his plan for his creation to this people, who have demonstrated that they will give God many opportunities to forgive them. His selection of them is dependent, not on their repeated faithfulness, but on his condescending loyalty.

Upon hearing the word of the Lord through Nathan, David recognizes God's condescension and grace toward him, praying,

> Who am I, O Sovereign LORD, and what is my family, that you have brought me this far? And as if this were not enough in your sight, O Sovereign LORD, you have also spoken about the future of the house of your servant. Is this your usual way of dealing with man, O Sovereign LORD? (2 Sam. 7:18–19)

This is exactly the way God commonly deals with humanity, in mercy and grace, not according to what they deserve. God seems to take pleasure in choosing people such as David, who was tending his father's sheep when God called him, and using them to accomplish his plan in the world.

But as for the temple, David will not be the one to build it. David later explains the reason for God's rejection of his offer: "This word of the LORD came to me: 'You have shed much blood and have fought many wars. You are not to build a house for my Name, because you have shed much blood on the earth'" (1 Chron. 22:8). Later he says it again: "But God said to me, 'You are not to build a house for my Name, because you are a warrior and have shed blood'" (28:3). David's violence was offensive to God and made him unsuitable to construct the temple.[6]

The Kingdom under Solomon

Solomon, David's son and successor as king, begins to build the temple 480 years after the exodus (1 Kings 6:1) and completes it seven years later (6:38).[7] Upon its completion, the ark is brought into the furnished building, and Solomon offers a prayer of dedication. In this prayer, Solomon affirms God's condescension to his people, to David, to Solomon, and to the temple he built.

> O Lord, God of Israel, there is no God like you in heaven above or on earth below—you who keep your covenant of love with your servants who continue wholeheartedly in your way. You have kept your promise to your servant David my father; with your mouth you have promised and with your hand you have fulfilled it—as it is today. . . .
>
> But will God really dwell on earth? The heavens, even the highest heaven, cannot contain you. How much less this temple I have built! Yet give attention to your servant's prayer and his plea for mercy, O Lord my God. Hear the cry and the prayer that your servant is praying in your presence this day. May your eyes be open toward this temple night and day, this place of which you said, "My Name shall be there," so that you will hear the prayer your servant prays toward this place. Hear the supplication of your servant and of your people Israel when

---

6. It could be David's role as commander of the armies of Israel that is in view. It is more likely David's vengeful and vindictive use of violence that offends God. See, for example, his anger toward Nabal (1 Sam. 25:22), or his annihilation of the Philistines ("he did not leave a man or woman alive, but took sheep and cattle, donkeys and camels, and clothes," 1 Sam. 27:9), or, most disturbing, his treatment of the Moabites (2 Sam. 8:2–4). What makes the latter so disconcerting is that David himself was a descendant of Moab through his great-grandmother Ruth.

7. Solomon's palace took thirteen years to build (1 Kings 7:1), perhaps partly because it was much larger than the temple (see 6:2; 7:2).

they pray toward this place. Hear from heaven, your dwelling place, and when you hear, forgive. (8:23–24, 27–30)

Solomon affirms the God of Israel in the heavens. He cannot be contained in a building on earth. Yet God condescends to meet his people at this place and, in some sense, makes his dwelling in that temple. The temple does not contain God, but God does make the temple his dwelling place. In so doing, God has condescended to establish his residence in Jerusalem, in anticipation of the eternal state, when God will live on the earth in the New Jerusalem (Rev. 21:2).

The Lord appears to Solomon.[8] He does actually come down from heaven to meet with this human king. The Lord says, "I have heard the prayer and plea you have made before me; I have consecrated this temple, which you have built, by putting my Name there forever. My eyes and my heart will always be there" (1 Kings 9:3). Yet the Lord also reminds Solomon of his responsibility to obey God; otherwise,

I will cut off Israel from the land I have given them and will reject this temple I have consecrated for my Name. Israel will then become a byword and an object of ridicule among all peoples. And though this temple is now imposing, all who pass by will be appalled and will scoff. (vv. 7–8)

Solomon's story, which begins so well, ends in tragedy. This wisest man who ever lived (see 3:12) becomes a fool. He accumulates many foreign wives—seven hundred of royal birth and three hundred concubines—"and his wives led him astray" (11:3). He follows his wives in their worship of foreign gods. He does "evil in the eyes of the LORD"; he does not "follow the LORD

8. This is the second time in Scripture that God appears to Solomon. The first time was at the beginning of his reign, when God promised him wisdom, riches, and, if he walked in obedience to God, long life (1 Kings 3:12–14).

completely, as David his father had done" (v. 6). He even builds places of worship to other gods (vv. 7–8).[9] This angers the Lord, who says to Solomon,

> Since this is your attitude and you have not kept my covenant and my decrees, which I commanded you, I will most certainly tear the kingdom away from you and give it to one of your subordinates. Nevertheless, for the sake of David your father, I will not do it during your lifetime. I will tear it out of the hand of your son. Yet I will not tear the whole kingdom from him, but will give him one tribe for the sake of David my servant and for the sake of Jerusalem, which I have chosen. (vv. 11–13)

Having chosen to bless David and to make Jerusalem his dwelling place, God has obligated himself to bless. Even Solomon's folly will not cause God to change his mind. For the sake of David, Solomon and the Israelites will continue to receive blessing. God will eventually judge this rebellious people and send them into exile, but even then he preserves a remnant because of his promise to David. God's faithfulness to his word, his loyalty to David, and his gracious and merciful character result in great blessing on Solomon and on the rebellious kings that follow him.

God's Condescension through Two Prophets

The kings that follow Solomon, with several notable exceptions, fail to obey God. Instead, most of them do "evil in the eyes of the LORD" (1 Kings 15:26). Yet, in the midst of this succession of evil, there are remarkable cases of divine grace, of God's condescension to specific people—several of whom were not even Israelites.

9. It is more than a little ironic that David is forbidden to build the temple because of his violent past, while his son Solomon is chosen to be the builder even though he becomes an idolater. The only explanation for the choice of Solomon seems to be God's grace. Surely idolatry is not less offensive to God than violence.

Ahab reigns over Israel for twenty-two years, and he does "more evil in the eyes of the LORD than any of those before him" (16:30). He does "more to provoke the LORD, the God of Israel, to anger than did all the kings of Israel before him" (16:33). During Ahab's reign, God decrees a famine through the word of the prophet Elijah. God miraculously preserves his prophet by sending ravens to feed him by a brook east of the Jordan (17:5–6). When the brook dries up, the LORD sends Elijah to Zarephath of Sidon, to the home of a widow (v. 9), in the territory ruled by the father of Ahab's wife, Jezebel (see 16:31). During the years of the famine, the God of Israel provides this Sidonian widow with an endless supply of flour and oil. When the woman's son dies, Elijah raises him from the dead (17:7–24).

Similarly, under Joram, Ahab's son, God provides for two widows through the prophet Elisha. In one case, a prophet dies and his widow is unable to pay his creditors. Her sons are about to be sold into slavery. Elisha asks her to pour the little oil she has left into as many empty jars as she can find. The oil multiplies and provides enough income to satisfy her debts (2 Kings 4:1–7). Another woman, from Shunem, gives birth to a son, who is taken ill and dies. Elisha raises him from the dead (vv. 8–37). Like Elijah, Elisha is an instrument of God's grace in the midst of God's judgment on Israel.

But perhaps the most striking illustration of the compassion of the God of Israel in the era of the prophet Elisha is found in the story of Naaman. The commander of the army of Aram, Naaman is successful because of the blessing of the Lord (2 Kings 5:1).[10] But he is not a believer in the God of Israel. He is, rather, the leader of Israel's enemy (v. 2).

Naaman gave a young, unnamed Israelite girl to his wife to be her servant. When he contracts leprosy, this young girl

10. God blesses the leader of the enemy of Israel. As a means of judging his people, God blesses their oppressor.

tells her mistress, "If only my master would see the prophet who is in Samaria! He would cure him of his leprosy" (v. 3). This is a remarkable act of faith and compassion. This servant girl, who appears to be a victim of human trafficking, becomes a means of healing and mercy to her captor.[11] Rather than rejoicing in his suffering and looking forward to his demise, she acts redemptively, selflessly, and sacrificially. She forgives the man who is responsible for her enslavement and acts to preserve his life.

Naaman trusts the word of this servant girl.[12] He travels to Israel, arrives at Elisha's house, and receives instructions through a messenger that he will be healed if he washes seven times in the Jordan (vv. 4–10). Reluctant to submit to this requirement, he at first refuses, but eventually follows the advice of his servants, washes in the Jordan, and is cleansed of leprosy. Healing comes to Naaman, the enemy of Israel, as a gracious gift of God.

Naaman then returns to Elisha and offers to pay him. The prophet refuses to accept payment. But after Naaman leaves, the prophet's servant, Gehazi, runs after him and falsely claims that Elisha has changed his mind. When Gehazi returns to Elisha, the prophet rebukes him and strikes him with leprosy for his deception and dishonesty.[13]

These stories of God's blessing of Gentiles are used by Jesus to rebuke the Jews of his day. In response to the request of the

11. Human trafficking remains a problem in our day. One organization working to bring it to an end is Free the Captives, LLC, founded by Julie Waters. See http://www.freethecaptiveshouston.com.

12. Apparently this unnamed young woman has demonstrated that she is trustworthy by her service to Naaman's household.

13. Gehazi and his descendants forever were struck with Naaman's leprosy (2 Kings 5:27). Just as Achan's family shared in the guilt of his sin (Josh. 7), so Gehazi's family shared in his. These two stories illustrate that God "punishes the children and their children for the sin of the fathers" (Ex. 34:7). In both stories, a Gentile family receives the blessing of God while an Israelite family suffers. See Frank Anthony Spina, *The Faith of the Outsider: Exclusion and Inclusion in the Biblical Story* (Grand Rapids: Eerdmans, 2005), 52–93.

crowd in Nazareth—"Do here in your hometown what we have heard that you did in Capernaum" (Luke 4:23)—Jesus says,

> I tell you the truth, . . . no prophet is accepted in his hometown. I assure you that there were many widows in Israel in Elijah's time, when the sky was shut for three and a half years and there was a severe famine throughout the land. Yet Elijah was not sent to any of them, but to a widow in Zarephath in the region of Sidon. And there were many in Israel with leprosy in the time of Elisha the prophet, yet not one of them was cleansed—only Naaman the Syrian. (vv. 24–27)

When they hear this, the crowd is furious and tries to kill Jesus, but he walks through the crowd and goes on his way (vv. 28–30). In short, according to Jesus, God intentionally went outside of Israel in the days of Elijah and Elisha to bless Gentiles while, within the land of Israel, widows and lepers suffered and died without relief. God is God of the nations, the God who condescends to help the widows and the sick. As Jesus makes clear, and as extensive human experience verifies, God does not always help every widow nor heal every sick person. But he does condescend to help some, and to withhold blessing from some while showering blessing on others is his sovereign right.

God's Condescension in the Psalms: A Response of Worship

In the Psalms, the hymnbook of Israel, poets often worship God for his condescension. David recognizes that the transcendent Creator of the universe has condescended to care for his creatures: "O LORD, our Lord, how majestic is your name in all the earth! You have set your glory above the heavens. From the lips of children and infants you have ordained praise" (Ps. 8:1–2). Although God is majestic, with glory in the heavens, he has condescended to make his majestic name known on the earth, and this is done through the lips of children and infants. David then continues with a worshipful response.

> When I consider your heavens,
>   the work of your fingers,
> the moon and the stars,
>   which you have set in place,
> what is man that you are mindful of him,
>   the son of man that you care for him?
> You made him a little lower than the heavenly beings
>   and crowned him with glory and honor. (vv. 3–5)

But more than that,

> You made him ruler over the works of your hands;
>   you put everything under his feet:
> all flocks and herds,
>   and the beasts of the field,
> the birds of the air,
>   and the fish of the sea,
>   all that swim the paths of the seas. (vv. 6–8)

The Creator has condescended to put humans in charge of the other creatures he created (see Gen. 1:26–28), and it is through those who bear his image that his name is made majestic in all the earth (Ps. 8:1, 9).

According to several psalms, the Creator of the universe condescends to care for the helpless and hopeless. In Psalm 12, David quotes God as saying, "Because of the oppression of the weak and the groaning of the needy, I will now arise. . . . I will protect them from those who malign them" (v. 5). David writes in Psalm 34, "This poor man called, and the LORD heard him; he saved him from all his troubles" (v. 6). And in Psalm 41 he says,

Blessed is he who has regard for the weak;
 the LORD delivers him in times of trouble.
The LORD will protect him and preserve his life;
 he will bless him in the land
 and not surrender him to the desire of his foes.
The LORD will sustain him on his sickbed
 and restore him from his bed of illness. (vv. 1–3)

David describes God's condescension to deliver him in his time
of need.[14] David has experienced God's care for him personally.

In my distress I called to the LORD;
 I cried to my God for help.
From his temple he heard my voice;
 my cry came before him, into his ears. . . .
He parted the heavens and came down;
 dark clouds were under his feet. . . .
He reached down from on high and took hold of me;
 he drew me out of deep waters. . . .
He brought me out into a spacious place;
 he rescued me because he delighted in me. (18:6, 9, 16, 19)

David says to his God, "You stoop down to make me great" (v. 35).
God's condescension to come to earth, care for David, and lift
him up is the basis of his praise.

 Psalm 113 praises the name of the Lord "from the rising of
the sun to the place where it sets" (v. 3). The psalmist describes
the Lord as "exalted over all the nations, his glory above the
heavens" (v. 4). He then asks a rhetorical question: "Who is like
the LORD our God, the One who sits enthroned on high, who
stoops down to look on the heavens and the earth?" (vv. 5–6).

 In Psalm 118, the psalmist expresses his confidence that the
Lord is present with him.

---

14. See also the comparison of the Lord to a shepherd in Psalm 23.

> In my anguish I cried to the LORD,
>   and he answered by setting me free.
> The LORD is with me; I will not be afraid.
>   What can man do to me?
> The LORD is with me; he is my helper.
>   I will look in triumph on my enemies.
> It is better to take refuge in the LORD
>   than to trust in man. (vv. 5–8)

That the Lord is the psalmist's helper clearly does not indicate his inferiority to the human writer, for this helper is infinitely superior to the one in need. God condescends to help one who is under attack.

Finally, in Psalm 144, David pleads with God to act on his behalf, to come to his aid.

> Part your heavens, O LORD, and come down;
>   touch the mountains, so that they smoke.
> Send forth lightning and scatter the enemies;
>   shoot your arrows and rout them.
> Reach down your hand from on high;
>   deliver me and rescue me
> from the mighty waters,
>   from the hands of foreigners
> whose mouths are full of lies,
>   whose right hands are deceitful. (vv. 5–8)

God's Condescension in the Prophets: Hope for the Future Because of God's Faithfulness

A prophet is one who speaks for God (Deut. 18:17–20). God chooses to speak through prophets not out of an inability to speak for himself (see Gen. 1). In choosing to speak through prophets, he entrusts to these human spokesmen his message to humanity in an act of condescension. This is what the Israelites requested at Sinai (Deut. 5:22–29). He mediates his message through human spokesmen, risking that some might speak presumptuously, misleading his people or even leading them away from worship of the true God.

The Call of the Prophets

Several of the prophets of Israel describe their call to ministry in a way that emphasizes divine condescension. When the word of the Lord comes to Jeremiah, he hears these words: "Before I formed you in the womb I knew you, before you were born I set you apart; I appointed you as a prophet to the nations" (Jer. 1:5). When Jeremiah objects, the Lord says to him, "You must go to everyone I send you to and say whatever I command you. Do not be afraid of them, for I am with you and will rescue you" (vv. 7–8). Then the Lord extends his hand to touch the mouth of the prophet, saying, "Now, I have put my words in your mouth" (v. 9). Jeremiah's call to speak for God is accompanied by an appearance of God and the intimate act of God's touching his mouth.

The prophet Isaiah describes a vision of the Lord seated on a throne. Isaiah is in the temple in Jerusalem when he sees the highly exalted Lord. The train of his robe fills the temple (Isa. 6:1), and Isaiah hears the angelic beings cry, "Holy, holy, holy is the LORD Almighty; the whole earth is full of his glory" (v. 3). Then Isaiah says, "The doorposts and thresholds shook and the temple was filled with smoke" (v. 4). Just as God's presence filled the tabernacle (Ex. 40:34–38), so the cloud of the Lord's presence is visible to Isaiah in the temple.

The sovereign and glorious Creator of the universe condescends to come to earth and make himself visible to the prophet Isaiah. In so doing, he veils himself to make himself visible, diminishing his glory to avoid incinerating Isaiah in his presence (see Ex. 33:20), and he humbles himself to come to the earth to call Isaiah into his service.

God's glory is visible, and his presence is terrifying to Isaiah. The prophet recognizes his sinfulness and that of his people and expresses his uncleanness in the presence of the King, the Lord Almighty. From the presence of the Lord, a seraph brings a live coal and cleanses Isaiah's mouth. His guilt is thereby taken away, and his sin is atoned for. Then Isaiah hears the call of God and is commissioned for a prophetic ministry (Isa. 6:6–7).

That God would condescend to come into Isaiah's world, meet him in the temple, forgive his sin, take away his uncleanness, and then call him into his service, evidences the degree to which God humbles himself to his creation. He does not call Isaiah up to where he is; he comes to Isaiah's world, to the very place where Isaiah met with the people to worship God. He chooses a sinful man, an unclean man, who lives in the midst of an unclean people. He cleanses him from his uncleanness. Then he condescends to use this human voice to speak his message to the people.

Later this prophet explicitly affirms that God has condescended to care for the weak and lowly: "For this is what the high and lofty One says—he who lives forever, whose name is holy: I live in a high and holy place, but also with him who is contrite and lowly in spirit, to revive the spirit of the lowly and to revive the heart of the contrite" (57:15). The Lord is the high and lofty one. There is none who can compare to him. He is eternal and holy and lives in a high and holy place. He is the transcendent one, separated from his creation. He dwells in unapproachable light (1 Tim. 6:16). But this one is also with any who are contrite and lowly in spirit. He is present with the humble and lowly ones. He condescends to come near to the lowest of the low. He does so without ceasing to be the transcendent and holy one. He does so without ceasing to be the elevated one. The God of Israel is a deity of condescension.

Here the reason for this humility of God is given as well. It is to revive the spirit of the lowly and the heart of the contrite. God comes to the aid of the contrite and needy in order to bring them life and health, to elevate them to where he is. He elevates, not from a distance, but by coming to them. This is a clear declaration of God's intention to condescend to his creatures, which has been seen in practice over and over again in the biblical story.

The New Covenant and the Hope of the Eternal Kingdom

In Jeremiah 31, God promises at some time in the future to make a new covenant with his people, the house of Israel and the house of Judah (v. 31). This future new covenant is contrasted with the covenant "made with their forefathers when I took them by the hand to lead them out of Egypt" (v. 32). That covenant, the Sinaitic or Mosaic covenant, was broken by the people; it was a fallible covenant with a fault (see Heb. 8:7–8). The new covenant will replace the old covenant.

This new covenant will include four major provisions: the internalization of the law of God ("I will put my law in their minds and write it on their hearts"), an intimate relationship between God and his people ("I will be their God, and they will be my people"), universal knowledge of God ("no longer will a man teach his neighbor, or a man his brother, saying, 'Know the LORD,' because they will all know me, from the least of them to the greatest"), and the removal of sin ("I will forgive their wickedness and will remember their sins no more") (Jer. 31:33–34). In short, God promises that in some future eschatological era, he will again condescend to enter into a covenantal relationship with his people through an eternal and unbreakable covenant.

This hope, that one day God will make things right, particularly solving the problem of sin and its effects, provides comfort, encouragement, and reason for living to the people of God. This eschatological hope will be a gracious gift of God, totally undeserved and unmerited. Jeremiah explains, "The people of Israel and Judah have done nothing but evil in my sight from their youth; indeed, the people of Israel have done nothing but provoke me with what their hands have made, declares the LORD" (32:30). He continues with a rehearsal of their idolatry; nevertheless, the Lord declares,

> I will surely gather them from all the lands where I banish them in my furious anger and great wrath; I will bring them back to this place and let them live in safety. They will be my people, and I will be their God. I will give them singleness of heart and action, so that they will always fear me for their own good and the good of their children after them. I will make an everlasting covenant with them: I will never stop doing good to them, and I will inspire them to fear me, so that they will never turn away from me. I will rejoice in doing them good and I will assuredly plant them in this land with all my heart and soul. (32:37–41)

God likewise rebukes his people through the prophet Ezekiel for their idolatry and rebellion. Their conduct is reprehensible to him; they profane God's name everywhere they go, and their exile from the land is a further profanation of that name (Ezek. 36:16–23). So their promised return to the land is not a result of their righteousness, but a gracious gift of God. God promises to cleanse them ("I will sprinkle clean water on you, and you will be clean"—v. 25), to give them a new heart and a new spirit (v. 26), and to "increase the fruit of the trees and the crops of the field" for them (v. 30). Then, after God has done this, they will repent of their sins and return to him (v. 31). Ezekiel's oracle concludes,

> I will make a covenant of peace with them; it will be an everlasting covenant. I will establish them and increase their numbers, and I will put my sanctuary among them forever. My dwelling place will be with them; I will be their God, and they will be my people. (37:26–27)

On the island of Patmos, the apostle John also hears this promise of God's condescension to dwell eternally with his people:

> Now the dwelling of God is with men, and he will live with them. They will be his people, and God himself will be with them and be their God. He will wipe every tear from their eyes. There will be no more death or mourning or crying or pain, for the old order of things has passed away. (Rev. 21:3–4)

The promise that God will make his dwelling with his people on earth is the eschatological hope of the people of faith. When that happens, the word of the one seated on the throne will be realized on earth: "I am making everything new!" (v. 5).

Elijah Must Come before the New Heaven and the New Earth

But before this day will come, there will be the day of the Lord, a day of judgment. The Hebrew Scriptures conclude with the reminder that the day of the Lord's judgment is coming (Mal. 4:1). The final words in the Old Testament canon promise,

> See, I will send you the prophet Elijah before that great and dreadful day of the LORD comes. He will turn the hearts of the fathers to their children, and the hearts of the children to their fathers; or else I will come and strike the land with a curse. (vv. 5–6)

That day will be a day of justice, darkness, death, and destruction (Amos 5:6–20). It will be a day of calamity (Hab. 3:16), of darkness, gloom, clouds, and blackness (Joel 2:2). It will be a day of destruction of the wicked and vindication of the righteous (Mal. 4:2–3). The new creation is coming, but before it does there will be a day of judgment. Before that day, however, will come one identified as the prophet Elijah. His message will be one of repentance, calling the people to "remember the law of my servant Moses, the decrees and laws I gave him at Horeb for all Israel" (v. 4).

As we turn the pages of Scripture to the New Testament, we meet John the Baptist, who is identified as Elijah. His birth and the coming of the Messiah are the subject of the next chapter.

6

THE EVERLASTING INCARNATION OF THE ETERNAL SON

I GREW UP in a Christian home, the first child of devout, churchgoing, Christian parents. From a young age, I was in Sunday school and worship services nearly every Sunday morning. I have vivid and mostly pleasant memories of those years. My testimony is similar to Philip Yancey's: "I first got acquainted with Jesus when I was a child, singing 'Jesus Loves Me' in Sunday school, addressing bedtime prayers to 'Dear Lord Jesus,' watching Bible Club teachers move cutout figures across a flannel board. I associated Jesus with Kool-Aid and sugar cookies and gold stars for attendance."[1]

Active involvement in the community of faith was valued in our home, and I am grateful for that heritage. Yet, as I reflect on those and subsequent years, I now see that my understanding of Christianity was more as a religion of morality than the amazing story of a God who became human, while remaining fully divine, in order to redeem his creation.[2] I remember being

1. Philip Yancey, *The Jesus I Never Knew* (Grand Rapids: Zondervan, 1995), 13.
2. It would require a great deal more space than I have to investigate the reasons for this misunderstanding. It is also not my intention to be overly critical of my Sunday

taught what to do, to choose to do good things and avoid bad things. I also recall being taught to avoid bad people.[3] Somehow I missed the incredible wonder of the mystery of incarnation, of God becoming one of us, of the transcendent God condescending to become a creature out of his great love for us (Eph. 2:4). As a result, my worship was deficient, and my view of ministry was truncated. Coming to understand how the doctrine of the incarnation impacts all of life and ministry is transforming me.

The Birth and Childhood of Jesus

There is limited biblical revelation of the childhood of Jesus. Only Matthew and Luke record his birth, and only Luke records an event that occurred when Jesus was twelve years old—the only inspired glimpse into his life between his infancy and his public ministry.

Each gospel birth narrative emphasizes different aspects of the incarnation. Matthew begins with a genealogy, narrates the conception and birth with a focus on Joseph, relates the coming of the magi some time later, and concludes with the family's flight to Egypt because of Herod's hatred and anger. Luke begins with two angelic announcements, one to Zechariah predicting the birth of John, and the other to Mary announcing the birth of Jesus. Then he tells the stories of these two births, first of John and then of Jesus. Then Luke relates two stories of Jesus' appearances in the temple, the first when he was eight days old and the second when he was twelve years old. In Luke's gospel, the genealogy of Jesus follows the introduction of the ministry of John the Baptist and the baptism of Jesus.

---

school teachers and other church leaders. My misunderstandings might not have been due to their failure to teach as much as to my failure to learn.

3. This had huge implications for my view of mission and ministry. It is hard to reach those who do not yet know the Savior by avoiding contact with them.

The Two Genealogies

The genealogies of Jesus clearly affirm his humanity.[4] In the incarnation, Jesus adds humanity to his divinity. Divinity is eternal; humanity has a beginning. An eternal being does not have a genealogy.

Jesus is the son of David (see Rom. 1:3) and the seed of Abraham (see Gal. 3:16); the genealogies establish this lineage. The ordinariness of his family tree is made clear, particularly in Matthew's genealogy. Rather than ignoring the disreputable characters in Jesus' heritage, Matthew names them. These include Tamar, the Canaanite woman who pretended to be a prostitute to entice Judah to keep his promise (Gen. 38); Rahab, another Canaanite woman with prostitution in her background, who negotiated the salvation of her family during the conquest of Jericho (Josh. 2); and Ruth, the Moabite who joined the family by marrying Boaz (Ruth 4). Another woman is mentioned, although her name is not given. Instead, Bathsheba is called "Uriah's wife" (Matt. 1:6; see also 2 Sam. 11–12). The reader recalls the sordid details of David's adultery, deception, murder, and attempted cover-up. Throughout that story, Uriah the Hittite manifests righteous behavior, while the unrighteousness of God's chosen and covenanted king of Israel is made clearer by contrast.

When Matthew names these characters, those familiar with their stories remember the shameful details. Perhaps more importantly, we remember that in all of these stories, God shows his grace and mercy to people who are outside the community of faith. These sinners who receive divine grace make it into the community of faith. These women are part of Jesus' family.

4. On the two genealogies, see D. S. Huffman, "Genealogy," in *Dictionary of Jesus and the Gospels*, ed. Joel B. Green and Scot McKnight (Downers Grove, IL: InterVarsity Press, 1992), 253–59. Huffman discusses the problem of the discrepancies between the two genealogies and concludes, "A final solution to the intricate issues involved in comparing the two lists may never be found, but enough is known to show that the apparent discrepancies are not insoluble" (p. 258).

This child comes from a long line of unlovely people. When he comes to earth, when he becomes human, he identifies with these outcasts in order to save those who are like them (see Heb. 2).

The Birth of Jesus in Matthew

The Virgin Birth. According to Matthew, Joseph and Mary are pledged to be married, but prior to their union Mary is "found to be with child through the Holy Spirit" (Matt. 1:18). Joseph, of course, knows that the baby is not his. Before Joseph is able to "divorce [Mary] quietly" (v. 19), an angel appears to him and tells him that the child is "from the Holy Spirit" and that he should marry Mary (v. 20). This child, the angel says, is to be named Jesus, "because he will save his people from their sins" (v. 21)—people like those named in his genealogy.

In the same way that Mary is chosen to bear the child, Joseph is selected to be his father. Unlike Mary, the boy's biological mother, Joseph is not his biological father. He is, nonetheless, Jesus' father.[5] Similar to Abraham, who did not name either of his first two sons (Gen. 16:11, 15; 17:19; 21:3), Joseph will not name Jesus (Matt. 1:21, 25; Luke 1:31). The heavenly Father of Jesus names his Son. Joseph willingly obeys—evidence that he is a righteous man (Matt. 1:19).

Matthew declares this virgin birth to be the fulfillment of prophecy and quotes from the prophecy of Isaiah: "'The virgin will be with child and will give birth to a son, and they will call him Immanuel'—which means, 'God with us'" (1:23; see also Isa. 7:14).[6] This child is not simply the son of Mary

---

5. That Joseph is not the biological father of Jesus does not make his fatherhood less significant. Joseph is Jesus' father, chosen by God to be the one to raise his son. Several conversations with parents of adopted children have helped me to see the importance of not using such demeaning language as "Joseph was not the real father of Jesus."

6. Like many prophecies, this one had a fulfillment both in Isaiah's day and in the future. See Walter C. Kaiser Jr., *The Messiah in the Old Testament* (Grand Rapids: Zondervan, 1995), 158–62. Kaiser explains, "Given the frequency with which OT and

and Joseph. He is the Son of God. He is God with us. He is Immanuel.

Jesus is not merely a sign that God is with us; he actually is God with us, the God who becomes human. A higher degree of condescension cannot even be conceived. The Creator of the universe has become a creature.

Matthew summarizes the birth of Jesus with the simple statement, "[Joseph] had no union with her until she gave birth to a son. And he gave him the name Jesus" (Matt. 1:25). Joseph, the righteous man, honors the Lord—not only by giving the child this name in obedience to the angel's instruction, but also by preserving the virginity of Jesus' mother.

The Visit of the Magi. Some time later, magi come from the east to Jerusalem to worship the child (2:1–2).[7] They have seen a star in the east and somehow know this means the king of the Jews has been born. The appearance of these magi disturbs Herod. He asks the chief priests and teachers of the law where the Christ is to be born (v. 4).[8] They are apparently unaware of Jesus' birth, because rather than tell Herod where the child is, they quote the prophet Micah's promise that the Messiah would be born in Bethlehem (v. 6; see also Mic. 5:2). The magi find the child and worship him (Matt. 2:11).

The king of the Jews is born in fulfillment of biblical prophecy, and the event is almost completely overlooked. The leaders

NT prophecy have both a now and a not-yet aspect to their predictions, Ahaz is granted evidence of this sign in his own day, even though the full impact of all that God has in mind will not be realized until the Messiah himself is born in a unique manner in fulfillment of this passage" (p. 160).

7. Tony Maalouf, *Arabs in the Shadow of Israel* (Grand Rapids: Kregel, 2003), 183–218, argues that the magi were from Persia and that the star was a precursor of God's presence on earth in the kingdom.

8. Herod does not ask where the Messiah has been born, but where he is to be born. That the chief priests and teachers of the law are unaware that Jesus has been born seems clear; they do not declare that the child has been born in Bethlehem.

of Israel, the experts in the Old Testament Scriptures, miss this significant event that begins to fulfill all the expectations of the prophets. When the Creator humbles himself to become a human, when the invisible God takes on flesh and blood, he does so without a great deal of fanfare or attention.[9]

The apostle John says, "He was in the world, and though the world was made through him, the world did not recognize him. He came to that which was his own, but his own did not receive him" (John 1:10–11).[10] When the Creator becomes a creature, his deity is so well hidden, so disguised, that the creatures do not recognize him. In a manger in a small town, the Creator of the universe condescends to become a creature and come into his world. And most of creation misses it.

But some do recognize him, such as the magi who make a long pilgrimage from the east. Called by God through special revelation, these Gentiles leave their homeland to make a long and dangerous journey to worship this boy who would be king. When God warns them that the child's life will be at risk if they return to Herod, they return to their country by another route (Matt. 2:12), demonstrating again their faith in the revealed word of God and in God himself.

How will God respond to Herod's threat to Jesus? Rather than destroy Herod or otherwise use power against him, God chooses a less active or confrontational approach. As he did prior to the birth of the child, the angelic messenger again appears to Joseph and tells him to flee to Egypt with his family. God waits for Herod to die before bringing his Son back to Israel. This passive approach results in the death of many boys "two years old and under" in Bethlehem (v. 16). Destroying the wicked king

9. It might seem odd that no one has apparently heard the message of the shepherds (Luke 2). We will return to this question later.

10. The "world" is the creation. The Creator came to his creation, and the creation did not recognize him. Similarly, "his own" is the world that he made, including the creatures who inhabit it.

Herod would have allowed Jesus to grow up in Bethlehem or even in Nazareth, not to mention saving the lives of many babies in Bethlehem, but God had a different plan.[11]

The Infancy Narrative in the Gospel of Luke

The Angelic Announcements. Luke's infancy narrative begins with an angelic announcement to a priest named Zechariah. Although both Zechariah and his wife, Elizabeth, are righteous, she is barren.[12] Even at their advanced age, they continue to pray for a child. The angel appears to Zechariah and tells him that his prayer has been heard—Elizabeth will bear him a son (Luke 1:11–13). Named John by God, he will be great and will bring many people back to the Lord their God. The angel declares, "He will go on before the Lord, in the spirit and power of Elijah, to turn the hearts of the fathers to their children and the disobedient to the wisdom of the righteous" (v. 17). John will be Elijah, the one promised by the prophet Malachi (Mal. 4:5–6).

Zechariah finds this message unbelievable, due to his age and that of his wife (Luke 1:18).[13] The angel, Gabriel, gives him a sign to confirm the message.[14] Zechariah will be unable to speak until the day the child is born (vv. 19–20). Yet the plan of

11. God's patience almost always has both positive and negative effects. He is patient, "not wanting anyone to perish, but everyone to come to repentance" (2 Peter 3:9), resulting in the salvation of some while the wicked prosper and continue to thrive in their rebellion.

12. Both Zechariah and Elizabeth are descendants of Aaron, the brother of Moses and the first high priest of Israel (Luke 1:5).

13. On the one hand, Zechariah's incredulity is understandable. Although we do not know his exact age, it is implied that he and Elizabeth are beyond childbearing age. But he surely knows that the God of Abraham, Isaac, and Jacob has a history of bringing life out of death, of giving offspring to barren women and to those beyond childbearing age.

14. In addition, the sign appears to be a judgment on Zechariah's unbelief. The angel tells him, "And now you will be silent and not able to speak until the day this happens, because you did not believe my words, which will come true at their proper time" (Luke 1:20).

God still requires this righteous man and woman to act upon their faith, since this child is not to be "virgin born."[15] The child is conceived, and Elizabeth recognizes this as a sign of divine favor (v. 25).

In the sixth month of Elizabeth's pregnancy, the angel appears to Mary, a virgin pledged to be married to Joseph, a descendant of David (v. 27).[16] Mary hears the incredible news that she will bear a son who will be named Jesus (v. 31). The angel's message concludes, "He will be great and will be called the Son of the Most High. The Lord God will give him the throne of his father David, and he will reign over the house of Jacob forever" (v. 33).

In language very similar to Zechariah's, Mary asks, "How will this be . . . since I am a virgin?" (v. 34).[17] Mary apparently understands that this child will not be conceived in the normal way, that the conception will occur prior to her marriage while she remains a virgin. Mary knows this is not the normal way things work.

As he did with Zechariah, the angel gives Mary an explanation and a sign:[18]

> The Holy Spirit will come upon you, and the power of the Most High will overshadow you. So the holy one to be born will be called the Son of God. Even Elizabeth your relative

15. As Abraham and Sarah needed to engage in sexual intercourse to fulfill the promises God made to them (Gen. 17–18), so also Zechariah and Elizabeth need to both trust God and obey him. Faith and works come together in perfect harmony, as is always the case.

16. Throughout the early chapters of his gospel, Luke consistently identifies Joseph as the son of David (1:27; 2:4). Joseph is not the biological father of Jesus, but he is his father by divine choice.

17. Zechariah says, "How can I be sure of this? I am an old man and my wife is well along in years" (1:18). Mary similarly says, "How will this be . . . since I am a virgin?" (v. 34). Both seem to imply the impossibility of the angel's message coming true and give biological reasons for believing so.

18. Unlike Zechariah's sign, this sign comes without a rebuke.

is going to have a child in her old age, and she who was said to be barren is in her sixth month. For nothing is impossible with God. (vv. 35–37)

Mary's son will be conceived by the Holy Spirit. This is the extent of the explanation of the process. Unlike the child of Zechariah and Elizabeth, this child will not be conceived through sexual intercourse. The child will be conceived miraculously, through the overshadowing work of the Holy Spirit of God. Those who believe in him will also be born (again) by the Spirit of God (see John 1:12–13).

That Mary understands the message about Elizabeth as a sign seems clear. She immediately hurries to the hill country of Judea to see Elizabeth (Luke 1:39). Upon hearing Mary's greeting, the baby in Elizabeth's womb leaps for joy, and Elizabeth is filled with the Holy Spirit (vv. 41–44).[19] Both Elizabeth (v. 45) and Mary (vv. 46–55) recognize the miraculous blessing of God in their midst.

The Birth of John. Mary remains with Elizabeth until Elizabeth gives birth to a son. He is given the name John, as the angel commanded (Luke 2:57–66). Zechariah is immediately filled with the Holy Spirit and empowered to prophesy the ministry that his son will have (vv. 67–79). This forerunner of the Messiah (Isa. 40:3–5; Matt. 3:3) is Elijah (Mal. 3:1; 4:5–6; Matt. 11:14; 17:12), the promised messenger who will proclaim the coming kingdom and prepare the way for the coming king. Zechariah calls his son "a prophet of the Most High" who "will go on before the Lord to prepare the way for him, to give his people the knowledge of salvation through the forgiveness of their sins, because of the tender mercy of our God" (Luke 1:76–78).

19. The leaping of the baby in her womb might imply that both Elizabeth and her unborn child are filled with the Spirit.

The Birth of Jesus. According to Micah 5:2, the Messiah will be born in Bethlehem, the city of David. Joseph and Mary are in Nazareth (Luke 1:26; 2:4). How will this pregnant, unmarried woman make the trip from Nazareth to Bethlehem, and perhaps more importantly, why?[20] God uses the Roman emperor, Caesar Augustus, to accomplish his plan. The emperor issues a decree that a census should be taken, requiring everyone in Israel to return to their hometowns to register (2:1–3). Since Joseph is of the line of David, he must return to Bethlehem. Mary accompanies him. While they are in Bethlehem, the baby is born (vv. 4–6). God condescends to use the decisions of this Roman ruler to accomplish his plan. In an ordinary way, through the normal process of an ungodly ruler's carrying out of his agenda of self-promotion and conquest, the mother and father of the Son of God make their way to the place where the prophet predicted the Messiah would be born.

The Announcement to Shepherds. Another amazing act of condescension occurs on the night of Jesus' birth. There are shepherds keeping watch over their flocks in the fields outside Bethlehem (v. 8). This is not unusual—shepherds regularly watch over flocks. But it is unusual that "an angel of the Lord appeared to them, and the glory of the Lord shone around them" (v. 9). The shepherds are, understandably, terrified (v. 9). The angel encourages them: "Do not be afraid. I bring you good news of great joy that will be for all the people. Today in the town of David a Savior has been born to you; he is Christ the Lord" (vv. 10–11).

These shepherds were not the well-groomed, clean, mannerly men and women who appear in church Christmas pageants

---

20. The trip of around a hundred miles would likely have taken at least a week. Anna Dintaman Landis, "Hiking the Nativity Trail from Nazareth to Bethlehem," Jesus Trail, December 18, 2010, http://www. http://jesustrail.com/blog/hiking-the -nativity-trail-from-nazareth-to-bethlehem.

today.[21] First-century shepherds were dirty; they spent their time outside, in all kinds of weather, taking care of sheep. They were ceremonially unclean; caring for animals, they dealt with injuries, illnesses, and other matters related to animal husbandry. Leon Morris writes, "Shepherds had a bad reputation. The nature of their calling kept them from observing the ceremonial law which meant so much to religious people. More regrettable was their unfortunate habit of confusing 'mine' with 'thine' as they moved about."[22] Like the magi—although at the opposite end of the socioeconomic spectrum—the shepherds were outsiders in Israel. The gospel is good news for outsiders and the disenfranchised, and on the day of Jesus' birth this good news is announced to a representative group of this kind of people. At about the same time, the magi in the east see the sign of the star and begin their journey to Jerusalem.

Then, once again, an angel gives a sign to accompany its message: "You will find a baby wrapped in cloths and lying in a manger" (v. 12). Since there were surely other babies born around this time, perhaps even several more on this night, it is hard to see how the baby itself could be the sign. Since every baby in the first century was wrapped in cloths, the cloths could hardly be the sign. There were, after all, no disposable diapers to put on babies in the first century. Rather, the sign was the baby's lying in a manger. Babies are not usually born in animal stalls. And newborn infants seldom spend their first night sleeping in an animal's trough.

A king in an animal's feed trough? The Creator of the universe, the Son of almighty God, in a manger? This is where the shepherds are told to look for the Savior of the world, the son of David, the Son of God. This is an incredible act of

---

21. On the social status of the shepherds, see Leon L. Morris, *Luke*, Tyndale New Testament Commentaries (Downers Grove, IL: InterVarsity Press, 2008), 93.
22. Ibid.

condescension: from the heights of heaven God has come to an animal's stable.

Suddenly the angel is joined by a large angelic choir that is saying, "Glory to God in the highest, and on earth peace to men on whom his favor rests" (v. 14). Heaven has come to earth; the Creator has become a creature. In the story of God's plan of redemption, the gap between heaven and earth is beginning to close in anticipation of the day when heaven will become a place on earth. God has come to earth in the person of Jesus of Nazareth in anticipation of the time when God will make the earth his home forever. The triune God will condescend to come to earth to remain forever (Rev. 21:3–5).

The Response of the Shepherds and Mary. After watching the angels disappear into heaven, the shepherds decide to go into Bethlehem to look for the child. How could they do otherwise?[23] When they arrive in town, they find him, along with Mary and Joseph. The child is, as the angel said, lying in a manger (Luke 2:16). After worshipping him, they leave the stable and spread the word about what they have seen and heard, and "all who heard it were amazed at what the shepherds said to them" (v.18). Those who listened to the shepherds were surely those who shared their socioeconomic status; this is perhaps one reason they are amazed. The favor of God has come to those who were not generally understood in this culture to be recipients of blessing. The shepherds then return to their flocks, "glorifying and praising God for all the things they had heard and seen, which were just as they had been told" (v. 20).

Mary, on the other hand, treasures up these things and ponders them in her heart (v. 19). She keeps her thoughts to herself,

---

23. How will they find the child? How will they know where to look? In telling the story, Luke does not focus any attention on their search, but rather on their success. Everything is just as the angel had announced.

perhaps because she is unsure what to make of all this. From the angelic announcement, to the virgin conception, to the trip to Elizabeth, to the birth of her son in a stable, to the visit by the shepherds, Mary has experienced nine months of surprises.

Jesus' First Trip to the Temple

Eight days later, in accordance with the requirements of the law (Lev. 12:3), Mary and Joseph take their son to the temple to be circumcised. He is given the name Jesus in obedience to the message of the angel (Luke 2:21).[24] Then, when the time of purification is completed, thirty-three days later (Lev. 12:4–8), Joseph and Mary take the infant to the temple in Jerusalem to present him to the Lord (Luke 2:22–24). There they meet a righteous and devout man named Simeon, who has been waiting for "the consolation of Israel, and the Holy Spirit was upon him" (v. 25). On this day, the Spirit moves him to come into the temple courts, where he sees this child and his parents and recognizes that this one is the consolation of Israel (vv. 26–28). He takes the child in his arms and prays,

> Sovereign Lord, as you have promised,
>   you now dismiss your servant in peace.
> For my eyes have seen your salvation,
>   which you have prepared in the sight of all people,
> a light for revelation to the Gentiles
>   and for glory to your people Israel. (vv. 29–32)

This infant, Simeon knows, is the one for whom he has been looking, the one who is the Messiah of Israel. This is good news for Israel. But Simeon knows that the news is even better than that; this is good news for all people, for the Messiah is a light

24. The name was chosen by his Father, not by his parents. Like Abraham's two sons, and John, this child is named by God.

of revelation for the Gentiles too. The Messiah will not simply be the Savior of Israel; through him, Gentiles too will be blessed. This child is the one who will fulfill the promise that God made to Abraham (Gen. 12:1–3), the gospel of blessing for all nations (Gal. 3:8).

Jesus' parents marvel at this news, but then Simeon continues: "This child is destined to cause the falling and rising of many in Israel, and to be a sign that will be spoken against, so that the thoughts of many hearts will be revealed" (Luke 2:34–35). He concludes with these ominous words: "And a sword will pierce your own soul too" (v. 35). Jesus is a sign of good and bad, of obedience and disobedience, of submission and rebellion, of life and death. He will be the source of great joy and great heartache. He will bring families together and divide them.[25] He will be the source of unity and the cause of disunity. He will be a polarizing figure, the most polarizing person in human history. This is no ordinary child.

Another prophet then appears in the temple. Luke explains that Anna is "very old" (v. 36); she has lived in the temple for many years (v. 37).[26] At that very moment, she approaches the family. She too "gave thanks to God and spoke about the child to all who were looking forward to the redemption of Jerusalem" (v. 38). An elderly woman who spends every day in the temple, she declares the good news of redemption.

The shepherds spread the good news of the promise of peace on earth because of what they have seen. Surely some people in Bethlehem have heard the news. Simeon declares the son

25. Jesus himself said, "Do not suppose that I have come to bring peace to the earth. I did not come to bring peace, but a sword. For I have come to turn a man against his father, a daughter against her mother, a daughter-in-law against her mother-in-law—a man's enemies will be the members of his own household" (Matt. 10:34–36; see also Mic. 7:6).

26. It is unclear whether she was eighty-four years old or had been a widow for that long, although the former appears more probable (Luke 2:37).

born to Mary and Joseph to be the consolation of Israel and the light of revelation for all nations. Surely some people in the temple listen to him. Anna proclaims the hope of redemption to everyone who looks forward to it. Surely some people listen to her. After all, Simeon and Anna are in the temple in Jerusalem, the center of worship of the God of Israel. Yet when the magi appear in Jerusalem some time later, apparently no one knows or remembers that the Messiah Jesus has been born in Bethlehem. How could this be?

Perhaps by this time Simeon and Anna have both died, but even if they lived only for a short time after the events of Luke 2, more than several people had heard the news. Could it be that no one believed them? Could it be that there was so great a cultural divide between the shepherds and the rest of society that no one involved in the cultic practices of Israel trusted the word of these keepers of sheep? Could it be that so few were "looking forward to the redemption of Jerusalem" (v. 38) that the teachers of the law and the chief priests had never heard? Or could it be that these leaders of Israel's religion were not looking forward with hope to the coming of the Messiah?

The teachers of the law are unaware of the birth of the Messiah when the magi arrive in Jerusalem (see Matt. 2:3–6). The incarnation of the Son of God, God come to earth in Jesus of Nazareth, was one of the best-kept secrets of human history. This secret could have been kept only if Jesus' humanity appeared ordinary to those who saw this child. And, to be clear, this is exactly the point. His humanity was, and is, like ours. He is "of the same reality as we ourselves as far as his humanness is concerned; thus like us in all respects, sin only excepted," as the Definition of Chalcedon expresses it.[27] The Creator humbled himself to become a creature, fully God and fully human.

27. "Definition of Chalcedon," accessed September 26, 2011, http://www.creeds.net/ancient/chalcedon.htm.

Jesus at Twelve Years of Age

Very little is known of Jesus' childhood, of his growth and development, of his life between his birth and his appearance as a rabbi at the age of thirty (Luke 3:23). From Matthew's gospel, we learn that Jesus and his family flee to Egypt, so we know that Jesus spends his early years growing up in the land where his forebears were oppressed and enslaved. He returns from Egypt after the death of Herod (Matt. 2:13–20), an event that in some sense reenacts the exodus (v. 15).

After the family returned to Nazareth, the son of Joseph and Mary "grew and became strong; he was filled with wisdom, and the grace of God was upon him" (Luke 2:40). Then Luke tells a story that takes place when Jesus is twelve years old. Luke concludes that account, "And Jesus grew in wisdom and stature, and in favor with God and men" (v. 52).

Every year Jesus' parents traveled to Jerusalem for the Feast of the Passover (Luke 2:41). The Passover introduced the Feast of Unleavened Bread (Lev. 23:5–8), one of the feasts when all the men of Israel were required "to appear before the Sovereign Lord" (Ex. 23:14–17). Jesus is twelve years old this time—thus he has been part of this family celebration about a dozen times (Luke 2:42).

When the feast is over, the family begins the return trip to their home, as they do each year. This time, however, Jesus does not accompany the family. Instead, he remains in Jerusalem. When his parents realize he is not with the caravan, they return to Jerusalem, and "after three days they found him in the temple courts, sitting among the teachers, listening to them and asking them questions" (v. 46).[28]

Luke records two reactions to Jesus' behavior in the temple. Luke says of those in the temple, "Everyone who heard him was

---

28. Was it three days' journey or three days spent looking for him? Either is possible.

amazed at his understanding and his answers" (v. 47). Jesus is well trained in the law of God. His answers indicate significant insight and perception. His parents have a different reaction: "They were astonished" (v. 48). Although it is possible that "amazed" and "astonished" indicate the same attitude, his mother's rebuke implies that their response is a bit less positive than those who observed Jesus in the temple. "Son, why have you treated us like this? Your father and I have been anxiously searching for you," she says (v. 48). His mother appears exasperated, disappointed, and frustrated with him.

For years, I had a hard time understanding this text. How could Mary, who knew that Jesus was the Son of God even before he was conceived, have been surprised at his behavior or unhappy with him? Surely she understood that he was a perfect child. As she watched him grow up and compared him to her ordinary children, surely she was able to see the difference. Anyone who was in the presence of God in the flesh would recognize his deity, I thought. I now believe that this story reveals to us that Jesus' deity was well concealed.

Apparently, the difference between Jesus and her other children was not as obvious to Mary as I had thought.[29] Jesus never sinned, never rebelled against her; he never behaved in a depraved way. But surely he acted as a child while he was a child. He cried when hungry, struggled to understand Hebrew, learned what it meant to be the son of Joseph. He was immature, and immaturity is not sin. And this seems to be the point that Luke is making: Jesus' growth and development was normal, like our own. Donald Macleod writes,

> The evangelist records that the child Jesus grew in wisdom just as he grew in physical stature. He observed and learned and

29. What I had learned in Sunday school was that Jesus is God. What I had not learned was that he is fully human.

remembered and applied. This would have been impossible if he had been born in possession of a complete body of wisdom and knowledge. Instead, he was born with the mental equipment of a normal child, experienced the usual stimuli and went through the ordinary processes of intellectual development.[30]

The significance of belief in Jesus' humanity is stated clearly by John Walvoord.

> Though the doctrine of the deity of Christ is generally recognized as the indispensable fundamental of Christology, the doctrine of His true humanity is equally important. . . . Those who deny the true humanity of Christ, such as modern Christian Science, are just as effective at destroying the Christian faith as those who deny the deity of Christ.[31]

As his parents interact with Jesus and his siblings, they seem not to understand what it means for Jesus to be Immanuel, God in flesh. As parents do, they sometimes confuse immaturity with rebellion, ignorance with disobedience, and childishness with defiance.

Jesus' response to his mother's question expresses surprise. "Why were you searching for me? . . . Didn't you know I had to be in my Father's house?" (Luke 2:49). Jesus assumes they will know and understand. They do not (v. 50).

In what is perhaps the most surprising detail of this story, and a poignant illustration of Jesus' submission to his parents, Luke says that "he went down to Nazareth with them and was obedient to them" (v. 51). He is not merely submissive to them— he is obedient, and for an extended period of time. In the culture of his day, Jesus is transitioning at twelve years of age into

30. Donald Macleod, *The Person of Christ* (Downers Grove, IL: InterVarsity Press, 1998), 164.
31. John Walvoord, *Jesus Christ Our Lord* (Chicago: Moody, 1969), 109.

adulthood.[32] He is no longer under any obligation to live with his parents and submit to their authority. But he does submit to them until he begins his public ministry. He returns to Nazareth with his parents and remains obedient to them.

The writer of Hebrews asserts, "Although he was a son, he learned obedience from what he suffered and, once made perfect, he became the source of eternal salvation for all who obey him" (Heb. 5:8–9). Throughout his life, Jesus practices obedience, not only to his heavenly Father, but also to his parents. In so doing, he grows to maturity; he learns what it means to be submissive, to obey. In a similar way, we learn obedience through suffering; we grow toward maturity through obedience and become godly through submission to God and one another (see Phil. 2:5–11).

Conclusion

In the incarnation, the Creator of the universe condescends to enter into the world he created. But he does not merely come to visit as a divine being; he humbles himself by adding to his complete deity complete humanity, not temporarily but permanently. The Creator becomes a creature while still remaining fully divine. Jesus' life and ministry, both what he says and what he does, reveal this humility and condescension. It is to his teaching about true greatness that we now turn.

32. Further evidence of his adulthood is seen in his presence in the temple with the teachers of the law.

7

JESUS' TEACHING ON GREATNESS

DURING THE PASSOVER meal on the night of his arrest, Jesus rises from the table, takes off his outer clothing, wraps a towel around his waist, pours water into a basin, and begins to wash his disciples' feet (John 13:5). In that group is Judas, who, in a few minutes, leaves the room to accept the money he has been promised to betray Jesus (vv. 21–30). Lest any of them miss the significance of his actions, Jesus explains to the disciples,

> You call me "Teacher" and "Lord," and rightly so, for that is what I am. Now that I, your Lord and Teacher, have washed your feet, you also should wash one another's feet. I have set you an example that you should do as I have done for you. (vv. 13–15)

Jesus does not merely talk about servanthood; he lives it.[1] He shows his disciples what it looks like to humble oneself for the sake of others, thereby redefining greatness for them.

1. On the parallels between John 13 and Philippians 2, see Greg Perry, "To Know and Be Known: How Christ's Love Moves Us into Intimacy, Humility and Risk: A Sermon on John 13:1–17," in *All for Jesus: A Celebration of the 50th Anniversary of Covenant Theological Seminary*, ed. Robert A. Peterson and Sean Michael Lucas (Ross-shire, UK: Mentor, 2006), 375–76.

The people who know him best, the men he chose to be his disciples, struggle with the way Jesus defines greatness. According to their standard, greatness is defined by positions of power and influence, by fame and prestige. In the Gospels, we see the disciples arguing among themselves about which of them is the greatest, and Jesus tells them repeatedly how unbecoming their behavior is. Again and again they miss the point that the greatest of all is in their midst; were they to pay attention to him, they would understand true greatness.

Throughout the centuries since, Jesus' disciples have continued to struggle with this concept. Jesus' teaching on greatness is counterintuitive, countercultural, counterproductive, and counter to our desires. It is opposite to the way things work in a fallen world. Kings don't wash their subjects' feet as Jesus did.

This chapter will survey the ministry of Jesus, particularly his public and private teaching on greatness in the gospel of Matthew.[2] His example of condescension creates a new understanding of greatness for his followers, one that is further explained in his teaching.

The Public Ministry of Jesus

Jesus' Baptism

Many people have responded to the message of John the Baptist: "Repent, for the kingdom of heaven is near" (Matt. 3:2). Upon confession of sin, they submit to John's baptism of repentance (v. 6; see also v. 11). Jesus, too, offers himself to John for baptism (v. 13). Of course, Jesus does not need to repent or confess his sins, so there is no apparent reason for him to be baptized. Even John recognizes this: "I need to be baptized by you, and do you come

2. In the interest of continuity and in view of the need to be selective, most of the content of this chapter is taken from the gospel of Matthew.

to me?" (v. 14). But Jesus insists, "Let it be so now; it is proper for us to do this to fulfill all righteousness" (v. 15).

Jesus submits to John's baptism, not because he needs to repent, but because it is God's plan. Jesus' baptism honors and elevates John, endorsing his ministry. The Father is delighted with this act; as Jesus is being baptized, heaven opens, the Spirit descends, and a voice declares, "This is my Son, whom I love; with him I am well pleased" (v. 17).[3] Jesus' baptism, which inaugurates his public ministry, is an act of condescension. The greater one, Jesus, submits to the prophet and, in so doing, brings pleasure to his Father in heaven.

Jesus' Temptations by the Devil

Immediately after his baptism, Jesus is led by the Spirit into the desert to be tempted by the Devil (4:1). In three representative temptations, Jesus is victorious over the adversary. When tempted to turn stones into bread, Jesus responds by quoting Deuteronomy 8:3: "It is written: 'Man does not live on bread alone, but on every word that comes from the mouth of God'" (Matt. 4:4). When tempted to test God's promise of protection by throwing himself from the highest point of the temple, Jesus responds with Deuteronomy 6:16: "It is also written: 'Do not put the Lord your God to the test'" (Matt. 4:7). When tempted to bow down and worship the tempter, Jesus responds with Deuteronomy 6:13: "For it is written: 'Worship the Lord your God, and serve him only'" (Matt. 4:10). In all three cases, Jesus submits himself to the law of God and uses it to rebuke Satan. Rather than exercise his authority as Creator, he submits to the Word of God. After the final temptation, he responds, "Away from me, Satan!" (v. 10). In so doing, he demonstrates the power of the Scriptures and models resistance, providing an example of the

3. One reason for the Spirit's descent on Jesus is so that John will know the identity of the Messiah (John 1:32–34).

approach his brother James will later advise: "Resist the devil, and he will flee from you" (James 4:7). The Devil then leaves him (Matt. 4:11).

In submitting to the baptism of John, Jesus fulfils all righteousness (3:15). In submitting to the temptation of the Devil, Jesus identifies with us as our high priest, "who has been tempted in every way, just as we are—yet was without sin" (Heb. 4:15). In submitting to the Word of God, Jesus demonstrates the authority of the Scriptures (2 Tim. 3:16–17). In all three temptations, he condescends to the limitations of humanity. Rather than using the power of his deity, he humbles himself as one of us.

Jesus Begins His Public Ministry

Jesus begins his public ministry after John is imprisoned (Matt. 4:12). He returns to Galilee in order to fulfill Isaiah 9:1–2, to proclaim to the Gentiles that "the people living in darkness have seen a great light; on those living in the land of the shadow of death a light has dawned" (Matt. 4:16).[4] From that time on, Matthew says, Jesus preaches a simple and singular message: "Repent, for the kingdom of heaven is near" (v. 17). This message is identical to John's (see Matt. 3:2), the message that Malachi predicted would come from the prophet Elijah: "Remember the law of my servant Moses, the decrees and laws I gave him at Horeb for all Israel" (Mal. 4:4).[5]

The Preaching of Jesus: The Sermon on the Mount

Like other religious leaders of his day, Jesus selects disciples to travel with him. In a mixture of instruction and practice, through life-on-life and flesh-on-flesh mentoring, Jesus teaches

4. Thus, from the beginning of his account of Jesus' ministry, Matthew emphasizes that he came to bring hope for all nations (see Gen. 12:3).
5. Jesus declares that John was the fulfillment of Malachi 3:1 (Matt. 11:10). The messenger (Mal. 3:1) is named Elijah in Malachi 4:5. Thus, John the Baptist is Elijah.

his disciples to follow him. Matthew's gospel records several extended teaching discourses of Jesus. In each of these, he calls people to follow him, to serve others as he served, and to become part of his kingdom.

In the Sermon on the Mount, Jesus teaches his disciples about his kingdom. A series of beatitudes pronounces blessing on the poor in spirit, the mourners, the meek, and those who hunger and thirst for righteousness; all their desires will be met in the kingdom (Matt. 5:3–6). Jesus explains that the kingdom is characterized by mercy, purity, peacemaking, and persecution (vv. 7–10). The latter might seem out of place in such a list. How could the kingdom of God be characterized by persecution and suffering? The answer is that this kingdom is radically different from the dominant culture, from the ways things work in a fallen world, from the kingdoms of the Gentiles. As Jesus goes on to explain, "Blessed are you when people insult you, persecute you and falsely say all kinds of evil against you because of me. Rejoice and be glad, because great is your reward in heaven" (vv. 11–12).

Jesus uses two simple analogies from the created order to picture the role of his disciples in this kingdom. "You are the salt of the earth. But if the salt loses its saltiness, how can it be made salty again? It is no longer good for anything" (v. 13). Similarly, "You are the light of the world. A city on a hill cannot be hidden. Neither do people light a lamp and put it under a bowl" (vv. 14–15). Jesus' disciples are to shine in the world, "that they may see your good deeds and praise your Father in heaven" (v. 16). In short, the disciples of Jesus are to be immersed in the world—visible, present, and actively manifesting the character of the King and his kingdom. Jesus' disciples are not to hide from the world, separate from it, or limit their interaction with it. They are to be in it, actively involved with it, and making a redemptive difference in it, just as salt flavors food and as light exposes the deeds of darkness (see Eph. 5:11).[6]

Salt preserved in a hermetically sealed container is as worthless as salt that has lost its saltiness. In the latter case, it is no longer good for anything except to be thrown out. In the former case, it is not good for anything because it is not fulfilling its function. Salt is not meant to be preserved from harm; it is to be used. Salt, a relatively inexpensive food additive, makes the food to which it is added taste better. No one, when eating a nice cut of prime rib, praises the salt. But without the salt, the diner might complain to the chef about the tastelessness of the meat. In the same way, disciples of Jesus give themselves for the sake of others. The salt deserves no reward for doing its job; the honor is not to the servant, but to the master (see Luke 17:10).

As the light of the world, Jesus' disciples will penetrate the world with goodness and righteousness. Light drives out the darkness, exposing what it is hidden in the dark (Eph. 5:8–14). Light is of little value if collected, preserved, or isolated from the darkness. A small light in the presence of a great deal of light has little impact, but that same small light appears quite bright when it shines in darkness, driving it out.

As salt and light, followers of Jesus are in the world. They do not separate themselves in some self-protective attempt at self-preservation, instead giving themselves for the sake of others. In short, they are like Jesus, who left the glory of heaven to come to earth.

The Miracles of Jesus

After the Sermon on the Mount, Matthew records several healing miracles. They function as living parables, examples of

6. On the redemption of culture by cultivation and creation, see Andy Crouch, *Culture Making: Recovering Our Creative Calling* (Downers Grove, IL: InterVarsity Press, 2008).

Jesus' teaching. In the first, Jesus heals a man with leprosy. In doing so, Jesus does the unthinkable: he "reached out his hand and touched the man" (Matt. 8:3), and the leper is cured. Jesus does not avoid contact with this unclean man. At great personal cost to himself, in violation of social and hygienic mores, Jesus touches an unclean man. He condescends to care about the man with leprosy, disregarding what others think of him or his own health. This man, who because of his illness is an outcast who has not experienced human touch for some time, receives the compassionate touch of the Son of God.

Then, in Capernaum, Jesus meets a centurion who asks Jesus to heal his paralyzed servant. When Jesus agrees to go to this man's house to heal him, the centurion expresses his faith and humility by saying, "Lord, I do not deserve to have you come under my roof. But just say the word, and my servant will be healed" (v. 8). Jesus is astonished at this and observes to those around him,

> I tell you the truth, I have not found anyone in Israel with such great faith. I say to you that many will come from the east and the west, and will take their places at the feast with Abraham, Isaac and Jacob in the kingdom of heaven. But the subjects of the kingdom will be thrown outside, into the darkness, where there will be weeping and gnashing of teeth. (vv. 10–12)

In this countercultural statement, Jesus predicts that people of privilege will be rejected while the outcasts and disenfranchised will be honored (see 22:1–14). Entrance to his kingdom is not based upon family heritage, knowledge, or ethnic identity. It is only by faith. A Gentile who has faith will get in and be seated at the feast with Abraham, Isaac, and Jacob, while some of Abraham's biological descendants will be cast outside into the darkness.

Finally, Jesus enters into the home of Peter's mother-in-law, who is sick in bed with a fever. Jesus touches her, and she is healed

(8:14–15). That evening, many others come to Jesus to be healed, and he heals them.

In these three stories, Jesus heals a leper, a Gentile, and a woman. These three categories of outsiders experience the healing touch of the King and are brought inside his kingdom. In so doing, Jesus demonstrates the kingdom of heaven to be radically different from the kingdoms of this world. Kingdoms of this world marginalize these people, but such people are the focus of Jesus' ministry.

As Jesus travels through the towns and villages to proclaim the good news of the kingdom and to demonstrate its presence through healing miracles, he is filled with compassion (9:35–36). Compassion motivates his mission of mercy. Because he sees the crowds "harassed and helpless, like sheep without a shepherd" (v. 36), Jesus asks the disciples to join him in praying for workers in the harvest (vv. 37–38). Then he sends out his disciples to do what he has been doing, "to drive out evil spirits and to heal every disease and sickness" (10:1). They become the answer to their own prayer, serving those in need.

Then, in one of the most shocking statements thus far in Matthew's gospel, Jesus explains to his disciples his reason for coming: "Do not suppose that I have come to bring peace to the earth. I did not come to bring peace, but a sword" (v. 34). He quotes Micah 7:6, which describes hatred and conflict within families, and then summarizes,

> Anyone who loves his father or mother more than me is not worthy of me; anyone who loves his son or daughter more than me is not worthy of me; and anyone who does not take his cross and follow me is not worthy of me. Whoever finds his life will lose it, and whoever loses his life for my sake will find it. (Matt. 10:37–38)

This is the first reference to the cross in Matthew. This kingdom is unlike any kingdom on earth. It brings conflict, not peace;

hatred, not love; a cross, not a crown; death, not life; and enmity, not friendship. Yet Jesus promises his followers great reward at a future day.

> He who receives you receives me, and he who receives me receives the one who sent me. Anyone who receives a prophet because he is a prophet will receive a prophet's reward, and anyone who receives a righteous man because he is a righteous man will receive a righteous man's reward. And if anyone gives even a cup of cold water to one of these little ones because he is my disciple, I tell you the truth, he will certainly not lose his reward. (vv. 40–42)

But until that day, they are to lay down their lives for others.

The Kingdom Parables

In another extended discourse, Jesus tells a series of parables about the kingdom, explaining how it will grow until that day of reward. In the first, a parable about a sower of seeds, he describes a variety of responses to the message of the kingdom (13:1–9). Then, in the parable of the weeds, he compares the kingdom to a farmer's field. A farmer sows good seed, but his enemy sows weeds. When the farmer's servants ask if they should remove the weeds, their master tells them to allow the wheat and the weeds to grow together until the harvest. At that time, he says, the Son of Man will send angels into the kingdom to separate the wheat (the righteous) from the weeds (wicked). The wicked will be taken and thrown into the fiery furnace, while the righteous will be left behind to shine in the kingdom (vv. 24–30, 37–43). Thus, the current age of the kingdom will end with judgment. The wicked will be taken, and the righteous will be left behind to enjoy life on the earth.

Jesus tells two parables to picture the growth of the kingdom from humble and small beginnings into a worldwide phenomenon. He says the kingdom is like a mustard seed that grows into a big tree, like yeast that expands into the whole dough (vv. 31–33). The kingdom starts small and grows large. It starts in one spot and expands to fill the whole earth. These analogies are rooted in the vision of Nebuchadnezzar in Daniel 2. Just as the rock that destroys the statue grows into a mountain that fills the whole earth (Dan. 2:35), so the kingdom in Jesus' parables grows from a small seed into a large tree, like a small amount of yeast permeating the whole dough.

Two parables compare the kingdom to valuable things. The kingdom is like a treasure hidden in a field. A wise person will sell everything he has to get that field. The kingdom is also like a pearl of great price. A wise person will sell everything to buy that jewel. In short, the kingdom is worth whatever it costs; nothing is more valuable than the kingdom (Matt. 13:44–46).

One final parable reinforces the point of the parable of the wheat and the weeds. Jesus compares the kingdom to fishermen pulling their net onto the shore. Just as they throw the bad fish away and keep the good, so angels will come to earth at the end of the age to take the wicked—throwing them into the fiery furnace—and leave the righteous behind to experience the kingdom (vv. 47–50).

In these parables, Jesus teaches that the kingdom message will be hidden from those who do not have ears to hear and will be revealed to those who do. Those who hear the message and see it come to pass are blessed by God (vv. 16–17). At the end of the age, the wicked will be separated from the righteous. The wicked will be taken in judgment, while the righteous will be left behind to enter into the kingdom on earth (vv. 40–43, 49–50). The kingdom starts out small, in one location, but will grow to fill the whole earth; it is valuable, worth whatever it costs. This kingdom will be characterized by righteousness, peace, and prosperity that last forever. And it will be located on the earth, under the reign of King Jesus. The time is coming when these servants of the king will be rewarded. Until that day, Jesus' followers serve others, as Jesus himself did.

Jesus Is the Christ

When Jesus arrives in Caesarea Philippi, he asks his disciples how people identify him. He asks that question, not because he is unsure of his own identity, but in order to teach the disciples. Some think he is John the Baptist, others Elijah, and others Jeremiah or one of the prophets, the disciples reply. "But," Jesus asks, "what about you? Who do you say I am?" (Matt. 16:15). In a pivotal moment in this gospel, Peter boldly declares, "You are the Christ, the Son of the living God" (v. 16).

Peter speaks the truth. He also speaks more than he understands. He speaks as a prophet, a mediator of divine revelation. All of this is made clear when Jesus declares to him, "Blessed are you, Simon son of Jonah, for this was not revealed to you by man, but by my Father in heaven" (v. 17). In short, Peter could not have known who Jesus was by any means other than divine revelation. And that he does recognize him as the Messiah is a demonstration of divine blessing. No one can come to Jesus unless drawn to him by the Father (see John 6:44).

From that time on, Jesus begins to teach the disciples that "he must go to Jerusalem and suffer many things at the hands of the elders, chief priests and teachers of the law, and that he must be killed and on the third day be raised to life" (v. 21). Peter, probably representing all the disciples, takes Jesus aside to rebuke him. "This shall never happen to you!" Peter says (v. 22). What kind of kingdom would it be if the king were to die? If the kingdom is present now ("from the days of John the Baptist"), would not the death of the king mean the end of the kingdom? How could an eternal kingdom come to an end? It is not hard to understand Peter's confusion, even if it is jarring to hear him rebuke the one he has just called "the Christ, the Son of the Living God."

Jesus' response is curt and direct: "Get behind me, Satan! You are a stumbling block to me; you do not have in mind the things of God, but the things of men" (v. 23). In the space of several sentences, Peter has gone from receiving a gracious commendation to being called Satan and hearing a harsh condemnation. He still does not understand the mission of Jesus, does not recognize the nature of the kingdom, and has not grasped the submission of the Son of God to the force of evil in this world.

In his rebuke of Peter, Jesus contrasts the things of God with the things of men. As the gospel of Matthew unfolds, these two views of the kingdom seem to be at the heart of Jesus' teaching of his disciples. Their kingdom view needs to be readjusted in order to understand God's kingdom.

Requirements for Disciples

Having just declared that his ministry is heading toward death, apparently soon, Jesus tells his disciples what they can expect if they follow him. He reminds them what he told them previously, that "a student is not above his teacher, nor a servant above his master" (10:24). Now he goes into more graphic detail, calling them to a life that, just as his, ends at the cross.

> If anyone would come after me, he must deny himself and take up his cross and follow me. For whoever wants to save his life will lose it, but whoever loses his life for me will find it. What good will it be for a man if he gains the whole world, yet forfeits his soul? Or what can a man give in exchange for his soul? For the Son of Man is going to come in his Father's glory with his angels, and then he will reward each person according to what he has done. (16:24–27)

This age of the kingdom will culminate in judgment when the Son of Man returns with his angels (see 13:37–43, 47–50). Then the wicked will be judged and the righteous will receive their reward; the wicked will be taken, while the righteous will be left behind to populate the earth. In the meantime, the kingdom will be characterized by the cross, self-denial, and death and loss. If the disciples are to follow Jesus, they must follow him all the way to the cross (see 1 Peter 2:21).

After healing a demon-possessed boy, Jesus again reminds his disciples of his fate: "The Son of Man is going to be betrayed into the hands of men. They will kill him, and on the third day he will be raised to life" (Matt. 17:22–23). The King is facing death. His kingdom is characterized by suffering before glorification. But death does not have the last word; it will be conquered by the resurrection.

The disciples are filled with grief at this teaching (v. 23). They still do not understand; otherwise they would not have come to Jesus with this question: "Who is the greatest in the kingdom of heaven?" (18:1). Jesus calls a little child and says to the disciples, "I tell you the truth, unless you change and become like little children, you will never enter the kingdom of heaven" (v. 3). Earlier he had rebuked them for their little faith (see Matt. 17:20). Now he tells them that they are in danger of not even being part of the kingdom. In short, rather than trying to figure out how to be the greatest in the kingdom, they should be asking how to participate in the kingdom. They are in danger of being left out.

According to Jesus, one enters the kingdom by becoming like a little child. "Therefore," Jesus continues, "whoever humbles himself like this child is the greatest in the kingdom of heaven" (18:4). Humility is the characteristic of the kingdom. Greatness in this kingdom is found through humility—like the king, who is humility incarnate.

Demonstrating that he still does not really understand this teaching, Peter asks Jesus how many times he needs to forgive his brother (v. 21). Peter is asking a bookkeeping question. He assumes, probably thinking he is being generous, that perhaps the number seven would establish a perfect standard. Jesus responds that the number is not seven but seventy-seven, or maybe seventy times seven (v. 22). The exact number is irrelevant; in fact, this is the point: the person who is counting the number of times does not understand forgiveness. Forgiveness is not only an obligation, but also an opportunity. It is in granting forgiveness that we are most like God (see Eph. 4:32). Since God's forgiveness is unlimited, ours should be too.

Jesus illustrates this in a parable about forgiveness and the kingdom of heaven (Matt. 18:23–35). A king decides to settle his accounts with his servants. One of his servants owes him a huge sum, more than he could ever repay. The servant pleads for time, promising to pay back what he owes eventually.[7] The king extends mercy to him, canceling the debt and releasing him from any obligation. As the servant leaves the king, he finds a fellow servant who owes him a much smaller sum of money.[8] He demands repayment. When this servant asks for more time, the forgiven servant refuses and has him thrown into debtor's prison. When other servants, distressed by what has happened, tell the king, he calls the first servant to him and says, "You wicked servant, . . . I canceled all that debt of yours because you begged me to. Shouldn't you have had mercy on your fellow servant just as I had on you?" (v. 33).[9]

7. That the debt is insurmountable makes this naive promise almost laughable. The servant fails to understand his need for grace.

8. The original debt is ten thousand talents (Matt. 18:24). This man owes a hundred denarii (v. 28). If a denarius is a day's wage, this is still a significant debt, but small when compared to the first man's obligation.

9. At the heart of this rebuke seems to be the Golden Rule (see Matt. 7:12): we should treat others the way we would like to be treated.

146

In anger, the king has the first servant tortured until he can repay the debt.[10]

Jesus concludes, "This is how my heavenly Father will treat each of you unless you forgive your brother from your heart" (v. 35). This is a very hard saying, but it is not the only time Jesus speaks this way about forgiveness.[11] At the conclusion of the Lord's Prayer, Jesus says, "For if you forgive men when they sin against you, your heavenly Father will also forgive you. But if you do not forgive men their sins, your Father will not forgive your sins" (6:14–15). Surely this does not mean that God grants forgiveness, but takes it back if we do not respond appropriately. That would make forgiveness operate according to the law of karma, not grace. It would make forgiveness, the heart of the gospel, dependent upon works. That cannot be true (see Eph. 2:8–10).

It seems, rather, that the parable is confronting Peter's misunderstanding of forgiveness. According to Jesus, forgiven people forgive, recipients of grace mediate grace to others, and the people of God demonstrate godliness in their behavior. In short, the parable emphasizes that a truly forgiven person does not keep a ledger of the number of times he has forgiven another person; rather, he forgives and forgives and forgives— without limit. That is, after all, what God has promised to do for his children (see 1 John 1:9); how could they not treat one another the same way (see Eph. 4:32)?

10. That this is a parable should give us pause before we attribute torture to God. I do not think Jesus is endorsing torture or is teaching that God is a torturer. Rather, this is a parable in which a king acts in anger and punishes a servant harshly for his lack of mercy to a fellow servant. Eternal judgment in hell is an act of justice, not cruelty.

11. Walter C. Kaiser, Jr., Peter H. Davids, F. F. Bruce, and Manfred T. Brauch, *Hard Sayings of the Bible* (Downers Grove, IL: InterVarsity Press, 1996), 386. The conclusion of these authors is that "if some of those to whom this admonition was addressed (and it is addressed to all Christians at all times) should persist in an unforgiving attitude toward others, could they even so enjoy the assurance of God's forgiveness? If Jesus' teaching means what it says, they could not" (p. 388).

The Nature of the Kingdom

On another occasion, the crowd brings children to Jesus for him to pray for them (Matt. 19:13). The disciples of Jesus rebuke the crowd. Jesus had earlier told his followers that they needed to become like little children to gain admittance to the kingdom (see 18:3). Again he rebukes his disciples: "Let the little children come to me, and do not hinder them, for the kingdom of heaven belongs to such as these" (19:14). Once more Jesus affirms and elevates children, even using them to admonish his disciples. The kingdom belongs to those who are like children, those who are characterized by vulnerability, dependence, and humility. Jesus is endorsing childlikeness, not childishness.

In a story that sets the context for a powerful teaching moment for Jesus' disciples, a rich young man comes to him and asks, "What good thing must I do to get eternal life?" (v. 16). Jesus does not reject his question, but reminds him that obedience to the law is the way to life (see Lev. 18:5).[12] When the man insists that he has kept the commandments, Jesus tells him that he lacks one thing: "If you want to be perfect, go, sell your possessions and give to the poor, and you will have treasure in heaven. Then come, follow me" (Matt. 19:21).

Jesus is surely not saying that this man, or anyone else, would be made perfect by something he does. Selling his possessions would not solve his problem of innate depravity. Rather, Jesus is asking this man to be like him, to give himself away for the sake of others.

The young man goes away sad because he has much wealth (v. 22). Holding on to his wealth is his greatest priority. Jesus, on the other hand, who has much greater wealth, gives himself for the sake of humanity (Phil. 2:6–8), for the joy set before him

---

12. This is not salvation by works, for salvation has always been by grace through faith. But it has also always been the case that faith works, so faithfulness is evidence of faith.

(Heb. 12:2). This man, by walking away, demonstrates that he is not a follower of Jesus; he does not believe. If he believed, he would do what Jesus requires. His giving away his possessions would not, in itself, have made him a follower of Jesus, but refusing to act like Jesus demonstrates that he is not following Jesus.

Jesus then turns to his disciples and shatters another of their cultural ideals. In a world that measures the blessing of God by material prosperity, Jesus says, "I tell you the truth, it is hard for a rich man to enter the kingdom of heaven" (Matt. 19:23). He tells them just how hard it is: "I tell you, it is easier for a camel to go through the eye of a needle than for a rich man to enter the kingdom of God" (v. 24). In short, it is not possible for a rich man to be saved apart from the grace of God. "With man this is impossible, but with God all things are possible" (v. 26).

Demonstrating that he is still not thinking correctly about the kingdom, Peter says, "We have left everything to follow you! What then will there be for us?" (v. 27). Peter's question indicates that he still has a mercenary's motivation, not a servant's heart.

Jesus reminds Peter that this stage of the kingdom is not the end; there is much more yet to come—"at the renewal of all things, when the Son of Man sits on his glorious throne," there will be restitution and reward (v. 28). Jesus says that the disciples will in that day "sit on twelve thrones" and "will receive a hundred times as much" as they gave up; furthermore, they will receive "eternal life" (vv. 28–29).

There will be judgment one day. The wicked will be taken. The righteous will be left behind and rewarded. Then, in the regeneration of all things, the kingdom of righteousness, peace, and prosperity will cover the earth in all its fullness. When that day comes, "Many who are first will be last, and many who are last will be first" (v. 30). In a parable that illustrates this principle, Jesus compares the kingdom to a farmer who hires workers for his vineyard. He hires some early in the day and some at the third hour, at the sixth, the ninth, and, finally, even at the eleventh hour. At the end of the day, the workers come to receive their pay. Those hired at the end of the day receive a denarius, as does everyone else. Although they have not worked the same number of hours, they each receive the same pay. Those who worked all day object the most, because "you have made them equal to us" (20:12).

The landowner answers,

> I am not being unfair to you. Didn't you agree to work for a denarius? Take your pay and go. I want to give the man who was hired last the same as I gave you. Don't I have the right to do what I want with my own money? Or are you envious because I am generous? (vv. 13–15)

The rhetorical questions pack an emotional punch. Of course the landowner can do whatever he wants with his money. He promised those he had hired in the morning a denarius. He paid what he had promised. We should note that only the first group had contracted for a wage. To the others, he had said, "I will pay you whatever is right" (vv. 4–5). But to those he hired last, in the final hour, there was no discussion of compensation. Thus, he was not unjust to anyone, but he did not pay all the workers what they had earned. He paid them all the same wages even though they had not done the same amount of work. The latter question gets to the heart of the matter. This landowner operated outside the law of sowing and reaping. Instead, he was generous. He asked them, "Are you envious because I am generous?" Of course they were.[13]

Even those of us saved by grace through faith (Eph. 2:8–9) sometimes struggle with the concept of generosity. Donald McCullough explains,

13. See Glenn R. Kreider, "The Unfair Payment," DTS, July 2, 2014, http://www.dts.edu/media/play/the-unfair-payment-kreider-glenn/.

If we find it difficult to accept grace for others, how much more unwilling are we to have it handed to others! When someone gets off the hook too easily, aren't you uncomfortable? When someone does something bad—steal money from a grandmother, say, or abuse an invalid, or commit a crime—don't you want that person to receive what's rightfully coming? Don't you have a primal, visceral instinct that wants others to get their just desserts? Don't you want wrongdoers to get the full measure of punishment they deserve, at least enough to make them really, really sorry? I mean, if you play by the rules, (most of the time), and you see someone else breaking them, don't you want that person to be held accountable? Don't you want what's *fair*? Well, grace is not fair. And that's the problem.[14]

According to Jesus, "The last will be first, and the first will be last" (Matt. 20:16). Jesus then tells his disciples what is awaiting him.

We are going up to Jerusalem, and the Son of Man will be betrayed to the chief priests and the teachers of the law. They will condemn him to death and will turn him over to the Gentiles to be mocked and flogged and crucified. On the third day he will be raised to life! (vv. 18–19)

The King of kings is on his way to die. The Son of Man and Son of God will be put to death. The Creator of the universe will submit himself to his creatures. The giver of life will die at the hands of those who he created and to whom he grants life. God will condescend to allow his enemies to do what they want to him.

The disciples still do not understand. The mother of two of Jesus' inner circle of disciples, the sons of Zebedee, comes to Jesus with a request. "Grant that one of these two sons of mine

14. Donald McCullough, *If Grace Is So Amazing, Why Don't We Like It?* (San Francisco: Jossey-Bass, 2005), 6–7.

may sit at your right and the other at your left in your kingdom," she asks, with her sons present (v. 21). This mother is asking Jesus to take care of her sons, promote them, honor them, and give them important and prominent roles in the kingdom. And this comes on the heels of the explicit revelation that the King is on his way to suffer and die.

"You don't know what you are asking," Jesus says to them (v. 22). Jesus turns his attention from a mother's request to the sons who are making a foolish appeal through her. In order to demonstrate that they really have no idea what they are asking and, perhaps, to give them the opportunity to admit it, Jesus asks the two sons, "Can you drink the cup I am going to drink?" (v. 22). Surely they have heard Jesus talking about his impending death. Surely they have understood the predictions of his death by crucifixion. Surely they will at least ask what he means by "the cup," but they do not. Instead, their response is, "We can" (v. 22).

Jesus' response is direct: "You will indeed drink from my cup, but to sit at my right or left is not for me to grant. These places belong to those for whom they have been prepared by my Father" (v. 23). Since he has told the disciples repeatedly that they will be treated the same as he, it is not surprising to hear Jesus tell James and John that they will drink his cup. But he also claims not to have the authority to grant positions in the kingdom. Even if there is an organizational chart of positions in the kingdom, King Jesus apparently does not get to decide who fills them. The king of this kingdom does not even get to choose his staff or reward those who serve with him. His Father makes those decisions.

When the rest of the disciples hear about the request of James and John, they are indignant, probably because these two tried to gain an inside track in the kingdom. Jesus calls them together to give them the strongest statement about condescension to date.

You know that the rulers of the Gentiles lord it over them, and their high officials exercise authority over them. Not so with you. Instead, whoever wants to become great among you must be your servant, and whoever wants to be first must be your slave—just as the Son of Man did not come to be served, but to serve, and to give his life as a ransom for many. (vv. 25–28)

The contrast between Gentiles and disciples is clear. Gentiles are concerned about positions and influence, are obsessed with being served, are ambitious about climbing the ladder of success, are interested in making an impact, and desire to change the world. They want to be recognized for their greatness, receive the trappings of power, and be praised and honored by their subjects. Their desire is to accumulate property and people, climb the ladder of success, and be famous and important in the eyes of the world. But of his disciples, Jesus says, "Not so with you." Instead, disciples are servants. They look for opportunities to give, not to take; to serve, not to lord it over others; to be anonymous, not to be famous; to lift others up, not to elevate themselves. In short, they look to be like God, who created the world and turned it over to those created in this image, knowing they would rebel against him.

The greatest in this kingdom is a slave with no rights, property, prerogatives, privileges, prestige, fame, or subjects. In short, the model of greatness is Jesus, who lays down his life as a ransom for sinners.

The Passion of the Christ

As the Passover approaches, Jesus prepares for his upcoming death. Again he tells his disciples that the end is coming: "As you know, the Passover is two days away—and the Son of Man will be handed over to be crucified" (26:2). The chief priests and the elders plot to kill him (vv. 3–5), a woman anoints his body in advance of his burial (vv. 6–13), and Judas agrees to betray him (vv. 14–16). Although it looks from an earthly or human perspective that the scheming of these people is in opposition to the will of God, they are actually the means by which God's will is carried out.

Jesus celebrates the Passover with his disciples and institutes the Lord's Supper. During the meal, Jesus gives them a graphic illustration of servanthood when he gets up from the table and washes his disciples' feet (John 13).

Jesus then takes his disciples to Gethsemane. He asks them to wait while he prays. Deeply sorrowed and troubled, he prays, "My Father, if it is possible, may this cup be taken from me. Yet not as I will, but as you will" (Matt. 26:39), and then, "My Father, if it is not possible for this cup to be taken away unless I drink it, may your will be done" (v. 42). He also prays a third time (v. 44). In this deeply painful series of prayers, Jesus reaffirms his submission to the will of the Father for the sake of his enemies. He submits his will to the will of the Father, no matter what the cost.

As Jesus finishes praying, Judas arrives with a crowd armed with swords and clubs. One of the disciples of Jesus takes out his sword and cuts off the ear of the servant of the high priest.[15] Jesus restores the man's ear (Luke 22:51) and rebukes Peter (Matt. 26:52):

> Do you think I cannot call on my Father, and he will at once put at my disposal twelve legions of angels? But how then would the Scriptures be fulfilled that say it must happen in this way? (vv. 53–54)

Jesus submits to the betrayer, the crowd, and his enemies because he has submitted to the Father and the Scriptures. In so doing, he sets an example for his disciples to follow.

---

15. Matthew does not identify the culprit. John, however, says it is Peter (John 18:10).

Even though there are many false witnesses, the chief priests and the Sanhedrin cannot find sufficient evidence to put Jesus to death.[16] Finally two witnesses declare that Jesus claimed he would destroy the temple of God and rebuild it in three days. Jesus remains silent until the high priest says to him, "I charge you under oath by the living God: Tell us if you are the Christ, the Son of God" (v. 63). Jesus replies, "It is as you say. But I say to all of you: In the future you will see the Son of Man sitting at the right hand of the Mighty One and coming on the clouds of heaven" (v. 64). At that, the high priest tears his clothes and proclaims Jesus guilty of blasphemy. Jesus allows them to spit in his face, strike him with their fists, and beat and mock him (vv. 67–68).

Pilate finds Jesus guilty of nothing, but condemns him to die, as Jesus had predicted (Matt. 27:11–26). After being mocked, tortured, humiliated, and shamed, Jesus is crucified under a sign which, ironically, proclaims the truth: "THIS IS JESUS, THE KING OF THE JEWS" (v. 37).

Finally, Jesus cries in a loud voice and surrenders his spirit (v. 50). His death is not caused by what he suffers; it is his gift.[17] The giver of life is not subject to the actions of his creatures unless he chooses to put himself in their hands. And this is what Jesus does. He allows them to have their way with him, in submission to the will of the Father and to the Word of God, and he lays down his life.

At that moment, the curtain of the temple is torn in two, the earth shakes, tombs open, and the bodies of many saints are raised to life. They come out of their tombs and appear to

16. Matthew puts it this way: "The chief priests and the whole Sanhedrin were looking for false evidence against Jesus so that they could put him to death. But they did not find any, though many false witnesses came forward" (26:59–60). In John's gospel, Pilate repeatedly affirms Jesus' innocence, but then has him flogged and killed (John 18–19).

17. See his own words in John's gospel: "The reason my Father loves me is that I lay down my life—only to take it up again. No one takes it from me, but I lay it down of my own accord. I have authority to lay it down and authority to take it up again. This command I received from my Father" (10:17–18).

many in the holy city after Jesus' resurrection (vv. 52–53). These resurrected bodies are a foretaste of the coming day, when all who are in the graves will come forth (Matt. 22:31–32; see also John 5:28–29).

Jesus is buried in a tomb provided by Joseph of Arimathea. Guards are stationed in front of the tomb to prevent anyone from stealing the body. And all creation waits three long days (Matt. 27:57–66).

The Resurrection of Jesus

Then, on the first day of the week, Jesus conquers death. An earthquake shatters the silence of the early morning and the entrance to the tomb. An angel appears. When the women come to care for Jesus' body, the angel sends them away to testify to the disciples that Jesus is alive (28:1–10). This event provides hope. Because he lives, we too shall live.

The Great Commission

Matthew concludes his gospel with the Great Commission. To his worshipping, yet doubting, disciples, Jesus says, "All authority in heaven and on earth has been given to me. Therefore go and make disciples" (vv. 18–19). The one who has all authority has chosen not to use it himself. The one who has all power has chosen to give it away. The one who has just conquered sin, death, and the grave has turned over the next stage of the kingdom to this group of fearful and doubting followers, who have demonstrated over and over again that they are more concerned about themselves than about Jesus, about their agendas than about the kingdom, about their reputations than about "the least of these," and about greatness than about servanthood. Yet it is to these men that Jesus gives the responsibility to make disciples. The gospel is entrusted to them. The mission of the church is given to them. The fate of the poor, the needy, and the oppressed is delegated to these followers who, even in the presence of the resurrected Jesus, continue to doubt. And that continues to be God's plan. It is through the church that the kingdom grows and spreads over the earth.

Conclusion

In his life and death, as well as in his teaching, Jesus showed his disciples what greatness looks like. He corrects their cultural understanding that positions of power and privilege are the prerogatives of greatness. Instead, he repeatedly corrects their misunderstandings and gives them a graphic demonstration of humility and condescension through submission to death on a cross. But death cannot defeat Life itself. After three days, Jesus comes back to life. The lives of the disciples are forever changed through his resurrection from the dead. And ours too are transformed by it.

8

CONDESCENSION IN THE TEACHING OF THE APOSTLES

IN THE MID-NINETEENTH CENTURY, Scottish hymn writer Christian H. Bateman composed "Come, Christians, Join to Sing." The first stanza calls Christians to join their voices in praise to Christ the King. The third stanza expresses the hope of everlasting life and looks forward to an eternity to praise Christ. The second focuses on Christ as a condescending guide and friend: "Come, lift your hearts on high, Alleluia! Amen! Let praises fill the sky; Alleluia! Amen! He is our Guide and Friend; To us he'll condescend; his love shall never end. Alleluia! Amen!"[1]

That the eternal king of the universe condescended to become our guide and friend and, through his resurrection from the dead, to provide the hope of eternal life and the re-creation of all things is the good news, the gospel. Christians join together to sing the song of salvation, the song of praise to the Creator and Redeemer.

---

1. Christian H. Bateman, "Come, Christians, Join to Sing," 1843. This familiar hymn is usually sung to a traditional Spanish melody.

The Gospels tell the story of the coming of Christ to earth, his death, and his resurrection, but the biblical story does not end with the first coming. It culminates in his return to the earth. The triune God will condescend to make the earth his eternal home, to dwell forever with redeemed humanity on a re-created earth.

The Acts of the Apostles

The Promise of the Spirit

In the Acts of the Apostles, Luke picks up the story of Jesus after his resurrection. Over a period of forty days, Jesus continues to speak to his disciples about the kingdom of God (Acts 1:3).[2] One time, while eating with them, he reminds them to stay in Jerusalem until the coming of the Spirit: "Do not leave Jerusalem, but wait for the gift my Father promised, which you have heard me speak about. For John baptized with water, but in a few days you will be baptized with the Holy Spirit" (vv. 4–5)."[3] The disciples respond with a question: "Lord, are you at this time going to restore the kingdom to Israel?" (v. 6).

This question expresses two major misunderstandings held by the disciples, and Jesus' answer addresses both of them. These have implications for understanding the ministry of Jesus and his condescension. First, the disciples still seem to think that

---

2. Luke explicitly refers to his former book in the beginning of Acts: "In my former book, Theophilus, I wrote about all that Jesus began to do and to teach until the day he was taken up to heaven, after giving instructions through the Holy Spirit to the apostles he had chosen" (Acts 1:1–2).

3. Jesus' eating seems to imply that his condescension continues even after the resurrection. Surely the resurrected and glorified Christ does not need to eat for survival. Luke's gospel does not include the extensive promise of the coming of the Spirit found in John 14–16. Since John wrote after Luke, it is not that Luke is referring to the teaching of John, but he does assume that Theophilus is aware of the promises that Jesus made about the coming of the Spirit.

the ultimate focus of the kingdom is the nation of Israel. The kingdom certainly includes Israel, but it is much broader than one nation. The redemption of God is for all peoples, not just for Israel (Gen. 12:3).[4] Second, even though Jesus repeatedly insisted that the time of the end of the age cannot be known, the disciples seem to think that he really does know. In the Olivet Discourse, Jesus told them that "no one knows about that day or hour" (Matt. 24:36). It will come suddenly and unexpectedly, like the flood in Noah's day (vv. 38–39). "You do not know on what day your Lord will come" (v. 42). He will come like a thief (v. 43), "at an hour when you do not expect him" (v. 44). The master "will come on a day when [the servant] does not expect him" (v. 50).[5] The implication is that the end of the age will come suddenly and without warning.[6] It is hard to hear the disciples' question, "Are you at this time going to restore the kingdom to Israel?" (Acts 1:6), other than as expressing their hope that Jesus will establish a Jewish kingdom and will tell them when it will happen.

Jesus' response to his disciples addresses both these misunderstandings.

4. In Acts 3:25, Peter makes this point explicitly as he quotes the promise that God made to Abraham: "Through your offspring all peoples on earth will be blessed." But it is only after the vision of the sheet with unclean animals and his experience in the house of Cornelius that Peter really understands that the gospel is for all peoples (Acts 10). Paul calls the promise to bless all nations the gospel (Gal. 3:8).

5. One of the many mysteries of the incarnation is how the attributes of humanity and deity can both be present in one person without separating, dividing, confusing, or mixing them. Robert Reymond puts it well: "Jesus expressly stated that he did not know the day or the hour of his return (Matt. 24:36; Mark 13:32). That is to say, he emphatically disavowed knowledge as a man of the 'when' of his parousia" (*A New Systematic Theology of the Christian Faith* [Nashville: Thomas Nelson, 1998], 1007).

6. Herman Bavinck summarizes the teaching of Jesus on this point succinctly: "His intent is not to inform his disciples of the precise moment of his parousia, but to urge them to be watchful. . . . Taking notice of the signs of the times is a duty for Jesus's disciples; the calculation of the precise time of his coming is forbidden to them and also impossible" (*Holy Spirit, Church, and New Creation*, vol. 4 of *Reformed Dogmatics*, ed. John Bolt, trans. John Vriend [Grand Rapids: Baker, 2008], 687–88).

It is not for you to know the times or dates the Father has set by his own authority. But you will receive power when the Holy Spirit comes on you; and you will be my witnesses in Jerusalem, and in all Judea and Samaria, and to the ends of the earth. (vv. 7–8)

He encourages them to have a forward-looking perspective that results in an expansion of the kingdom, rather than a backward-looking perspective that longs for the good old days. He reminds them that the time of the end is set by the Father; it is not for the disciples to know. Then he sends them out as witnesses, not just in Jewish territory, but to the ends of the earth, to all peoples.[7] The mission of the disciples of Jesus is to all peoples, as God announced in the gospel in advance to Abraham (Gal. 3:8).

The Ascension and the Promise of Return

When Jesus finishes speaking, he disappears. He ascends to heaven. But the ascension is not the end of Jesus' relationship to the earth. Two angelic figures promise the disciples that "this same Jesus, who has been taken from you into heaven, will come back in the same way you have seen him go into heaven" (Acts 1:11). In the age to come, in the eschatological kingdom, the King will be on the earth.

The embodied Son of God is coming back to the earth. Thus, the hope of the followers of Jesus is not just that they will go to be with him, but that he will come to them—that he will return to the earth and make things right when he lives on the earth forever.[8] In short, the hope of redeemed humanity is not heaven, but earth. Heaven is a temporary home until the day of resur-

7. On the mission of the church, see John Piper, *Let the Nations Be Glad: The Supremacy of God in Missions*, 3rd ed. (Grand Rapids: Baker, 2010).
8. That he "must remain in heaven until the time comes for God to restore everything" (Acts 3:21) implies that at that time he will return to the earth and make his dwelling here. See Revelation 21–22 for the culmination of this hope.

rection, when heaven will come down to earth and the God of heaven will make the earth his home (Rev. 21:3).[9] When the work of redemption is completed, the triune God will condescend to dwell eternally on this planet.

The Coming of the Spirit

In the meantime, as the firstfruits of the age to come (Rom. 8:23), the Spirit of God descends and fills the believers in Jesus on the day of Pentecost (Acts 2:1–4), as Jesus had promised (1:4). He empowers his disciples in Jerusalem to speak in such a way that the people who had gathered there from many nations say in amazement, "We hear them declaring the wonders of God in our own tongues!" (2:11).

The confusion of tongues at Babel (Gen. 11) is now being redeemed, at least in its beginning stages. In the future, a great multitude of people "from every nation, tribe, people and language" will worship in Spirit and truth, in unity "before the throne and in front of the Lamb" (Rev. 7:9). Pentecost gives a foretaste of that day. The gift of the Spirit, and the kingdom, is for all peoples, "for all whom the Lord our God will call" (Acts 2:39); people who speak many different tongues receive this blessing on this day.

The Preaching of the Gospel

In the book of Acts, we see a difference in the way the good news of Jesus' resurrection is communicated by the apostles. The ethnic makeup of the crowd seems to be determinative. The message of a humble Savior is consistent; how it is communicated differs. With a Jewish audience, the preaching begins with the Scriptures, demonstrating from the Law and the Prophets that

9. See N. T. Wright, *Surprised by Hope: Rethinking Heaven, the Resurrection, and the Mission of the Church* (New York: HarperOne, 2008).

Jesus is the Messiah (13:16–41). With a Gentile audience, with people not familiar with the Scriptures, the approach is different (see 14:14–18). An example of the latter is found in Paul's sermon in Athens in chapter 17.

Paul's Sermon in Athens

In Athens, Paul is invited to speak at the Areopagus because the philosophers who meet there are curious about his strange ideas (17:19–20). The message of the resurrected Jesus sounds odd to them (v. 18). At their request, Paul addresses the crowd.

> Men of Athens! I see that in every way you are very religious. For as I walked around and looked carefully at your objects of worship, I even found an altar with this inscription: TO AN UNKNOWN GOD. Now what you worship as something unknown I am going to proclaim to you. (vv. 22–23)

Paul begins his sermon by claiming that he has investigated the cultural setting of Athens. He has walked around the city and looked carefully at the objects of worship (v. 23). Rather than separating from this pluralistic culture, Paul admits publicly that he has spent significant time in it. Rather than avoiding any contact with the false religions of Athens, Paul has visited the places of worship and looked carefully at their artifacts. Rather than evading any interaction with the culture, Paul intentionally immerses himself in it. Paul is able to bring the gospel into the culture of Athens because he condescends to act like Jesus.

Then, in several short paragraphs, Paul tells the metanarrative of God's work of creation and re-creation.

> The God who made the world and everything in it is the Lord of heaven and earth and does not live in temples built by hands.

> And he is not served by human hands, as if he needed anything, because he himself gives all men life and breath and everything else. (vv. 24–25)

Like Moses in the opening words of Scripture (Gen. 1:1), Paul begins with the assertion that God exists. He does not provide an argument or apologetic for God's existence. He assumes it to be true.[10] The God who created everything is before everything, the cause of everything and the Lord of everything. He does not live within temples built for him.[11] He is not dependent upon creatures. They, rather, are dependent upon him. He is the source of their existence and of everything else.

Paul continues,

> From one man he made every nation of men, that they should inhabit the whole earth; and he determined the times set for them and the exact places where they should live. God did this so that men would seek him and perhaps reach out for him and find him, though he is not far from each one of us. "For in him we live and move and have our being." As some of your own poets have said, "We are his offspring." (Acts 17:26–28)

According to Paul's anthropology, every human who has ever lived is descended from one man, from the first man, from the man who God created.[12] God is not only the source of

---

10. The apologetic for God's existence is creation. To those who believe, no argument is necessary. To those who do not believe, no argument is sufficient (see Rom. 1:18–25).

11. Paul does not say it explicitly here, but God might choose to dwell in a temple, as he did in the one built by Solomon. Paul's claim seems to be about God's independence, not his location. In short, the creatures do not determine where God dwells; rather, the Creator determines where the creatures dwell.

12. The historicity of Adam is a basic precondition for Paul's anthropology and soteriology (see Rom. 5). Much Pauline theology collapses if the historicity and the special creation of Adam are rejected. See C. John Collins, *Did Adam and Eve Really Exist? Who They Were and Why You Should Care* (Wheaton: Crossway, 2011).

all humanity, but also the one who determines when they live—and even the "exact places" where they live. And he does this for a purpose: so humans might find him. The God who is, in contrast to the nonexistent gods of the Athenians, is transcendent. He is outside of his creation and independent of it. But God has made himself knowable and known in the world he has made. He is present in the world he created; he is not far from us.

Then Paul quotes from some philosopher-poets known to the Athenians in order to support his claim. Paul believes that truth about God can be found in the words of those who do not believe in him, do not worship him as God, and have no intention to reveal the truth about him. John Calvin put it this way: "Since all truth comes from God, if any ungodly person has said anything that is true, we should not reject it, for it also comes from God."[13]

Consistent with his preaching elsewhere, Paul tells the biblical story. But in Athens, he does it without quoting the Bible. Since his audience does not accept the Bible as a sacred text, he would gain nothing by citing Bible verses. But he does proclaim the truth of Scripture. When he does quote sources, it is the poets of the Athenians.[14]

Then Paul applies the truth about God.

> Therefore since we are God's offspring, we should not think that the divine being is like gold or silver or stone—an image made by man's design and skill. In the past God overlooked such ignorance, but now he commands all people everywhere to repent. For he has set a day when he will judge the world with

---

13. John Calvin, *1 and 2 Timothy and Titus*, Crossway Classic Commentaries (Wheaton: Crossway, 1998), 187.

14. Phillip J. Long has an excellent discussion of Paul's use of these poets in "Acts 17—Paul and the Poets," *Reading Acts: Some Thoughts on the Book of Acts and Pauline Theology* (blog), March 20, 2013, http://readingacts.wordpress.com /tag/acts-17/.

justice by the man he has appointed. He has given proof of this
to all men by raising him from the dead. (vv. 29–31)

This powerful, transcendent Creator has condescended to make
himself present and known in the world he created. He has overlooked ignorance for a time. But he is a God of justice and judgment, and the day of reckoning is coming.

What God declared about himself (see Ex. 34:6–7) has now
received proof in the incarnation. The one who lived, died, and
was resurrected has been appointed judge of the entire world.
The one who condescended to come to earth has been exalted
and will sit in judgment (see Phil. 2:6–11).

The audience's response to this message is typical and common: some believe, some sneer, and some are curious to hear
more (Acts 17:32–34).[15] When the gospel is proclaimed, God seldom
grants universal acceptance, although sometimes there seems
to be little response at all. Generally, some believe the gospel,
some emphatically reject it, and others are willing to hear more
at a later time.

Paul's Message to the Ephesian Elders

When Paul calls the elders of the church in Ephesus in Acts
20 to meet with him at Miletus, he describes his ministry among
them as one of serving the Lord "with great humility and with
tears" (v. 19). Paul's ministry style is consistent with the character
of God. He condescends to deal mercifully and lovingly with
these men. He then tells the elders of his uncertainty about
what will happen to him, but he appears fairly sure that he will

15. Some have argued that Paul's approach here was a dismal failure and a mistake
he learned not to repeat. Rather, as Lane G. Tipton argues, "Paul's address to the
Athenian philosophers on Mars hill, recorded in Acts 17:16–34, presents us with the
locus classicus for understanding the Pauline apologetic" ("Resurrection, Proof, and
Presuppositionalism," in *Revelation and Reasons: New Essays in Reformed Apologetics*,
ed. K. Scott Oliphint and Lane G. Tipton [Phillipsburg, NJ: P&R Publishing, 2007], 42).

not see them again (v. 25). He gives them instructions about
shepherding the community entrusted to their care (v. 28). He
asks them to emulate his style of ministry—one that he learned
from Jesus himself: "In everything I did, I showed you that by
this kind of hard work we must help the weak, remembering
the words the Lord Jesus himself said: 'It is more blessed to give
than to receive'" (v. 35).

In this saying of Jesus, which is not recorded in the Gospels,
Paul finds a summary of the attitude and lifestyle of Jesus and his
followers. In the same way that Jesus came to serve and not to be
served, those who follow him are blessed when they give. Jesus
humbled himself, became one of us, and laid down his life for
his enemies, thus establishing a model to be followed. Christian
ministry must focus on serving others, empowering and elevat-
ing others, providing for the needs of others, and encouraging
others to grow in godliness. This is the means of true blessing,
both for the minister and for those who are served.

The Book of Romans

In the prologue of his letter to the Romans, the apostle
Paul expresses his confidence in the gospel, the center of his
life and ministry. The gospel, he says, is concerned with Jesus
Christ our Lord, descended from David in his human nature
and, through the Spirit of holiness, declared to be the Son of
God by his resurrection from the dead (Rom. 1:2–4). Thus, the
gospel is about Jesus Christ in his condescension—becoming
human for the sake of fallen humanity, laying down his life
for his enemies, and rising from the dead to give them hope
of life everlasting.

Paul asserts his confidence in the gospel when he writes,

> I am not ashamed of the gospel, because it is the power of God
> for the salvation of everyone who believes: first for the Jew, then

for the Gentile. For in the gospel a righteousness from God is revealed, a righteousness that is by faith from first to last, just as it has been written: "The righteous will live by faith." (1:16–17)

The gospel is the power of God for salvation. It reveals the only way a sinner can be justified before God.

God's Revelation in Creation

Before he explains how the gospel provides justification, Paul insists that "the wrath of God is being revealed from heaven" (v. 18). This statement stands in stark contrast to the previous one: "in the gospel a righteousness of God is revealed" (v. 17). Two strongly juxtaposed ideas are found here, one negative and the other positive. What connects the two is that both righteousness and wrath are revealed by God, are presently experienced, and have future implications.

At the heart of this revelation is God's revelation of himself. Paul claims that "God's invisible qualities—his eternal power and divine nature—have been clearly seen" (v. 20). God's wrath is justified because he has made himself visible.[16] When we look at the world, we see the God who created it. Not just his effects, not just his fingerprints, not just evidence of him once having been present, not shadows or images of him, and not a twisted or corrupted picture of him, but God's "eternal power and divine nature" are clearly seen. Even in a fallen and broken world, God is revealed. When Paul says that the gospel reveals the righteousness of God, he is not implying that the righteousness of God has never before been seen. The gospel is not the solution to the hiddenness of God. Rather, it is the

16. Paul says that more than evidence of God is seen. He says that God's invisible qualities have been seen—his eternal power and divine nature. In short, the invisible God has become visible in his creation. This is not pantheism; God is not his world. But he is present in it and thus can be seen.

solution to the sinfulness of humanity. It is the revelation of righteousness to the unrighteous.

As Paul continues in this section, he explains the unrighteousness for which the gospel is the only solution. God has revealed his eternal power and divine nature; he has made it "plain to them" (v. 19), and it was "clearly seen" (v. 20). Humans are not ignorant.[17] Paul explains that humans "suppress the truth by their wickedness" (v. 18), "knew God" (v. 21), "exchanged the glory of the immortal God for images made to look like mortal man and birds and animals and reptiles" (v. 23), and "exchanged the truth of God for a lie" (v. 25). Rebellion, not ignorance, is humanity's condition. We are unrighteous and worthy of condemnation because we rejected and continue to reject the presence of God in the world he made. God's wrath is rightly revealed because of our rebellion against him. That is why the gospel is such good news; it reveals the only way by which unrighteous people can become righteous.[18]

Our parents in the garden of Eden rebelled against God (Gen. 3), and so do their children. Since no one consistently and clearly observes God's eternal power and divine nature when he observes the world, it seems that Paul has all humanity in view here. All of us find it difficult, at least at times, to see the attributes of God in what he created.

Further, as we read through the catalog of evil behaviors that characterize the lives of the rebellious (vv. 24–32), we should see ourselves.[19] Could anyone really honestly claim to have avoided

17. K. Scott Oliphint, *Reasons {for Faith}: Philosophy in the Service of Theology* (Phillipsburg, NJ: P&R Publishing, 2006), 133, writes: "What is Paul telling us in this passage? Notice, first of all, that we *all*, born as we are into our sinful state by virtue of our wickedness, nevertheless *know* God" (emphasis original).

18. In Romans, Paul defends the imputation of righteousness through the gospel. In 2 Corinthians 5:21, Paul asserts that we "become the righteousness of God" in Christ.

19. Paul's intention in Romans 1:24–32 is not to give a hierarchy of sins or describe a downward declension away from God, but rather to present a catalog of sinfulness. Thus, the list serves as a mirror, so that everyone can clearly see himself or herself as

every kind of wickedness? Surely there is no one among us who has not disobeyed his parents, at least once. So, rather than looking at this first chapter of Romans as if it applied only to other people, either those who lived long ago or those who are really bad, we should see ourselves in the mirror of God's Word (see James 1:22–25) and should walk away changed by it. As further evidence that all humanity is in view, Paul's words in the next chapter are particularly convicting: "You, therefore, have no excuse, you who pass judgment on someone else, for at whatever point you judge the other, you are condemning yourself, because you who pass judgment do the same things" (Rom. 2:1).[20] In short, the person who claims to be neither on this list nor in the intended audience of this passage will have condemned himself.[21]

Two significant conclusions follow from this important text. First, God is not revealed for the first time in his Son. The attributes of deity have been plain and have been clearly seen from the beginning of the world. God is not hiding; he desires to be known. God has condescended to reveal himself in what he has made. He is not the god of deism, which asserts that although God created the world, he has no normative contact with it.[22] He is not the god of pantheism, which views the world as divine.[23]

---

a sinner. That, after all, is Paul's conclusion: "For all have sinned and fall short of the glory of God" (3:23).

20. It is easy for me to look at the catalog of sins in Romans 1 and think, "I've not done every one of these, and I've done none of them as badly as someone else I know." And then I can walk away feeling (self) justified. But when I realize that my heart is wicked, that I envy, that I am arrogant and boastful, and that I disobeyed my parents, yet that God has made a way for me to be justified, I walk away humbled and deeply grateful for the gospel.

21. The person who claims to be innocent of any sin is condemned by Romans 3:10–20.

22. For an excellent introduction to deism, see Gerald R. McDermott, "Deism," in *The Encyclopedia of Protestantism*, ed. Hans J. Hillerbrand (New York: Routledge, 2004), 2:568–74.

23. For an excellent, yet a bit technical, treatment of pantheism, see Alasdair MacIntyre, "Pantheism," in *The Encyclopedia of Philosophy*, ed. Paul Edwards (New York: Macmillan, 1967), 6:31–35.

He is the Creator of all that is and is also omnipresent in his world. So he is actually there. Even in a corrupted, fallen world populated by evil creatures who are in rebellion against him, God is present and active.

Second, if God is revealed in his Word and his world, and if the incarnate Word came into this world to redeem it for himself and to re-create it into a world where he can live forever, we cannot ignore what we learn about God from his world. The study of science, literature, music, and other cultural forms of revelation is not optional for Christian theologians.[24] Of course, the world is corrupted and fallen, but so are we. So any study of God's revelation, even of the Scriptures, must be undertaken in dependence upon the Spirit of truth, who indwells us and empowers us to know God more accurately.

Justification by Grace

All humans, Jews and Gentiles alike, are sinners and can be justified only by grace through faith. This statement summarizes the next couple of chapters of Romans. God is the God of both Jews and Gentiles, and Abraham, the non-Jew, stands as a clear example of this good news. He is the father of all who believe (4:17). He is the father of the promised seed, the one through whom all nations will be blessed (see Gen. 12:3).

In Adam, all die. His one act of rebellion brought decay, destruction, and death into the world. All humans are born guilty of his sin and thus die. Life is found only in Christ. The good news is that we can have peace with God through Christ—not because of us, but because of him. "While we were still sinners, Christ died for us" (Rom. 5:8). God's love is a condescending love. God's love is gracious. God gives to his enemies. God's love comes to them. And God saves them: "When we were God's enemies,

24. See Herman Bavinck, *The Philosophy of Revelation* (1909; repr., Eugene, OR: Wipf and Stock, 2003).

172

we were reconciled to him though the death of his Son" (v. 10).[25] God has given to these former enemies an incredible hope, the resurrection from the dead: "If we have been united with him like this in his death, we will certainly also be united with him in his resurrection" (6:5). Death does not have the final word for us.

The Hope of All Creation

In another pivotal section of this book, Paul reminds us that "our present sufferings are not worth comparing with the glory that will be revealed in us" (8:18). What God has already done for us, what he has given us, is not the end of his promises and blessings. Rather, these current blessings pale in comparison to what is to come. God has great and precious promises for us (2 Peter 1:4), and we wait for them. We join creation, Paul says, in waiting in eager expectation for those promises: "The creation was subjected to frustration, not by its own choice, but by the will of the one who subjected it, in hope that the creation itself will be liberated from its bondage to decay" (Rom. 8:20–21).

We remember that when Adam and Eve sinned, God cursed the ground (Gen. 3:17), and an animal died to provide clothing for them (v. 21). When God sent the flood on the earth to curse the ground, all animals died except those in the ark with Noah and his family (Gen. 6:17–21; 7:21–23). The fate of the creatures was undeserved; they suffered and died because of human sin. Creation, Paul says, hopes that it will be set free, that it will be redeemed in conjunction with humanity's redemption (Rom. 8:21). In short, the substitutionary atonement of Christ provides redemption not just for humanity, but for all creation.

"We know," Paul continues, "that the whole creation has been groaning as in the pains of childbirth right up to the present time" (v. 22). These words echo what Jesus taught about wars

---

25. The apostle John explains that we know what love is because of what God has done (1 John 3:16).

between nations, famines, and earthquakes: "All these are the beginning of birth pains" (Matt. 24:8). Creation's birth pains have been ongoing since the fall. And we, the elect, "who have the firstfruits of the Spirit, groan inwardly as we wait eagerly for our adoption as sons, the redemption of our bodies" (Rom. 8:23). Creation groans; we also groan. We join creation in looking forward to the resurrection of the dead, the redemption of our bodies. This is our common hope, a hope that creation and humanity share. This is the good news found in the gospel. This is also the hope that Jesus has, that one day his body (the church) will be complete when the saints are raised to experience and enjoy the new creation with him. Since he has become one of us, his future is tied to ours, and ours is tied to his.

Because of his love for us, God has granted us the firstfruits of the Spirit. The Spirit is not the end of God's blessings to us, but merely the beginning. The Spirit was not given to us to satisfy us, to be the solution to our longing. Instead, he was given for two major purposes. He groans within us (v. 23) and prays and intercedes for us (vv. 26–27).

The Holy Spirit, the third person of the Godhead, indwells us, intercedes for us, and will never leave us. The God who loved us eternally, who provided redemption through the death and resurrection of Jesus, permanently indwells the saints (see v. 9). God condescends to save, indwell, and live forever with creatures who, even though his "eternal power and divine nature are clearly seen," consistently choose to exchange that glory for images they create of things that are made. What amazing love! What transforming grace! What condescending mercy and compassion!

Love One Another

After giving an admonition to serve God through transformation that comes through renewing of the mind (Rom. 12:2), Paul tells the Romans to think of themselves "with sober judgment, in accordance with the measure of faith God has given you" (v. 3). He specifically tells them to reject pride: "Do not be proud, but be willing to associate with people of low position. Do not be conceited" (v. 16). He encourages them to submit to authority, especially to the "governing authorities, for there is no authority except that which God has established" (13:1).

But it is love, Paul says, that most clearly evidences godliness. All the commandments of God are summed up in one: "Love your neighbor as yourself" (v. 9). Jesus summed up the Law and the Prophets in two commandments: love God and love your neighbor (Matt. 22:37–40); Paul sums them up in one: "Love does no harm to its neighbor. Therefore love is the fulfillment of the law" (Rom. 13:10). Jesus treats the two commandments not as hierarchical, but as complementary. In short, love for others involves love for God, and love for God involves love for others. The apostle John expresses it this way:

> We love because he first loved us. If anyone says, "I love God," yet hates his brother, he is a liar. For anyone who does not love his brother, whom he has seen, cannot love God, whom he has not seen. And he has given us this command: Whoever loves God must also love his brother. (1 John 4:19–21)

How does love summarize the law? Again, the apostle John is helpful in taking us to the heart of the matter. "God is love," he says twice (vv. 8, 16). If God is love, then those who are godly are also characterized by love. In fact, John explains, we are dependent upon divine revelation even to know what love is. Love is not just an ethical standard or a theoretical principle. It is active and practical and concrete.

> This is how we know what love is: Jesus Christ laid down his life for us. And we ought to lay down our lives for our brothers. If anyone has material possessions and sees his brother in need

but has no pity on him, how can the love of God be in him?
Dear children, let us not love with words or tongue but with
actions and in truth. This then is how we know that we belong
to the truth, and how we set our hearts at rest in his presence
whenever our hearts condemn us. (3:16–20)

The implication is clear: Were it not for the work of Christ, we
would not know what love is. Because God is love, God acts in
love. And because God is love and acts in love, we now know what
love is, because God the Son condescended to lay down his life
for us. Love acts. Those who love act in love. Those who belong
to God act like God, caring for others in need—not simply feeling
pity for them, but acting to meet their needs. And this acting in
love, John says, is the way we know that we belong to the truth,
that we are God's children, that we are Christians.

John returns to this theme a little later in this epistle.

Dear friends, let us love one another, for love comes from God.
Everyone who loves has been born of God and knows God.
Whoever does not love does not know God, because God is love.
This is how God showed his love among us: He sent his one
and only Son into the world that we might live through him.
This is love: not that we loved God, but that he loved us and
sent his Son as an atoning sacrifice for our sins. Dear friends,
since God so loved us, we also ought to love one another. (4:7–11)

God's initiative in showing love is the revelation of love to
us and a model of how we are to treat one another. This love for
others, John says, is evidence that we belong to the God of love,
a basis of our assurance of salvation. "God is love," he reminds
us. "Whoever lives in love lives in God, and God in him. In this
way, love is made complete among us so that we will have confidence on the day of judgment, because in this world we are
like him" (vv. 16–17).

The First Letter to the Corinthians

The apostle Paul gives an extended description of love in 1 Corinthians 13. Love is countercultural, radically unlike what is valued and respected in a fallen world. It rejects ambition, respect, accumulation, prestige, power, and similar values of the fallen world.

> Love is patient, love is kind. It does not envy, it does not boast, it is not proud. It is not rude, it is not self-seeking, it is not easily angered, it keeps no record of wrongs. Love does not delight in evil but rejoices with the truth. It always protects, always trusts, always hopes, always perseveres.
> Love never fails. (1 Cor. 13:4–8)

The parallel to God's description of himself in Exodus 34:6–7 is striking.[26] God declares there that he is compassionate and gracious; love is patient and kind. God declares that he is slow to anger; love is not easily angered and keeps no record of wrongs. God declares that he abounds in love and faithfulness and forgives wickedness, rebellion, and sin; love always protects, trusts, hopes, and perseveres. Love never fails.

The Book of Ephesians

Paul's description of our deliverance from sin in Ephesians 2:1–10 emphasizes God's condescending love. He asserts that we were "dead in . . . transgressions and sins" (v. 1), following "the ways of this world and of the ruler of the kingdom of the air" (v. 2), "gratifying the cravings of our sinful nature" (v. 3), and "by nature objects of wrath" (v. 3). But "because of his great love for us, God, who is rich in mercy, made us alive with

26. According to Paul House, "Perhaps no better summation of Yahweh's true nature appears in the Old Testament" (*Old Testament Theology* [Downers Grove, IL: InterVarsity Press, 1998], 123).

Christ even when we were dead in transgressions" (vv. 4–5). Our salvation is God's work for us, not dependent upon us in any way. "It is," as Paul puts it, "by grace you have been saved" (vv. 5, 8). Salvation is unmerited, unearned, undeserved—a gracious gift from God. For reasons known only to him, God has condescended to love his enemies, to turn rebels into obedient servants, and to adopt into his family those who hate and detest everything about him. Salvation is by grace through faith, and even the faith that is required is a gift of God (v. 8).

Having created this new man made up of Jews and Gentiles together (vv. 11–16), this new people made up of fellow citizens of his people and members of his household (v. 19), God has made this building (v. 21) into a temple, a "dwelling in which God lives by his Spirit" (v. 22). The church is the dwelling place of God. God has condescended to dwell in this people, that through them "he might show the incomparable riches of his grace" (v. 7) and his "manifold wisdom" (3:10).

In this letter to the church in Ephesus, Paul then encourages Christians to "live a life worthy of the calling you have received" (4:1). He explains what this means as he continues: "Be completely humble and gentle; be patient, bearing with one another in love" (v. 2). Since God is humble, gentle, patient, and loving, those in whom he dwells should look like him. So, Paul says, "make every effort to keep the unity of the Spirit through the bond of peace" (v. 3). Why? "There is one body and one Spirit . . . one Lord, one faith, one baptism; one God and Father of all, who is over all and through all and in all" (vv. 4–6). The one God is over all, but he has condescended to be in all and through all, and his presence is manifested in those he indwells. The transcendent one is also immanent in those he has chosen.

Paul also instructs Christians to

> Be imitators of God, therefore, as dearly loved children and live
> a life of love, just as Christ loved us and gave himself up for us
> as a fragrant offering and sacrifice to God. (5:1–2)

In short, his admonition can be summarized this way: love as Christ loved. Christ loved by giving himself for us. Christ loved by condescending to offer himself for his enemies. Love gives—that's what it does—and the primary or ultimate example of love is Christ's selfless, humble condescension. And, Paul says, this is how we imitate God. Godliness is condescending love.

When Paul exhorts Christians to be filled with the Spirit (v. 18), he lists several manifestations of the Spirit in those who are filled.

> . . . addressing one another in psalms and hymns and spiritual
> songs, singing and making melody to the Lord with your heart,
> giving thanks always and for everything to God the Father in
> the name of our Lord Jesus Christ, submitting to one another
> out of reverence for Christ. (vv. 19–21 ESV)

A person who is filled with the Spirit is submissive to others. Since to be filled with the Spirit means to be controlled or ordered by the indwelling Spirit, submission to one another is produced by the Spirit. Thus the Spirit too manifests divine condescension, and his power and presence in Christians is revealed in our submission to one another.

Conclusion

The coming of the Spirit introduced a new age. It transformed the apostles into a band of men who witnessed to the resurrected Christ in Jerusalem and then toward the ends of the earth (see Acts 1:8). Through a miraculous confrontation by the risen Christ, Saul of Tarsus was transformed from a persecutor of Christians into a missionary to the Gentiles (ch. 9). These men taught others what they had learned from Jesus: love as he loved; serve as he served; pour out your life for others because of the hope of Jesus' return to the earth. This final act of the biblical story is the focus of the next chapter.

9

THE NEW CREATION: THE FINAL CHAPTER IN THE BIBLICAL STORY

ROBERTSON MCQUILKIN served as president of Columbia Bible College and Seminary (now Columbia International University) from 1968 to 1990. When his wife, Muriel, was diagnosed with Alzheimer's disease, McQuilkin knew the time would come when he would have to make difficult decisions about her care. As the disease progressed, she became more and more agitated and fearful when he was absent. When he was present, however, she was content and happy. Often, after he left the house, Muriel would walk the mile from their house to the campus to be with him, sometimes as many as ten times a day.[1] It became increasingly clear that Muriel would need constant care. Should her husband find a caregiver for her, perhaps through institutional care, or should he resign from his position of ministry to be her primary caregiver? McQuilkin explained his decision in his resignation speech.

1. Robertson McQuilkin, "CT Classic: Living by Vows," *Christianity Today*, February 1, 2004, http://www.christianitytoday.com/ct/2004/februaryweb-only/2-9-11.0 .html?start=3.

I haven't in my life experienced easy decision making on major
decisions. But one of the simplest and clearest decisions I've
had to make is this one, because circumstances dictated it.
Muriel, now in the last couple of months, seems to be almost
happy when with me, and almost never happy when not with
me. In fact she seems to feel trapped, becomes very fearful,
sometimes almost terror, and when she can't get to me there can
be anger, she's in distress. But when I am with her she's happy
and contented. And so I must be with her at all times. And you
see, it's not only that I promised in sickness and in health, till
death do us part, and I am a man of my word, but as I have said,
I don't know with this group, but I have said publicly, it's the
only fair thing. She sacrificed for me for forty years, to make
my life possible. So if I cared for her for forty years, I would still
be in debt. However, there is much more. It's not that I have to,
it's that I get to. I love her very dearly, and you can tell it's not
easy to talk about. She is a delight. It's a great honor to care for
such a wonderful person.[2]

For the next thirteen years, McQuilkin cared for his wife.
During the last decade of her life, it seemed to him that she
no longer recognized him most of the time. Yet he served her,
bathed her, fed her, cared for her, loved her. After her death,
McQuilkin observed that during those years, "I would love her
but she couldn't love me back, and that's a painful thing."[3]

McQuilkin's loving care for his wife is a model of genuine,
self-sacrificial compassion. Because of his great love, he cared for

2. Roddy Clack, "Sacrificial Love," October 4, 2004, http://roddyclack.com
/sacrificiallove.html. The audio of the speech can be found at http://www.youtube
.com/watch?v=f6pXiphlqug, accessed 26 May 2011. I have watched my own father
lovingly care for my mother, who is suffering from Alzheimer's. He has been a model
of loyalty, patience, perseverance, and love for my sisters and me.
3. Stan Guthrie, "The Gradual Grief of Alzheimer's," *Christianity Today*, February 1,
2004, http://www.christianitytoday.com/ct/2004/february/8.64.html. See also Betsy
Childs, "Costly Grace and Christian Witness, Revisiting the Manhattan Declaration,"
Beeson, Spring 2011, 13.

her even though she could not repay him and perhaps, at least much of the time, was not even aware of what he was doing. In so doing, McQuilkin acted like Jesus, looking out not only for his own interests, but also for the interests of others (Phil. 2:4).

In our reading of the biblical story, we come now to the concluding chapter. From creation (Gen. 1–2) through the fall (Gen. 3) and its effects (Gen. 4–Rev. 20), the biblical story ends with re-creation (Rev. 21–22). Tim Keller summarizes the final act of the biblical story.

> How, then, will the story of human history end? At the end of the final book of the Bible, we see the very opposite of what other religions predict. We do not see the illusion of the world melt away nor do we see spiritual souls escaping the physical world into heaven. Rather, we see heaven *descending* into our world to unite with it and purify it of all its brokenness and imperfection. It will be a "new heavens and new earth." . . . When we look at the whole scope of this story line, we see clearly that Christianity is not only about getting one's individual sins forgiven so we can go to heaven. That is an important *means* of God's salvation, but not the final end or purpose of it. The purpose of Jesus' coming is to put the whole world right, to renew and restore the creation, not to escape it. It is not just to bring personal forgiveness and peace, but also justice and *shalom* to the world. God created both body and soul, and the resurrection of Jesus shows that he is going to redeem both body and soul. The work of the Spirit of God is not only to save souls but also to care and cultivate the face of the earth, the material world.[4]

The Hope of the Church

The hope of the church is Christ and his return to the earth. In several of his letters, Paul leads Christians in praise of God's

---

4. Tim Keller, *The Reason for God: Belief in an Age of Skepticism* (New York: Dutton, 2008), 222–23 (emphasis original).

blessing and then reminds us that our present experience is only a foretaste or deposit of what is to come.

> Praise be to the God and Father of our Lord Jesus Christ, who has blessed us in the heavenly realms with every spiritual blessing in Christ. . . .
>
> And you also were included in Christ when you heard the word of truth, the gospel of your salvation. Having believed, you were marked in him with a seal, the promised Holy Spirit, who is a deposit guaranteeing our inheritance until the redemption of those who are God's possession—to the praise of his glory. (Eph. 1:3, 13–14)

Paul also reminds Christians of the hope stored in heaven for us.

> We always thank God, the Father of our Lord Jesus Christ, when we pray for you, because we have heard of your faith in Christ Jesus and of the love you have for all the saints—the faith and love that spring from the hope that is stored up for you in heaven and that you have already heard about in the word of truth, the gospel that has come to you. (Col. 1:3–6)

Similarly, Peter explains that God has an incredible inheritance stored in heaven for us.

> Praise be to the God and Father of our Lord Jesus Christ! In his great mercy he has given us new birth into a living hope through the resurrection of Jesus Christ from the dead, and into an inheritance that can never perish, spoil or fade—kept in heaven for you, who through faith are shielded by God's power until the coming of the salvation that is ready to be revealed in the last time. (1 Peter 1:3–5)

But perhaps the clearest expression of the hope of the church is found in Titus 2, which refers to it as "the blessed hope." The apostle Paul asserts that "the grace of God that brings salvation has appeared to all men" (v. 11). In the incarnation, grace appeared on earth in the person of Jesus. The coming of Jesus revealed grace to the world to a degree never previously seen.[5]

Paul emphasizes that grace brings responsibility; it demands a lifestyle change. Grace "teaches us to say 'No' to ungodliness and worldly passions, and to live self-controlled, upright and godly lives in this present age" (v. 12). In short, the responsibilities of grace cannot be separated from the fruit of the Spirit (see Gal. 5:22–26).

But the goal of grace is not merely to avoid ungodliness, as important as that is. The goal of grace, the focus of godliness, is "the blessed hope—the glorious appearing of our great God and Savior, Jesus Christ, who gave himself for us to redeem us from all wickedness and to purify for himself a people that are his very own" (Titus 2:13–14).

We live between the two appearances of grace. The incarnation of grace has appeared, and he has promised to return. So we wait. We wait for our Savior to return. We wait for the hope of all creation. We wait for a person. We wait for the return of grace to the earth, when finally all will be made right. And we wait patiently.

When the Savior ascended to heaven, the angelic beings explained to the disciples that he would return "in the same way" (Acts 1:11). We thus expect him to return to the earth in his glorified body. Christians differ in their expectation of when and how Jesus will appear, but they all agree that he is our hope, and that his return will set things right.

Christ Is Our Hope

That Christ is our hope is a common theme in the New Testament. In his letter to the Philippian Christians, Paul encourages

---

5. Because God is gracious, his grace was visible previously. But in the incarnation, grace was more clearly revealed in the condescension of the Son of God. Grace and truth are found together in him; he is full of grace and truth (John 1:14, 17).

them to follow his example, to avoid those who live as enemies of the cross of Christ (Phil. 3:17–18). These enemies have their minds set on earthly things, while Christians have their focus on heavenly things: "And we eagerly await a Savior from there, the Lord Jesus Christ, who, by the power that enables him to bring everything under his control, will transform our lowly bodies so that they will be like his glorious body" (vv. 20–21). Our Savior is in heaven, but he will not remain there. Rather, he is coming to the earth to bring everything under his control (see 1 Cor. 15:27–28) and to transform our mortal bodies into the likeness of his glorified body (vv. 35–49).

In his first letter to the Thessalonians, Paul expresses his admiration for these believers, especially for their widespread positive reputation. These people have turned from idols to the living God and "wait for his Son from heaven, whom he raised from the dead—Jesus, who rescues us from the coming wrath" (1 Thess. 1:9–10). These believers are waiting for Christ's return and for the rescue and redemption that his return will bring.

The apostle Peter similarly looks forward to the return of Christ and the re-creation of all things. In his first epistle, Peter praises God:

> In his great mercy he has given us new birth into a living hope through the resurrection of Jesus Christ from the dead, and into an inheritance that can never perish, spoil or fade—kept in heaven for you, who through faith are shielded by God's power until the coming of the salvation that is ready to be revealed in the last time. (1 Peter 1:3–5)

Our hope is in Jesus. Through his resurrection, he provides an inheritance, kept in heaven with him until it is revealed at the last time. Jesus himself is the content of this hope. In short, the revelation of this inheritance and the experience of it on earth await the return of Christ.

In his second letter, Peter rebukes those who scoff at the promise of his coming with their derisive comments and mocking questions.[6] Their problem is not ignorance (see Rom. 1:18–25) but rebellion: "They deliberately forget that long ago by God's word the heavens existed and the earth was formed out of water and by water" (2 Peter 3:5). Peter responds to these scoffers by looking back to creation as evidence of the Creator's existence and character. These scoffers reject what they know about God and deliberately rebel against knowledge. Peter then moves from creation to the flood. The world, he says, was "deluged and destroyed" by water (v. 6). The word that created the world and sent judgment in the flood is preserving this world for judgment: "By the same word the present heavens and earth are reserved for fire, being kept for the day of judgment and destruction of ungodly men" (v. 7).

God Delays in Mercy

In contrast to the deliberate forgetfulness of the scoffers, Peter encourages his readers not to forget that "the Lord is not slow in keeping his promise, as some understand slowness. He is patient with you, not wanting anyone to perish, but everyone to come to repentance" (v. 9). It is unlikely that Peter intends to give a mathematical axiom comparing an earthly timescale to a heavenly one. Peter's point is that the long delay in the return of Christ, used by scoffers to mock the Christian hope, is, rather, consistent with God's character. Whereas on earth the focus is on the length of time passed, from God's perspective the focus is on mercy, compassion, and forgiveness. God is patient and compassionate. He does not want the judgment to come. He desires not destruction, but repentance and re-creation. He

---

6. Peter's expression emphasizes the scoffing when he says, "In the last days scoffers will come, scoffing" (2 Peter 3:3). Apparently this is what scoffers do—they scoff, and thus they are called scoffers.

does not want anyone to perish, but wants everyone to come to repentance.[7] God's compassion and patience are seen in the delay of the "last days."

The godly response to the delay in Christ's return is to be similarly compassionate and merciful toward unbelievers. Surely scoffing is ungodly, but perhaps so is an unbridled and even enthusiastic desire for God to destroy all his enemies—and soon. That the day of the Lord's judgment is a day of darkness, death, and destruction should lead godly people to a somber and compassionate attitude toward those who will experience such a terrible day. The prophet Amos issues a sobering warning:

> Woe to you who long
>   for the day of the LORD!
> Why do you long for the day of the LORD?
>   That day will be darkness, not light.
> It will be as though a man fled from a lion
>   only to meet a bear,
> as though he entered his house
>   and rested his hand on the wall
>   only to have a snake bite him.
> Will not the day of the LORD be darkness, not light—
>   pitch-dark, without a ray of brightness? (Amos 5:18–20)

The Lord Will Come

The "day of the Lord" will come. The end will eventually occur. Jesus Christ will return to the earth, and "the heavens

---

7. It could be that "everyone" is inclusive of all humanity (see 1 Tim. 2:4). But since only those who are called will respond (John 6:44–51), and only those foreknown and predestined will be justified and glorified (Rom. 8:29–30), "everyone" seems limited to the elect. In short, Peter is saying that as long as there are still elect on the earth who have not yet believed on the Son for eternal life, the return of Christ is delayed. Since no human knows who the elect are until they believe, we proclaim the good news of life in Jesus to anyone and everyone, trusting that God will have mercy on whom he will and compassion on whom he will (Rom. 9:15).

will disappear with a roar; the elements will be destroyed by fire, and the earth and everything in it will be laid bare" (2 Peter 3:10). Some interpreters believe that these words describe a cataclysmic, destructive fire that will annihilate the earth.[8] But Peter is comparing two acts of judgment, one by water in the time of Noah and another by fire at the last day. The water of the flood destroyed the earth (see v. 6) but did not consume it. When the floodwaters receded, the earth was still there. If these two judgments are parallel, the fire of judgment will not consume the earth. When the judgment is finished, the earth will remain. This is Peter's hope: "But in keeping with his promise we are looking forward to a new heaven and a new earth, the home of righteousness" (v. 13). In short, the hope expressed here by the apostle is not annihilation of the earth, but re-creation. The hope of the redeemed is not judgment that destroys the earth, but an earth that is habitable and no longer cursed by sin, a world in which things will be made new.

Herman Bavinck explains it this way:

> According to Scripture, however, the present world will neither continue forever nor will it be destroyed and replaced by a new one. . . . Peter, for example, expressly teaches that the old earth, which originated as a result of the separation of waters, was deluged with water and so perished (2 Pet. 3:6), and that the present world would also perish, not—thanks to the divine promise—by water but by fire. The world was not totally destroyed in the flood, and so we must no more think of a destruction of substance with fire than we would do with water: fire burns, cleanses, purifies but does not destroy. . . . The future blessedness of biblical hope, rooted in incarnation

---

8. For example, Jonathan Edwards believed that 2 Peter 3:7 means that "this world shall be set on fire, and be turned into a great furnace, wherein all the enemies of Christ and his church shall be tormented forever and ever" (*The Works of Jonathan Edwards*, ed. John F. Wilson, vol. 9, *History of the Work of Redemption* [New Haven: Yale University Press, 1989], 505).

and resurrection, is creational, this-worldly, visible, physical, bodily hope.[9]

Paul's personification of creation's hope, that it "will be liberated from its bondage to decay and brought into the glorious freedom of the children of God" (Rom. 8:21), expresses the expectation of re-creation. Annihilation could hardly be described as hope for liberation from bondage. Further, since we join creation in "groaning as in the pains of childbirth" (vv. 21–22), creation's hope and ours are the same. Since we hope for eternal life, not for annihilation, creation does too. We look forward to the resurrection of the body and the regeneration of all things (see Matt. 19:28). Michael Horton's conclusion is accurate and clear.

> If our goal is to be liberated *from* creation rather than the liberation *of* creation, we will understandably display little concern for the world that God has made. If, however, we are looking forward to "the restoration of all things" (Ac 3:21) and the participation of the whole creation in our redemption (Ro 8:18–21), then our actions here and now pertain to the same world that will one day be finally and fully renewed.[10]

The Final Chapter: The Book of Revelation

Like any good story, the Bible has a beginning, a middle, and an end. A world that was created good by a good God was corrupted and cursed by sin. In the midst of decay and death, God continued to act redemptively. At the midpoint of the

---

9. Herman Bavinck, *Reformed Dogmatics, Abridged in One Volume*, ed. John Bolt (Grand Rapids: Baker, 2011), 766–67 (emphasis original).

10. Michael Horton, *The Christian Faith: A Systematic Theology for Pilgrims on the Way* (Grand Rapids: Zondervan, 2011), 989–90 (emphasis original). See also N. T. Wright, *Surprised by Hope: Rethinking Heaven, the Resurrection, and the Mission of the Church* (New York: HarperOne, 2008).

story, the incarnate Son of God, Jesus Christ, came to earth. Christ died, was resurrected, and ascended to the Father. But that was not the end of the story. He is coming again to finish the work of redemption. In the Bible's final chapter, the book of Revelation, the suffering church is encouraged to persevere in the midst of sorrow and grief while waiting for that day.

The Revelation of Jesus Christ

The book of Revelation, written by the apostle John, is the revelation of Jesus Christ (Rev. 1:1). He is the focus and content of the book. It concerns the events that will soon take place, for the time is near (vv. 1, 3). The book's focus is on the return of Christ. Of that time, Jesus asserts that "no one knows about that day or hour, not even the angels in heaven, nor the Son, but only the Father" (Matt. 24:36). He compares his return to a flood that comes suddenly and sweeps away the wicked (vv. 37–41) and exhorts his followers to watchfulness, "because you do not know on what day your Lord will come" (v. 42). Using the illustration of a thief who does not announce the time of his coming (vv. 43–44), he concludes, "So you also must be ready, because the Son of Man will come at an hour when you do not expect him" (v. 44). He also tells a parable about wise and foolish virgins and concludes, "Therefore keep watch, because you do not know the day or the hour" (25:13). After his resurrection, he tells his disciples, "It is not for you to know the times or dates the Father has set by his own authority" (Acts 1:7). These texts teach that the time of Jesus' return is unknown—it could occur at any time. In short, he will return soon. Berkhof summarizes, "The exact time of the coming of the Lord is unknown, Matt. 24:36, and all attempts of men to figure out the exact date proved to be erroneous." He continues, "The only thing that can be said with certainty, on the basis of Scripture, is that He will return at the end of the world."[11] Since it has been nearly two thousand years since the promise of his near return, and God "is not slow in keeping his promise" (2 Peter 3:9), we continue to wait for his near return to earth. As trite as it may sound, his return is nearer today than it was yesterday.

In a book that describes a great deal of destruction and devastation, it is encouraging to read this greeting: "Grace and peace to you from him who is, and who was, and who is to come" (Rev. 1:4). This book promises grace and peace through the one who is to come: "Look, he is coming with the clouds, and every eye will see him, even those who pierced him; and all the peoples of the earth will mourn because of him" (v. 7), echoing Jesus' promise that when the sign of the Son of Man appears in the sky, "all the nations of the earth will mourn" (Matt. 24:30). The elect, on the other hand, will be gathered together (v. 31). The nations "will go away to eternal punishment, but the righteous to eternal life" (25:46); the wicked will be taken, and the righteous will be left behind. The focus of Revelation is on the near return of Christ, the culmination of all things, and the last days and completion of the work of judgment and redemption.

The Revelation of Heaven

John sees a door standing open in heaven and he travels "in the Spirit" into the throne room of God in heaven (Rev. 4:1–2). He sees incredible, wonderful sights and hears amazing songs of praise and thanksgiving to God. From a group of four living creatures, John hears a song: "Holy, holy, holy is the Lord God Almighty; who was, and is, and is to come" (v. 8). A second song comes from twenty-four elders, who probably represent the twelve tribes of Israel and the twelve apostles—thus, all the redeemed of all ages. These redeemed humans respond to the

---

11. Louis Berkhof, *Systematic Theology*, 4th ed. (Grand Rapids: Eerdmans, 1981), 703–4.

song of the creatures with their own song praising God for his work of creation: "You are worthy, our Lord and God, to receive glory and honor and power, for you created all things, and by your will they were created and have their being" (v. 11).

As John looks around the throne, he sees "in the right hand of him who sat on the throne a scroll with writing on both sides and sealed with seven seals" (5:1). This is the scroll of Daniel, who was told to "close up and seal the words of the scroll until the time of the end" (Dan. 12:4). The time of the end is here. John sees the scroll and hears a mighty angel saying, "Who is worthy to break the seals and open the scroll?" (Rev. 5:2).

John weeps "because no one was found who was worthy to open the scroll or look inside" (v. 4). He is sad, probably not because he is curious to see inside the scroll, but because he realizes that God desires the scroll to be opened. What a relief it must be for him to hear one of the elders say, "Do not weep! See, the Lion of the tribe of Judah, the Root of David, has triumphed. He is able to open the scroll and its seven seals" (v. 5). We can almost feel the release of John's tension. A lion—the king of beasts, a fierce and terrible creature—is on his way; all is well now. The conquering Lion of Jacob's paternal blessing has arrived.

> Judah, your brothers will praise you;
>> your hand will be on the neck of your enemies;
>> your father's sons will bow down to you.
> You are a lion's cub, O Judah;
>> you return from the prey, my son.
> Like a lion he crouches and lies down,
>> like a lioness—who dares to rouse him?
> The scepter will not depart from Judah,
>> nor the ruler's staff from between his feet,
> until he comes to whom it belongs
>> and the obedience of the nations is his.

He will tether his donkey to a vine,
>   his colt to the choicest branch;
he will wash his garments in wine,
>   his robes in the blood of grapes.
His eyes will be darker than wine,
>   his teeth whiter than milk. (Gen. 49:8–12)

If the Lion of the tribe of Judah is here—the one who will rule over his enemies and receive obedience from the nations, who will pour out the wine of judgment—all will be well. The powerful one will open the scroll.

This one is also the Root of David. He is the one of whom Isaiah spoke.

A shoot will come up from the stump of Jesse;
>   from his roots a Branch will bear fruit.
. . . .
He will not judge by what he sees with his eyes,
>   or decide by what he hears with his ears;
but with righteousness he will judge the needy,
>   with justice he will give decisions for the poor of the earth.
He will strike the earth with the rod of his mouth;
>   with the breath of his lips he will slay the wicked.
Righteousness will be his belt
>   and faithfulness the sash around his waist. (Isa. 11:1, 3–5)

We can sense the anticipation as John turns to see this roaring lion, this powerful ruler, this strong and mighty judge who will take vengeance on the enemies of God. We can also sense his surprise when he sees not a lion but a lamb. And this lamb still bears the marks of his execution; he is a lamb "looking as if it had been slain" (Rev. 5:6). Rather than strength, power, fierceness, and supremacy, John sees weakness, powerlessness, gentleness, and submission. The Lamb comes and takes the scroll from the hand of the one who sits on the throne (v. 7). This is no usurper or alien or interloper. This is the one who is worthy, who belongs here. He is worthy to open the scroll because of his death.

> You are worthy to take the scroll
>> and to open its seals,
> because you were slain,
>> and with your blood you purchased men for God
>> from every tribe and language and people and nation.
> You have made them to be a kingdom and priests to serve our
>> God,
>> and they will reign on the earth. (vv. 9–10)[12]

He is worthy to open the scroll because of his atoning sacrifice.

It is not power or might that makes Jesus worthy. It is not privilege or prestige that grants him the right to take the scroll. It is not fame or forcefulness that allows him the privilege to open the scroll. Rather, it is his weakness, death, submission, humiliation, powerlessness, shame, and dishonor; the scandal of the cross makes him worthy. And that he still bears the marks of his death implies that the shame of crucifixion has been turned into a mark of honor and worthiness.

The kingdoms of this world are based on power, privilege, prominence, prestige, and pleasure. The kingdom of the Messiah is grounded in submission, humility, weakness, and sacrifice. How will God defeat his enemies? How will the Creator of life conquer the last and greatest foe, death? He does it through not power but powerlessness, not elevation but degradation, not avoidance but immersion, not clinging to rights and prerogatives but giving them up and submitting to the power of death. Paul

12. Jonathan Edwards interpreted Revelation 5:10 as a reference to a future millennium, during which the saints would reign on the earth. See my summary in Glenn R. Kreider, *Jonathan Edwards's Interpretation of Revelation 4:1–8:1* (Lanham, MD: University Press of America, 2004), 145–74. As a premillennialist who believes in a re-created, eternal earth, I believe that Revelation 5:10 is fulfilled in the eternal state, when saints of all ages and the triune God will live and reign forever on the earth.

writes, "God made him who had no sin to be sin for us, so that in him we might become the righteousness of God" (2 Cor. 5:21). It is through submission to the enemy that Christ defeats death.

John sees a great multitude "from every nation, tribe, people and language, standing before the throne and in front of the Lamb" (Rev. 7:9), who cry out in one voice, "Salvation belongs to our God, who sits on the throne, and to the Lamb" (v. 10). The judgment on humanity at the tower of Babel (Gen. 11:8–9) has now been reversed. And the latter is better than the former; the diversity of voices in unity worshipping the one God together is better than the uniformity of one language. God's redemptive work makes things not only new, but better.

Judgment Poured Out on the Earth

In John's vision, the Lamb opens the seals to pour out judgment on the earth. Following the seals, John sees seven angels who sound seven trumpets. He sees two prophetic witnesses, earthquakes, beasts appearing on the earth, a variety of angelic beings, and then seven bowls of God's wrath. As a futurist, I interpret these as descriptive of a future time of judgment on the earth.[13]

The Return of Christ

This book is called "the revelation of Jesus Christ" (Rev. 1:1) and promises that he is coming back to earth (v. 7). In chapters 19 and following, John sees a vision of Christ's return, and the story of redemption comes to its culmination.

John hears a "great multitude" of saints shouting, "Hallelujah! For our Lord God Almighty reigns. Let us rejoice and be glad

---

13. For various interpretations of this book, see C. Marvin Pate, ed., *Four Views on the Book of Revelation* (Grand Rapids: Zondervan, 1998). See also my *Jonathan Edwards's Interpretation*, 37–88, for a survey of the history of the interpretation of the Apocalypse.

and give him glory! For the wedding of the Lamb has come, and his bride has made herself ready" (19:6–7). The wedding of the Lamb has come, and the bride is dressed appropriately, in wedding garments, in fine linen (v. 8; see also Matt. 22:11–14). John explains that the "fine linen stands for the righteous acts of the saints" (Rev. 19:8; see also 22:14).

John then sees heaven standing open and a sight that has been the hope of the church, and of all creation, since Jesus ascended to heaven. He sees a rider on a white horse. Although the rider is not named Jesus, he is called "Faithful and True" (19:11). He judges and wages war with justice (v. 11), has many crowns on his head (v. 12), is dressed in a robe dipped in blood (v. 13), is named "the Word of God" (v. 13; see also John 1:1–18) and "KING OF KINGS AND LORD OF LORDS" (Rev. 19:16), and has in his mouth a sharp sword to judge the nations (v. 15). This rider is the Son of Man, the Messiah, the Lord of all. He is accompanied by the armies of heaven, wearing white robes to identify them as saints (v. 8). When Jesus returns to the earth, he brings with him all those who have been in heaven with him.[14] When he is in heaven, they are there with him (see 2 Cor. 5:6–9), and when he returns to earth, the redeemed are with him.[15]

When he returns to earth, Christ's enemies on the earth are destroyed. In consistency with what Jesus teaches in Matthew 13 and 24 about the end of the age, the wicked are taken and the righteous are left behind. John sees "the beast and the kings of the earth and their armies gathered together to make

14. Many premillennialists believe that a coming of Christ in the air to receive the church (rapture) precedes a seven-year tribulation on the earth prior to the second coming. For a defense of this position, which I hold, see Craig A. Blaising, "Pretribulation Rapture," in *Three Views on the Rapture: Pretribulation, Prewrath, or Posttribulation*, ed. Alan Hultberg (Grand Rapids: Zondervan, 2010), 25–73. Unity among premillennialists, postmillennialists, and amillennialists can be found in our common hope of Christ's return to the earth.

15. The redeemed here would seem to be inclusive of all the redeemed in every age, all together as one people, with one Lord, one faith, one hope (Eph. 4:4–6).

war against the rider on the horse and his army" (Rev. 19:19). The beast and the false prophet are captured and thrown alive into the lake of burning sulfur (v. 20). The rest of the wicked are killed with the sword of the Word of the Lord (v. 21; see also v. 15). The wicked are taken, and the righteous are left behind on the earth. Thus, both the resurrected saints who come to the earth with Jesus and those mortals who are still alive are left behind to inhabit the earth.

Then John sees an angel coming down from heaven, who seizes, binds, and locks away the "ancient serpent," who is the Devil, or Satan (20:1–3). Satan is locked away from the earth for a millennium—one thousand years (vv. 2–3).[16] He is no longer able to deceive the nations, the inhabitants of the earth, until this millennium comes to an end (v. 3). Then John sees the resurrection of those who died during the reign of the beast (v. 4), another group of righteous people who are now raised to live and reign on the earth with the King (vv. 4–6). When the thousand years are over, Satan is released from his prison for a short time (v. 3), at which time he gathers the nations to oppose the King and his city.[17] In the shortest battle in history, "fire came down

16. Throughout the history of the church, this chapter has been interpreted variously. I respect the arguments for amillennial and postmillennial interpretations, but my own position is premillennial, that Christ's return to the earth is prior to a thousand-year period, during which he reigns on the earth, to be followed by an eternal reign of Christ on the earth. The millennium is not the goal or end of history; it is an intermediate stage between the current age and the age to come. On the differences between the views, see Darrell L. Bock, ed., *Three Views on the Millennium and Beyond* (Grand Rapids: Zondervan, 1999).

17. The contrasts within this chapter between a short time (Rev. 20:3), a thousand years (20:2, 3, 4, 5, 6, 7), and day and night forever and ever (20:10) seem to imply that the millennium is an intermediate length of time between "short" and "forever." Since "a thousand years" seems also to indicate a period of time rather than something else, it is better to take it as a reference to a period of time approximately one thousand years in length, rather than as a reference to some other period of time. I do, however, respect my brothers and sisters who see it differently. Although Jonathan Edwards's position is not premillennial, I find his argument defending the millennium as an actual period of a thousand years compelling. See *Jonathan Edwards's Interpretation*, 154–57.

from heaven and devoured them" (v. 9). The wicked are again taken in judgment; the righteous are left behind on the earth. The Devil is thrown into the lake of burning sulfur with the beast and the false prophet (v. 10), where they are joined, after a day of judgment at the great white throne, by all those whose names are not written in the book of life (vv. 11–14).

The metanarrative of Scripture now enters its final chapter. As it began with two accounts of creation, it ends with two accounts of re-creation. It began with a dark, empty, chaotic, water-covered earth. It ends with a glorious, heavenly city that descends to earth. The first act of the story ended with a man and his wife cast out of the garden. The second act will end with fire that destroys all the enemies of the Messiah gathered outside the city. And the third act will begin with the creation of a new heaven and a new earth, an eternal kingdom.

The New Heaven and the New Earth

> Then I saw a new heaven and a new earth, for the first heaven and the first earth had passed away, and there was no longer any sea. I saw the Holy City, the new Jerusalem, coming down out of heaven from God, prepared as a bride beautifully dressed for her husband. And I heard a loud voice from the throne saying, "Now the dwelling of God is with men, and he will live with them. They will be his people, and God himself will be with them and be their God. He will wipe every tear from their eyes. There will be no more death or mourning or crying or pain, for the old order of things has passed away." (Rev. 21:1–4)

The old order, and everything connected to it, is gone. A new order has come. The cursed earth, where everything is broken and every living thing eventually dies, is now gone. It is replaced by a new heaven and a new earth, where there is no death or decay, sadness or mourning, sickness or pain.

John then hears from the throne one last declaration: "I am making everything new! . . . Write this down, for these words are trustworthy and true" (v. 5). The old is gone; all has become new (see 2 Cor. 5:17). The Creator has moved onto the earth; he has made his dwelling place on earth. The Creator has moved into our neighborhood; he has condescended to come to us. No one, except the triune God, deserves to be here. Everyone other than God is here through inheritance, having been adopted as sons. Because of his great love, God adopts us into his family and allows us, through his grace, to live forever with him in his home, the earth he created.

When he created the world (Gen. 1–2), God gave to humans, those created in his image, the responsibility to care for it. But they consistently rebelled against him, destroying the earth he created. But God has not given up on us. He redeems us for his glory and re-creates the heaven and the earth, making it inhabitable for us forever. He then moves into our neighborhood.

The righteous are left behind eternally to live in this new home. The wicked, on the other hand, are taken to their eternal destiny in the fiery lake of burning sulfur (Rev. 20:10, 15). Elsewhere this place is described as blackest darkness (2 Peter 2:17; Jude 13), where the wicked are separated from the presence of the Lord and his majesty (2 Thess. 1:9). The horror of hell is that its inhabitants are forever separated from the joyous presence of God.[18]

The heavenly city, the bride, the wife of the Lamb (Rev. 21:9–10), is described as an ancient city with huge walls and multiple gates and foundations; it is a giant cube. In the vision, the city is constructed of pure gold, and its foundations are other precious minerals. This picturesque language seems to portray an extravagant, prosperous, safe, prestigious, and accessible city. It

18. See my "Sinners in the Hands of a Gracious God," *Bibliotheca Sacra* 163 (July–September 2006): 259–75. The allusion to the famous sermon by Jonathan Edwards, "Sinners in the Hands of an Angry God," is not unintentional.

is not a snapshot of the city, any more than the description of Jesus in chapter 19 is a portrait of the Savior. Unlike the ancient city of Jerusalem and most other cities in the ancient world, this city has no temple, no place of worship, "because the Lord God Almighty and the Lamb are its temple" (21:22). There also is no sun or moon, for the glory of God and the Lamb provide light (v. 23; see also Matt. 5:14–16). The nations walk in this light, and their kings bring splendor into the city (Rev. 21:24; see also Gen. 12:1–3).

There is a second description of the new earth, the great city:

> Then the angel showed me the river of the water of life, as clear as crystal, flowing from the throne of God and of the Lamb down the middle of the great street of the city. On each side of the river stood the tree of life, bearing twelve crops of fruit, yielding its fruit every month. And the leaves of the tree are for the healing of the nations. No longer will there be any curse. The throne of God and of the Lamb will be in the city, and his servants will serve him. They will see his face, and his name will be on their foreheads. There will be no more night. They will not need the light of a lamp or the light of the sun, for the Lord God will give them light. And they will reign for ever and ever. (Rev. 22:1–5)

In the original creation, two specific trees were mentioned, one of which gets almost all the attention (Gen. 2). Of the Tree of Knowledge of Good and Evil, God said, "You must not eat from [it], for when you eat of it you will surely die" (v. 17). No specific instructions were given about the Tree of Life, but it was surely included in the command, "You are free to eat from any tree in the garden" (v. 16). This tree has returned and produces a monthly harvest. The nations sit in its shade and are "healed." The "healing" clearly does not mean that the tree provides medical care. "Healing," rather, is salvation, salvation for the nations.

The Tree of Life represents the cross of Christ, for on that tree life was provided for all the redeemed.

The nations are at home in this city. There is no longer any curse; there is no death, sickness, pain, sorrow, decay, or any other effect of the fall. God reigns in this city from his throne. Everyone here belongs to him. They walk in the light and life that he provides.

Of course, these events have not yet occurred. The church continues to wait and watch for this hope. As the book of Revelation, and the entire Bible, ends, Jesus promises, "Behold, I am coming soon! Blessed is he who keeps the words of the prophecy in this book" (22:7). He says it again:

> Behold, I am coming soon! My reward is with me, and I will give to everyone according to what he has done. I am the Alpha and the Omega, the First and the Last, the Beginning and the End. (vv. 12–13)

How does the church respond? How should the church today respond to this hope? The Spirit and believers indwelt by the Spirit say, "Come!" (v. 17). "Amen. Come, Lord Jesus" (v. 20).

Conclusion

As the biblical story comes to an end, the work of redemption is completed. An earth that was created good is now even better. The original creation was subject to corruption and decay. This one will never be corrupted. The original humans were capable of sin, and their sin introduced death into God's world. The redeemed humans in this new world will never rebel. Sin is not possible here. The original creation was a place that God visited, walking with Adam in the cool of the day. This new creation is the dwelling place of the triune God. The Serpent had access to the original creation. Never will the Serpent be released from the lake of fire. He has no access to this new creation. The original creation was good. When God's work of redemption is completed, the new creation is much better. And surely what makes it particularly blessed is that it becomes home to the Trinity forever. The transcendent one who lives in heaven condescends to move onto the earth, a planet he created and hung in space. Our home becomes his home—a supreme act of condescension.

10

CONCLUSION

AT 10:25 A.M. on October 2, 2006, Charles Carl Roberts IV backed up his truck to the West Nickel Mines School, a one-room Old Order Amish schoolhouse in Nickel Mines, Pennsylvania. He ordered everyone to leave the building except ten young girls aged six to thirteen. A half hour later, he began shooting the girls and then shot himself. Three of the girls died at the scene, and two died later.

Events like this are horrifying and shocking—senseless, violent, meaningless, purposeless, and tragic; how could anyone do such a thing? And how can families of the victims and the community begin to cope with such calamity? In this tragedy, the response of the Amish community was a great surprise to the rest of the world and was a model of godly compassion. The grandfather of one of the victims said, "We must not think evil of this man." Another, a father of one of the victims, said of the shooter, "He had a mother and a wife and a soul, and now he's standing before a just God." Another said, "I don't think there's anybody here that wants to do anything but forgive, and not only reach out to those who have suffered a loss in that way, but to reach out to the family of the man who committed these acts."

And that is what the community did. They forgave the shooter and reached out to his family.[1]

Apparently Roberts's motivation for the killing was his anger at God. Nine years earlier, his wife had given birth to an infant daughter who died after only a few minutes. Before the shooting, he was heard saying, "I'm angry at God and need to punish some Christian girls to get even with him."[2] As one writer observed, "It's ironic that the killer . . . never forgave God for her death. Yet, after he cold-bloodedly shot 10 innocent Amish schoolgirls, the Amish almost immediately forgave him and showed compassion toward his family."[3]

In a book about this tragedy and its aftermath, *Amish Grace*, its writers observe, "The Nickel Mines Amish certainly didn't anticipate the horror of October 2. They were, however, uncommonly prepared to respond to it with graciousness, forbearance, and love." They continue, "Indeed, the biggest surprise at Nickel Mines was not the intrusion of evil but the Amish response. The biggest surprise was Amish grace."[4] Elsewhere they explain,

> If there's one thing we learned from the Nickel Mines story, it's this: the Amish commitment to forgive is not a small patch tacked onto their fabric of faithfulness. Rather, their commitment to forgive is intricately woven into their lives and their communities—so intricately that it's hard to talk about Amish forgiveness without talking about dozens of other things. . . . In a world where faith often justifies and magnifies revenge, and in a nation where some Christians use scripture to fuel retali-

1. Details taken from "Amish School Shooting and Grace," accessed July 6, 2011, http://www.800padutch.com/amishshooting.shtml; and "Amish School Shooting 2006," *Amish Country News*, last updated February 21, 2010, http://www.amishnews.com/publishersmessages/SchoolShooting.htm.
2. "Amish School Shooting and Grace."
3. "Amish Grace and Forgiveness," accessed July 6, 2011, http://www.800padutch.com/amishforgiveness.shtml.
4. Donald B. Kraybill, Steven M. Nolt, and David L. Weaver-Zercher, *Amish Grace: How Forgiveness Transcended Tragedy* (Indianapolis: Jossey-Bass, 2010), xi.

ation, the Amish response was indeed a surprise. Regardless of
the details of the Nickel Mines story, one message rings clear:
religion was not used to justify rage and revenge but to inspire
goodness, forgiveness, and grace. And that is the big lesson for
the rest of us regardless of our faith or nationality.[5]

This Christian community showed the world the power of
forgiveness. In response to horrifying tragedy, they put into
practice what they believed about God. Rather than pursuing
vengeance, they practiced peace. They put into action the
words of the apostle Paul:

> Get rid of all bitterness, rage and anger, brawling and slander,
> along with every form of malice. Be kind and compassionate to
> one another, forgiving each other, just as in Christ God forgave
> you. (Eph. 4:31–32)

Creation, Fall (and Redemption), and Re-creation

The biblical story begins with God's act of creation. In two
chapters (Gen. 1–2), Moses tells the story of how the earth came
to be. God created the heavens and the earth and gave humans,
created in his image, the responsibility to care for the world and
the creatures he made. These humans rebelled against him and
earned death (ch. 3). All their descendants come into the world as
sinners. But, thanks be to God, this is not the end of the story.[6]
Because of his compassion, mercy, and love, God has provided
a solution to our sin. In the incarnation, God the Son condescended to take on humanity, come to the earth, suffer, and die.
He was raised, ascended to heaven, and is coming back to the

5. Donald B. Kraybill, Steven M. Nolt, and David L. Weaver-Zercher, "Amish
Grace and the Rest of Us," *Christianity Today*, September 17, 2007, http://www
.christianitytoday.com/ct/2007/septemberweb-only/138-13.0.html.
6. From Genesis 3 through Revelation 20, God is acting redemptively in the midst
of a fallen world.

earth to make all things new. When the work of redemption is complete, the triune God will return to the earth to dwell with his creatures forever (Rev. 21–22).

How Then Should We Live?

Condescension, the voluntary humbling of oneself for the sake of others, is not merely an attitude but an action. It takes many forms, all of which can be summarized as gifts of love. Forgiveness, humility, and service are particularly good examples of condescension.

Forgiveness of Others

As he hung on the cross, Jesus looked at those responsible for his unjust suffering and prayed, "Father, forgive them, for they do not know what they are doing" (Luke 23:34). When Stephen was being stoned, he fell to his knees and prayed, "Lord, do not hold this sin against them" (Acts 7:60). When the Amish forgave the shooter, they were acting in line with these two great examples.

Thankfully, few of us will suffer the fate of Jesus or Stephen. But some might. Not all of us will suffer as the Amish families, Célestin Musekura, or Jennifer Thompson did. But many have. All of us, however, have been wronged and have wronged others. And all of us can be instruments of redemption through forgiveness.

One of the eyewitnesses of Stephen's act of forgiveness was the apostle Paul (see Acts 8:1). Later he wrote to the church in Colossae and encouraged them, "Bear with each other and forgive whatever grievances you may have against one another. Forgive as the Lord forgave you" (Col. 3:13). Having been forgiven by God, we should be like God and should grant that gift of forgiveness to others. Forgiveness is not easy, but it is a gift that transforms both those who give it and those who receive it.

Humility toward God and Humans

The prophet Micah summarizes God's requirements as "to act justly and to love mercy and to walk humbly with your God" (Mic. 6:8). From creation through the work of redemption, the Creator humbled himself for the sake of his creatures. Such humility should motivate us to respond in sacrificial love for him and others. The apostle Paul expresses it this way: "Therefore, as God's chosen people, holy and dearly loved, clothe yourselves with compassion, kindness, humility, gentleness and patience" (Col. 3:12).

Humility does not come naturally or easily to us. Confesses Gerald McDermott, "It is difficult for me to write about humility. . . . I feel as if I am describing a beautiful foreign country that I have never visited. I have seen it in pictures and even in the faces of people from that land, and I long to go there. But it remains foreign, essentially unknown to me."[7] But go there we must, for "God opposes the proud but gives grace to the humble" (James 4:6).

Condescension in Action

In this book, we have seen God's condescension as a common theme in the story of his dealing with his creation. Over and over again, he acts redemptively in response to the rebellion of creatures. The prophet Micah says of him, "You do not stay angry forever but delight to show mercy" (Mic. 7:18). He does get angry, and he does judge, but he is "slow to anger, abounding in love and faithfulness" (Ex. 34:6). His "mercy triumphs over judgment" (James 2:13).

The ultimate example of condescension is, of course, Jesus. Although he was the eternal God, he became human and came

---

7. Gerald McDermott, *Seeing God: Twelve Signs of True Spirituality* (Downers Grove, IL: InterVarsity Press, 1995), 142.

to earth, allowing himself to be captured and killed on a Roman cross. He conquered death through his resurrection and provided hope of eternal life to all who come to him in faith. Because of his resurrection, we too will be raised to live forever with him on a new earth (Rev. 21–22). In the meantime, we wait for our blessed hope, his return to earth (Titus 2:13).

While we wait for his return, we should have the same attitude as Christ Jesus. We should live as he lived, love as he loved, and serve as he served. In his introduction to the christological hymn in Philippians 2, Paul encourages those who have been united to Christ to be "like-minded, having the same love, being one in spirit and purpose" (Phil. 2:2). Such love, when we are united to one another in the Savior, leads to a humility that looks after the needs of others. Paul does not tell us to ignore our own needs; rather, he says, "Do nothing out of selfish ambition or vain conceit, but in humility consider others better than yourselves. Each of you should look not only to your own interests, but also to the interests of others" (vv. 3–4). As followers of Jesus, we do need to take care of our own interests. Otherwise we will be unable to care for others. Caring for my physical health gives me the stamina and strength to help others. Looking out for my emotional health allows me to be a stable support for the needs of others. Providing for my financial resources enables me to give generously to others.

Paul then uses Christ Jesus as the ultimate example for us: "Your attitude should be the same as that of Christ Jesus" (v. 5). He "did not consider equality with God something to be grasped," but gave himself by "taking the very nature of a servant" (vv. 6–7). He "became obedient to death—even death on a cross!" (v. 8). God then exalted him to the highest place and glorified him (vv. 9–11).

The Son of God humbled himself and became a servant of his rebellious creation. He submitted himself for the sake of his enemies. He left the glories of heaven to become a creature and to redeem all creation from the curse of sin and death. He became a creature and came to his creation to do for it, and for us, what we could never do for ourselves—to lift us up, provide us hope, and save us from ourselves. Paul's point is that since Jesus acts this way for us, we ought to emulate his example in our relationships with one another. For our condescension to one another pales in comparison to his condescension to us. We must remember what Jesus told his disciples when he washed their feet:

> I have set you an example that you should do as I have done for you. I tell you the truth, no servant is greater than his master, nor is a messenger greater than the one who sent him. (John 13:15–16)

And what is the result? "Now that you know these things, you will be blessed if you do them" (v. 17).

Cornelius Plantinga summarizes what this should look like in your life and mine.

> Take on self-denial, and trust that you won't be a fool to do it. Take on humility, and trust that humility is actually a sign of strength. Take on the form of a servant, and trust that real flourishing consists in causing others to flourish. In other words, get into the rhythm of God's great reversal and do some dying and rising of your own.[8]

---

8. "A Sermon for Advent: I Believe in Jesus Christ, God's Only Son, Our Lord," in *Exploring and Proclaiming the Apostles' Creed*, ed. Roger E. Van Harn (Grand Rapids: Eerdmans, 2004), 77.

QUESTIONS FOR STUDY AND REFLECTION

Chapter 1—Introduction

1. How familiar are you with the events of the genocide in Rwanda? Was this event covered by the news media where you lived? Why do you think much of the world was unaware of this tragedy?

2. ALARM is based on the conviction that reconciliation can occur only where there is forgiveness. Why is that the case? Why is it not possible for reconciliation to be based on justice?

3. How would you describe grace? Can you remember times when you were a recipient of grace from others? Do you remember times when you mediated grace to others?

4. How can forgiveness both be required (for a Christian) and be a gift of grace?

5. How are condescension and humility related? If condescension is an attribute of God, why do you think it is not usually emphasized in studies of divine attributes?

6. What are some specific ways in which your life would change if you were "to act justly and to love mercy and to walk humbly with your God" (Mic. 6:8)?

Chapter 2—Theological Foundations

1. In what ways could Mother Teresa serve as an example and model of godly servanthood?

2. What evidence can you see that we live in a fallen world, where things are not the way they are supposed to be? Are there concrete examples that you could cite?
3. What are some implications of the story of the good Samaritan? Why do you think Jesus shifted the question from "Who is my neighbor?" to "Which one of these acted as a neighbor to the man who was in need?"?
4. Have you read the Bible as the story of redemption? Why do you think God used stories to reveal himself? What are some implications of the Bible's narrative format?
5. What are implications of considering others better than ourselves? In what specific ways could you apply that command to your life?
6. How can you develop eyes to see all Scripture as being about Jesus? What does it mean that all Scripture points to him?

Chapter 3—God's Condescension in the Old Testament Stories, Part 1: From Creation to Abraham

1. What are some implications of God's preservation of Hagar and Ishmael? How does her naming of God impact the way you read this story?
2. What are implications of the two creation accounts in Genesis 1 and 2? Why do you think Moses recorded two stories?
3. The Bible does not begin with an argument for God's existence. Why is it important to observe this? What implications might this have for the way you read the Bible and interact with people and the world?
4. If humans were created to care for God's world and to mediate blessings to creatures God has blessed, how might this impact your concern and care for the environment today?
5. God chose Abram to be the means by which he would bless all nations on earth. If this is God's plan, if this is the heart

of the gospel, how might the church do a more effective job of blessing the nations?

6. Why is Melchizedek such an important character in the biblical story? Why do you think there is so little information recorded about him?

Chapter 4—God's Condescension in the Old Testament Stories, Part 2: From Isaac to the Conquest

1. What are some implications of Ishmael's being the seed of Abraham (Gen. 21:13), a recipient of promised blessings (17:20)?

2. Why do you think God chooses people like Jacob to be recipients of blessing? What are implications of the fact that he does?

3. Why do you think God used a series of plagues to deliver his people from Egypt? Why did he extend the process over a long period of time?

4. When God appeared to the Israelites on Mt. Sinai, the people were afraid. What are some implications of the fact that God's presence sometimes makes people afraid?

5. Moses acted as a mediator between God and his people. Jesus is the mediator between us and God. Through Christ, we are given the ministry of reconciliation (2 Cor. 5:19). What are some ways in which we can and should serve as mediators between God and man?

6. Both Rahab the Canaanite and Ruth the Moabite were blessed by God, were included in the people of God, and became part of the bloodline of the Messiah. What are some implications of God's grace to outsiders?

Chapter 5—God's Condescension in the Monarchy, Psalms, and Prophets

1. Can you identify with Jennifer Thompson? Have you ever struggled to forgive yourself for something you regretted? Have you ever received a gift of forgiveness from another

person, like she received from Ronald Cotton? Is there someone you should forgive?

2. Why do you think God chose David? Was it because of something God saw in David?

3. How could Solomon, a man of great wisdom, have become so foolish? How did things end up the way they did for him?

4. When Jesus pointed out to his opponents that God had blessed Gentiles through Elijah and Elisha, they were angry and offended. Why do you think this is? What are implications of God's blessing of outsiders?

5. In the Psalms, God's condescension to care for creatures is used to remind human beings of God's care for them. Jesus does something similar in Matthew 6:25–34. Why is worry such a problem for us? How can we learn not to worry by looking at God's care for his creation?

6. When God promises a new covenant, he implies that the old covenant was ineffective. The writer of Hebrews says the old covenant had a fault (8:8). Was the fault the covenant itself or the people with whom the covenant was made? Why did God make an inferior covenant, one that would need to be replaced by a better one?

Chapter 6—The Everlasting Incarnation of the Eternal Son

1. If you grew up in Sunday school, how has your view of God been shaped by those experiences? In what ways were the experiences positive? In what ways were they negative?

2. The New Testament emphasizes that Jesus was born to Mary, a virgin. Why is the virgin birth such an important doctrine? What is lost if the virgin birth is denied?

3. Why do you think we have such limited revelation of Jesus' childhood? What are some of the implications?

4. Why do you think there is such an emphasis on "signs" in the birth and infancy narratives of Jesus?

5. What are the implications of the birth announcements of Jesus to shepherds and magi from the east?

6. Luke emphasizes that Jesus grew and developed. What are some implications of his normal childhood, full humanity, and being like us in all respects, sin excepted?

Chapter 7—Jesus' Teaching on Greatness

1. Only John records the story of Jesus' washing of his disciples' feet. What are some of the implications of this event?

2. Why did Jesus submit to John's baptism?

3. Jesus was led by the Spirit into the wilderness to be tempted by the Devil. This was not an event outside of God's plan. What are some implications of this truth?

4. Jesus uses salt and light to illustrate how his followers should live in this world. What are the implications of this imagery?

5. The disciples seem to have struggled to understand greatness as taught by Jesus. Disciples today do too. How might your life change if you were to become more like Jesus in serving others?

6. What does childlike faith look like? How could you cultivate such faith?

Chapter 8—Condescension in the Teaching of the Apostles

1. Jesus taught that no one knows the time of his return. What are the implications of the promise of his return and the impossibility of predicting when it will be?

2. Paul quoted pagan poets in his sermon on Mars Hill. Does this establish a model that we should follow? How might you follow his example in communicating the truth of God's story of redemption in your life?

3. If God's invisible qualities and divine nature are clearly seen in creation, how might you train your eyes to see them more clearly?

4. The creation is groaning as in the pains of childbirth, in the hope that it will be set free from bondage to decay. We groan along with the creation. We share a common hope. What might be some implications of this truth?

5. God is love. Love is from God. Love is the summary of the requirements of the law. If love for God and love for others are the goals of the Christian life, how might you apply this truth to your life?

6. The church is the place where God dwells by his Spirit. Is it possible to know God, to be in relationship with him, apart from active involvement in the church? What are some of the implications of your answer?

Chapter 9—The New Creation: The Final Chapter in the Biblical Story

1. Robertson McQuilkin modeled sacrificial love in caring for his wife, Muriel. Do you know anyone like him? Has anyone you know modeled love in a similar way? Have you thanked him or her?

2. The blessed hope of the church is her Savior. How does it impact your hope to think of hope in a person rather than in a place or an inheritance?

3. According to 2 Peter 3, the delay in the return of Christ is due to God's patience and compassion. What implications does this have for Christians while we wait?

4. How would you describe the hope of all creation, the new heaven and the new earth? How will it be similar to the old creation, and how will it be different?

5. Revelation 21 and 22 describe the destiny of the righteous as living with God in a city that comes down from heaven. Is this an actual city, or does the city represent something else?

6. What is the significance of the presence of the Tree of Life in the new creation? What role does the Tree of Life play in the biblical story?

Chapter 10—Conclusion

1. How do you think the Amish families of the Nickel Mines shooting victims were able to forgive the shooter?
2. The shooter was angry with God. Although the way he dealt with his anger was inappropriate, is anger toward God ever appropriate?
3. Forgiveness is a gift from God. Has God prompted you to forgive someone as you have read these stories of forgiveness?
4. Why is it so difficult for us to forgive ourselves and to accept the gift of forgiveness from God or from people?
5. Salvation is by grace alone through faith alone in Christ alone. Have you accepted God's gracious gift of forgiveness through his Son?
6. What one or two things should be different about your life after you read this book?

Select Resources

Bavinck, Herman. *The Philosophy of Revelation.* 1909. Reprint, Eugene, OR: Wipf and Stock, 2003.

———. *Reformed Dogmatics: Abridged in One Volume.* Edited by John Bolt. Grand Rapids: Baker, 2011.

Bock, Darrell L., ed. *Three Views on the Millennium and Beyond.* Grand Rapids: Zondervan, 1999.

Bray, Gerald. *The Doctrine of God.* Downers Grove, IL: InterVarsity Press, 1993.

Burns, Lanier. *The Nearness of God: His Presence with His People.* Phillipsburg, NJ: P&R Publishing, 2009.

Calvin, John. *Institutes of the Christian Religion.* Edited by John T. McNeill. Translated by Ford Lewis Battles. 2 vols. Philadelphia: Westminster, 1960.

Clowney, Edmund P. *The Church.* Downers Grove, IL: InterVarsity Press, 1995.

Crouch, Andy. *Culture Making: Recovering Our Creative Calling.* Downers Grove, IL: InterVarsity Press, 2008.

Dumbrell, W. J. *Covenant and Creation: A Theology of Old Testament Covenants.* Nashville: Thomas Nelson, 1984.

Dyer, John. *From the Garden to the City: The Redeeming and Corrupting Power of Technology.* Grand Rapids: Kregel, 2011.

Edwards, Jonathan. *The Works of Jonathan Edwards.* Edited by John F. Wilson. Vol. 9, *History of the Work of Redemption.* New Haven: Yale University Press, 1989.

———. "Types of the Messiah." In *The Works of Jonathan Edwards.* Edited by Mason I. Lowance Jr. and David H. Watters. Vol. 11, *Typological Writings.* New Haven: Yale University Press, 1993.

Ferguson, Sinclair B. *The Holy Spirit*. Downers Grove, IL: InterVarsity Press, 1996.

Grudem, Wayne. *Systematic Theology: An Introduction to Biblical Doctrine*. Grand Rapids: Zondervan, 1994.

Hawthorne, Gerald F. *Philippians*. Word Biblical Commentary 43. Waco, TX: Word, 1983.

Horton, Michael. *The Christian Faith: A Systematic Theology for Pilgrims on the Way*. Grand Rapids: Zondervan, 2011.

———. *Introducing Covenant Theology*. Grand Rapids: Baker, 2009.

Hultberg, Alan, ed. *Three Views on the Rapture: Pretribulation, Prewrath, or Posttribulation*. Grand Rapids: Zondervan, 2010.

Jones, L. Gregory, and Célestin Musekura. *Forgiving As We've Been Forgiven: Community Practices for Making Peace*. Downers Grove, IL: InterVarsity Press, 2010.

Kaiser, Walter C., Jr. *The Messiah in the Old Testament*. Grand Rapids: Zondervan, 1995.

Kaiser, Walter C., Jr., Peter H. Davids, F. F. Bruce, and Manfred T. Brauch. *Hard Sayings of the Bible*. Downers Grove, IL: InterVarsity Press, 1996.

Keller, Tim. *The Reason for God: Belief in an Age of Skepticism*. New York: Dutton, 2008.

Kraybill, Donald B., Steven M. Nolt, and David L. Weaver-Zercher. *Amish Grace: How Forgiveness Transcended Tragedy*. Indianapolis: Jossey-Bass, 2010.

Kreider, Glenn R. *Jonathan Edwards's Interpretation of Revelation 4:1–8:1*. Lanham, MD: University Press of America, 2004.

———. "Jonathan Edwards's Theology of Prayer." *Bibliotheca Sacra* 160 (October–December 2003): 434–56.

———. "Sinners in the Hands of a Gracious God." *Bibliotheca Sacra* 163 (July–September 2006): 259–75.

Leith, John H., ed. *Creeds of the Churches: A Reader in Christian Doctrine from the Bible to the Present*. 3rd ed. Louisville: John Knox Press, 1982.

Maalouf, Tony. *Arabs in the Shadow of Israel*. Grand Rapids: Kregel, 2003.

Macleod, Donald. *The Person of Christ*. Downers Grove, IL: InterVarsity Press, 1998.

McCullough, Donald. *If Grace Is So Amazing, Why Don't We Like It?* San Francisco: Jossey-Bass, 2005.

Merrill, Eugene H. "A Theology of the Pentateuch." In *A Biblical Theology of the Old Testament*. Edited by Roy B. Zuck. Chicago: Moody, 1991.

Middleton, J. Richard. *The Liberating Image: The* Imago Dei *in Genesis 1*. Grand Rapids: Brazos, 2005.

Murray, John. *Redemption Accomplished and Applied*. Grand Rapids: Eerdmans, 1955.

Nichols, Stephen J. *For Us and for Our Salvation: The Doctrine of Christ in the Early Church*. Wheaton: Crossway, 2007.

Oliphint, K. Scott. *God with Us: Divine Condescension and the Attributes of God*. Wheaton: Crossway, 2011.

———. *Reasons {for Faith}: Philosophy in the Service of Theology*. Phillipsburg, NJ: P&R Publishing, 2006.

Oliphint, K. Scott, and Lane G. Tipton, eds. *Revelation and Reasons: New Essays in Reformed Apologetics*. Phillipsburg, NJ: P&R Publishing, 2007.

Packer, J. I. *Knowing God*. Downers Grove, IL: InterVarsity Press, 1977.

Pate, C. Marvin, ed. *Four Views on the Book of Revelation*. Grand Rapids: Zondervan, 1998.

Perry, Greg. "To Know and Be Known: How Christ's Love Moves Us into Intimacy, Humility, and Risk. A Sermon on John 13:1–17." In *All for Jesus: A Celebration of the 50th Anniversary of Covenant Theological Seminary*. Edited by Robert A. Peterson and Sean Michael Lucas. Ross-shire, UK: Mentor, 2006.

Piper, John. *Let the Nations Be Glad: The Supremacy of God in Missions*. 3rd ed. Grand Rapids: Baker, 2010.

———. *The Purifying Power of Living by Faith in Future Grace*. Portland, OR: Multnomah, 1995.

Plantinga, Cornelius, Jr. *Engaging God's World: A Christian Vision of Faith, Learning, and Living*. Grand Rapids: Eerdmans, 2002.

——. *Not the Way It's Supposed to Be: A Breviary of Sin.* Grand Rapids: Eerdmans, 1995.

——. "A Sermon for Advent: I Believe in Jesus Christ, God's Only Son, Our Lord." In *Exploring and Proclaiming the Apostles' Creed.* Edited by Roger E. Van Harn. Grand Rapids: Eerdmans, 2004.

Reymond, Robert L. *A New Systematic Theology of the Christian Faith.* Nashville: Thomas Nelson, 1998.

Ryrie, Charles C. *Basic Theology.* Wheaton: Victor, 1986.

Schaeffer, Francis A. *He Is There and He Is Not Silent.* Carol Stream, IL: Tyndale House, 1972.

Spina, Frank Anthony. *The Faith of the Outsider: Exclusion and Inclusion in the Biblical Story.* Grand Rapids: Eerdmans, 2005.

Thompson-Cannino, Jennifer, Ronald Cotton, and Erin Torneo. *Picking Cotton: Our Memoir of Injustice and Redemption.* New York: St. Martins Press, 2009.

Volf, Miroslav. *The End of Memory: Remembering Rightly in a Violent World.* Grand Rapids: Eerdmans, 2006.

——. *Free of Charge: Giving and Forgiving in a Culture Stripped of Grace.* Grand Rapids: Zondervan, 2006.

Wright, N. T. *Surprised by Hope: Rethinking Heaven, the Resurrection, and the Mission of the Church.* New York: HarperOne, 2008.

Yancey, Philip. *The Jesus I Never Knew.* Grand Rapids: Zondervan, 1995.

——. *Rumors of Another World: What on Earth Are We Missing?* Grand Rapids: Zondervan, 2003.

——. *What's So Amazing about Grace?* Grand Rapids: Zondervan, 1997.

INDEX OF SCRIPTURE

Genesis
1—5n7, 52n9, 53, 54, 55n14, 56n15, 106, 214
1-2—25, 26, 58, 183, 200, 207
1:1—50, 165
1:2—51
1:4—52, 56
1:8—52
1:9—56
1:10—52
1:12—56
1:18—56
1:21—56
1:22—53
1:25—56
1:26—53n11
1:26-28—53, 54, 104
1:28—53-54, 56, 57, 57n17
1:31—56
2—52, 52n9, 54n12, 55, 56n15, 201, 214
2:7—55
2:15—57n17
2:16—201
2:17—59, 201

2:18—56
2:19—52
2:22—56
2:23—56
2:25—58
3—170, 183, 207
3-Rev. 20—26, 58, 207
3:1—58
3:4—58
3:5—58
3:6—58
3:7—58-59
3:8—59
3:17—173
3:21—60, 173
3:22—60
4-Rev. 20—183
4:4-5—60-61
4:10-12—61
4:11—61
4:14—61
5:2—53
5:5—60
5:21-24—68n32
6:6—61
6:9—68n32
6:13—61-62, 62n27
6:17-21—173

7:2—62
7:21-23—173
8:21—62, 63, 64-65
9:12-15—63
9:16—63-64
9:25—89n12
11—163
11:8-9—196
12—67
12-14—67n31
12:1—67
12:1-3—65, 126, 201
12:2—48
12:3—48, 136n4, 161, 172
12:4—69n34
12:11-13—66
12:16—47
13—66
14—67n31
14:18—66
14:19-20—66
15—69n34
15:1—67, 67n31
15:2—67
15:3—67
15:4-5—48
15:5—67-68
15:6—68n32

15:8—68
15:13-16—77
15:18—68
16—69-70
16:1—47
16:3-4—47, 66
16:4—47
16:6—66
16:9—48
16:10—48
16:11—116
16:11-12—48-49
16:13—48n2, 49
16:14—49-50
16:15—50, 116
17-18—120n15
17:1—69n34
17:3—69, 69n35
17:5—65n30, 69
17:15-16—70
17:17—69, 69n35
17:19—116
17:20—215
17:20-21—75
18:1—70, 70n38
18:2—70, 70n38
18:17-18—70
18:21—71
18:24—71n40
18:24-25—71
18:26—71n40
18:28—71n40
18:30—71n40
18:31—71n40
18:32—71n40
19:1—70n38

19:37—91
20:11-13—66
21:3—116
21:13—49n4, 215
22:2-3—72
22:15-18—72
22:16-18—76n1
24:62—50n6
25:23—76
25:27-34—76
26:2-4—75-76
26:5—76n1
26:24—76
27—76
28:15—76
32:9-12—77
32:24—77n2
32:25—77
32:28—77
32:30—77n2
38—92, 115
49:8-12—193-94
49:10—96n4

Exodus
2:14-15—78
3:6—76, 78
3:12—79-80
3:14—78
3:15—78
3:19—79
3:19-20—78
4:13—79
4:14—79
12:21-30—90n13
14:21-31—79

19:5—86
19:16-19—80
20:12—62
23:14-17—128
32:1—80
32:4—81, 81n7
32:9-10—83
32:24—81n7
32:28—85
32:35—85
33:3-5—81
33:11—80
33:15-16—81
33:16—81
33:17—82
33:18—82
33:19—82
33:20—82, 107
34:1-3—82-83
34:5-7—83
34:6—81n8, 83, 209
34:6-7—14, 95, 167, 177
34:7—83, 84, 102n13
40:34-35—86
40:34-38—107
40:36-38—86

Leviticus
12:3—125
12:4-8—125
18:5—148
19:18—23n8
23:5-8—128

Numbers
13:31-33—87

14:11-12—87
14:17-19—87
14:22-23—87
14:29-30—87-88
14:34—88

Deuteronomy
5:22-29—106-7
5:28—80
6:5—23n8
6:13—135
6:16—135
7:7-9—88-89
8:2-4—88
8:3—135
18:17-20—106
20:16-17—89, 90
23:3—92
23:3-4—91
29:29—38, 51n8

Joshua
2—115
2:3—89
2:5—89
2:6—89
2:10—90
2:11-13—90
6:17—90
7—102n13
7:24-25—84n11
24:2—65

Ruth
1:16-17—91
2:6—91

4—115
4:12—91-92
4:17—92
4:22—92

1 Samuel
8:7—95
8:8—95
8:10-18—95
8:20—95
10:9-10—96
15:26-29—96
16:1-13—96
25:22—98n6
27:9—98n6

2 Samuel
2:4—96
7—92, 96n5
7:2—96
7:11-13—96
7:15-16—96-97
7:16—96n5
7:18-19—97
8:2-4—98n6
11-12—115
12:18—84n11

1 Kings
3:12—99
3:12-14—99n8
6:1—98
6:2—98n7
6:38—98
7:1—98n7
7:2—98n7

8:23-24—98
8:27-30—98-99
9:3—99
9:7-8—99
11:3—99
11:6—99-100
11:7-8—100
11:11-13—100
15:26—100
16:30—101
16:31—101
16:33—101
17:5-6—101
17:7-24—101
17:9—101

2 Kings
4:1-7—101
4:8-37—101
5:1—101
5:2—101
5:3—102
5:4-10—102
5:27—102n13

1 Chronicles
22:8—97
28:3—97

Nehemiah
9:17—84

Psalms—216
8:1—104
8:1-2—103
8:3-5—104

8:6-8—104
8:9—104
12:5—104
18:6—105
18:9—105
18:16—105
18:19—105
18:35—105
19:1—37
23—105n14
34:6—104
41:1-3—105
89—92
89:3—96, 96n5
89:29—97
89:36-37—97
89:38-52—97
90:2—51n7
103:8—84
110:4—67
111:4—84
113:3—105
113:4—105
113:5-6—105
113:7-9—91
118:5-8—106
144:5-8—106

Isaiah
6:1—107
6:3—107
6:4—107
6:6-7—108
7:14—116
9:1-2—136
11:1—194

11:3-5—194
40:3-5—121
57:15—108

Jeremiah
1:5—107
1:7-8—107
1:9—107
31:31—109
31:32—109
31:33-34—109
32:30—109-10
32:37-41—110

Ezekiel
36:16-23—110
36:25—110
36:26—110
36:30—110
36:31—110
37:26-27—110

Daniel
2:35—142
12:4—193

Joel
2:2—111
2:13—84

Amos
5:6-20—111
5:18-20—188

Jonah
1:1-3—84

4:2-3—84
4:4—84
4:10-11—85

Micah
5:2—117, 122
6:8—17, 209, 213
7:6—126n25, 140
7:18—209

Habakkuk
3:16—111

Malachi
3:1—121, 136n5
4:1—111
4:2-3—111
4:4—112, 136
4:5—136n5
4:5-6—111, 119, 121

Matthew—114-15, 134
1:5—92n16
1:6—115
1:18—116
1:19—116
1:20—116
1:21—116
1:23—116
1:25—117
2:1-2—117
2:3-6—127
2:4—117
2:6—117
2:11—117
2:12—118

228

2:13–20—128
2:15—128
2:16—118
3:2—134, 136
3:3—121
3:6—134
3:11—134
3:13—134
3:14—134–35
3:15—135, 136
3:17—135
4:1—135
4:4—135
4:7—135
4:10—135
4:11—136
4:12—136
4:16—136
4:17—136
5:3–6—137
5:7–10—137
5:11–12—137
5:13—137
5:14–15—137
5:14–16—201
5:16—137
6:12—14
6:14—14
6:14–15—147
6:25–34—216
7:12—146n9
8:3—139
8:8—139
8:10–12—139
8:14–15—139–40
9:35–36—140

9:36—140
9:37–38—140
10:1—140
10:24—144
10:34—140
10:34–36—126n25
10:37–38—140
10:40–42—141
11:10—136n5
11:12—143
11:14—121
13—197
13:1–9—141
13:16–17—142
13:24–30—141
13:31–33—142
13:37–43—141, 145
13:40–43—142
13:44–46—142
13:47–50—142, 145
13:49–50—142
16:15—143
16:16—143–44
16:17—143
16:21—143
16:22—143
16:23—144
16:24–27—144
17:12—121
17:20—145
17:22–23—145
17:23—145
18:1—145
18:3—145, 148
18:4—145
18:21—146

18:22—14, 146
18:23–35—146
18:24—146n8
18:28—146n8
18:33—146
18:35—147
19:13—148
19:14—148
19:16—148
19:21—148
19:22—148
19:23—149
19:24—149
19:26—149
19:27—149
19:28—64, 149, 190
19:28–29—149
19:30—149
20:4–5—150
20:12—150
20:13–15—150
20:16—151
20:18–19—151
20:21—151–52
20:22—152
20:23—152
20:25–28—153
22:1–14—139
22:11–14—197
22:19–21—54
22:31–32—156
22:36—23n8
22:37–40—175
22:40—23n8
24—197
24:8—174

24:30—192
24:31—192
24:36—161, 161n5, 191
24:37-41—191
24:38-39—161
24:42—161, 191
24:43—161
24:43-44—191
24:44—161, 191
24:50—161
25:13—191
25:46—192
26:2—153
26:3-5—153
26:6-13—153-54
26:14-16—154
26:39—154
26:42—154
26:44—154
26:52—154
26:53-54—154
26:59-60—155n16
26:63—155
26:64—155
26:67-68—155
27:11-26—155
27:37—155
27:50—155
27:52-53—155-56
27:57-66—156
28:1-10—156
28:18-19—156

Mark
2:7—14

10:43—20
13:32—161n5

Luke—114, 160n3
1:5—119
1:11-13—119
1:17—119
1:18—119, 120n17
1:19-20—119
1:20—119
1:25—120
1:26—122
1:27—120, 120n16
1:31—120
1:33—120
1:34—120, 120n17
1:35-37—120-21
1:39—121
1:41-44—121
1:45—121
1:46-55—121
1:76-78—121
2—118n9, 127
2:1-3—122
2:4—120n16, 122
2:4-6—122
2:8—122
2:9—122
2:10-11—122
2:12—123
2:14—124
2:16—124
2:18—124
2:19—124
2:20—124
2:21—125

2:22-24—125
2:25—125
2:26-28—125
2:29-32—125
2:34-35—126
2:35—126
2:36—126
2:37—126, 126n26
2:38—126-27
2:40-42, 42n43, 128
2:41—128
2:42—128
2:46—128
2:47—128-29
2:48—129
2:49—130
2:50—130
2:51—130
2:52—42, 42n43, 128
2:57-66—121
2:67-79—121
3:23—128
4:23—103
4:24-27—103
4:28-30—103
6:37—14
7:47—14
10:27—23
10:28—23
10:29—23
10:37—24
17:10—138
22:51—154
23:34—208
24—43
24:19-24—43

24:25–26—43
24:27—43–44
24:30-31—44
24:33-34—44
24:37—44
24:40-43—44
24:44-47—44

John—38
1:1–18—197
1:3—37, 5n7
1:10–11—118
1:12–13—121
1:14—34n28, 37, 70,
   185
1:17—185
1:18—37
1:32–34—135n3
3:16—37
4:9—23n9
5—39
5:10—39n37
5:15—39n37
5:16—39, 39n37
5:17—39
5:18—39, 39n37, 43
5:19—42
5:21—40
5:23—40
5:24-30—40
5:27—40
5:28-29—156
5:31-36—40
5:37-40—41
5:39—40, 43n44
5:40—39

5:45—41
5:45-47—40
5:46—41-42
5:46-47—40
6:44—143
6:44-51—188n7
10:17-18—155n17
11:25—40
13—133n1, 154
13:5—133
13:13-15—133
13:15-16—211
13:17—211
13:21-30—133
14-16—160n3
14:6—40
18-19—155n16
18:10—154n15
20:25—82
20:28—82
20:29—82

Acts
1:1–2—160n2
1:3—160
1:4—163
1:4–5—160
1:6—160-61
1:7—191
1:7-8—162
1:8—179
1:11—162, 185
2:1-4—163
2:11—163
2:39—163
3:21—162n8, 190

3:25—161n4
7:2-4—67
7:60—208
8:1—208
9—179-80
10—161n4
13:16-41—164
14:14-18—164
17—164
17:16-34—167n15
17:18—164
17:19-20—164
17:22-23—164
17:23—164
17:24-25—164-65
17:26-28—165
17:29-31—166-67
17:32-34—167
20:19—167
20:25—167-68
20:28—168
20:35—168

Romans—170n18
1—171n20
1:2-4—168
1:3—115
1:16-17—168-69
1:17—169
1:18—169, 170
1:18-20—30, 37
1:18-25—165n10,
   187
1:19—170
1:20—169, 170
1:21—170

1:23—170
1:24-32—170, 170n19
1:25—170
2:1—171
3:10-20—171n21
3:23—171n19
3:25—62n28
4:1-4—68n32
4:1-5—68n32
4:11—65, 68n32
4:11-12—70
4:17—69n36, 172
5—165n12
5:8—34, 37, 60, 172
5:10—172-73
6:5—173
6:23—22
8:9—174
8:18—173
8:18-21—190
8:18-34—37
8:19—64
8:20-21—173
8:21—64, 173, 190
8:21-22—64, 190
8:22—173
8:23—64, 163, 174
8:26-27—174
8:29-30—188n7
9:15—188n7
12:2—174
12:3—174-75
12:16—175
13:1—175
13:9—175
13:10—175

1 Corinthians
1:26-31—65
12—56
13:4-8—177
15—64
15:27-28—186
15:35-49—186

2 Corinthians
5—64
5:6-9—197
5:17—200
5:19—215
5:21—34n29, 170n18, 196

Galatians
3—70n37
3:6-14—68n32
3:8—65, 70, 126, 161n4, 162
3:9—65
3:16—115
3:16-29—67
3:29—66
5:22-26—185

Ephesians
1:3—184
1:13-14—184
2:1—177
2:1-10—177
2:2—177
2:3—177
2:4—78, 114
2:4-5—60, 83, 177-78
2:5—178

2:7—178
2:8—178
2:8-9—150
2:8-10—147
2:11-16—178
2:19—178
2:21—178
2:22—178
3:10—178
4:1—178
4:2—178
4:3—178
4:4-6—178, 197n15
4:31-32—207
4:32—146, 147
5:1-2—179
5:8-14—138
5:11—138
5:18—179
5:19-21—179
6:1-3—62

Philippians
2—32, 133n1
2:2—210
2:3—32
2:3-4—210
2:4—32, 183
2:5—33, 210
2:5-11—131
2:6—33, 35
2:6-7—33, 210
2:6-8—148
2:6-11—32, 167
2:7—33
2:8—210

2:9-11—210
3:17-18—186
3:20-21—186

Colossians
1:3-6—184
1:15-20—37
1:17—51n7
3:12—209
3:13—208

1 Thessalonians
1:9-10—186

2 Thessalonians
1:9—200

1 Timothy
2:4—188n7
2:5—72
6:16—108

2 Timothy
3:15—41
3:16—25
3:16-17—136

Titus
2—184
2:11—185
2:12—185
2:13—210
2:13-14—185

Hebrews
1:1-4—37

2—116
2:18—42n43
4:15—136
5:4-6—67
5:8—42n43
5:8-9—131
7:4—66
7:6-7—66
8:7-8—109
8:8—216
11:4—61n24
11:8-10—68n32
12:2—148-49

James
1:22-25—171
2:1-4—34n30
2:13—209
2:14-26—34n30
2:21-24—72
2:25—90
4:6—209
4:7—136
4:10—34

1 Peter
1:3-5—184
1:3-6—186
2:21—145

2 Peter
1:4—173
2:5—91n15
2:6-9—71
2:7—91n15
2:7-8—91

2:17—200
3—218
3:3—187n6
3:5—187
3:5-7—64
3:6—187, 189
3:7—187, 189n8
3:9—119n11, 187, 192
3:10—189
3:13—189

1 John
1:9—147
2:6—38
3:7—38
3:8—38
3:10—38
3:16—34, 37, 38,
   173n25
3:16-20—175-76
3:23-24—38
4:7—38
4:7-11—176
4:8—34, 175
4:9—34
4:9-10—37
4:12—37
4:16—34, 38, 83, 175
4:16-17—176
4:19—34, 37, 38
4:19-21—175
5:2-3—38
5:16—38

Jude
13—200

Revelation
1:1—191, 196
1:3—191
1:4—192
1:7—192, 196
4:1-2—192
4:8—192
4:11—193
5:1—193
5:2—193
5:4—193
5:5—193
5:6—194
5:7—194
5:9-10—195
5:10—195n12
7:9—56, 163, 196
7:10—196
19—201
19-22—196
19:6-7—196-97

19:8—197
19:11—197
19:12—197
19:13—197
19:15—197, 198
19:16—197
19:19—197-98
19:20—198
19:21—198
20:1-3—198
20:2—198n17
20:2-3—198
20:3—198, 198n17
20:4—198, 198n17
20:4-6—198
20:5—198n17
20:6—198n17
20:7—198n17
20:9—198-99
20:10—198n17, 199, 200
20:11-14—199

20:15—62, 200
21-22—25, 27, 162n8,
    183, 208, 210, 218
21:1-3—59
21:1-4—199
21:1-5—62
21:2—99
21:3—70, 163
21:3-4—111
21:3-5—124
21:5—111, 200
21:9-10—200
21:22—201
21:23—201
21:24—201
22:1-5—201
22:7—202
22:12-13—202
22:14—197
22:17—202
22:20—202

Index of Subjects and Names

Abel, 60–61

Abraham, Abram, 47–50, 65–66, 67–68, 69–72, 73, 75, 76, 90, 116, 120n15, 172

Abrahamic Covenant, 67–68, 69–70, 75

Adam, 26, 52, 53, 54, 56nn.15,16, 58, 59, 73, 165n12, 172, 202

ALARM, 12–13

Angel of the Lord, 48–50, 72, 77n2

Babel, 163, 196

Bateman, Christian H., 159

Bathsheba, 84n11, 115

Bavinck, Herman, 29, 57, 60n22, 64, 161n6, 189

Berkhof, Louis, 191–92

Boaz, 91–92, 115

Bray, Gerald, 28

Brooks, Phillips, 44–45

Cain, 60–62

Calvin, John, 28–29, 166

Canaanite, 66–67, 89–90, 92, 115

Christology, 43–45, 130

compassion, 14, 16, 17, 21, 22, 23, 59, 65, 73, 81n8, 82–83, 84–85, 86, 95, 101, 102, 140, 177, 187–88, 188n7, 207

condescension, 14–17, 24, 26, 27, 28–29, 31–32, 33, 34–36, 37, 38, 46, 49, 50, 53, 55, 57, 60–61, 62, 62n28, 65, 66–67, 70n38, 71n39, 73, 76, 77, 77n3, 78, 80–83, 85, 86, 90, 92, 95, 96–97, 98–99, 100, 103–6, 107–9, 111, 114, 117, 118, 122, 124, 131, 134, 135, 136, 139, 151–52, 157, 159–60, 160n3, 163, 164, 167, 168, 171, 174, 176, 177–79, 185n5, 200, 203, 207, 208, 209, 211

Cotton, Ronald, 93–95

covenant of works, 31

creation, 14–15, 16, 17, 21, 24, 25–26, 27, 29, 30, 31, 36, 37, 38, 38n36, 42–43, 50–51, 51n7, 52, 52n9, 54–58, 59, 60, 62, 64, 67–68, 72–73, 85, 96–97, 108, 113, 118, 118n10, 156, 164–66, 169n16, 173–74, 183, 185, 187, 190, 193, 197, 199, 201, 202–3, 207, 209–11

Crouch, Andy, 24

Dallas Theological Seminary, 10, 43n44

David, 49, 84n11, 92, 96–97, 98, 100, 103–6, 115
Davidic Covenant, 96–97, 100
Definition of Chalcedon, 127
deism, 171
diversity, 56–57, 196
Dyer, John, 61n26

Edwards, Jonathan, 78n4, 189n8, 195n12, 198n17
Elijah, 101, 103, 111–12, 119, 121, 136
Elisha, 101–3
Esau, 76–77

fall, 25, 25n14, 26–27, 31, 57, 58n19, 59, 60n22, 174, 183, 202
forgiveness, 12–14, 16, 17, 81, 81n8, 85, 87, 92, 94–95, 108, 109, 146–47, 147n11, 177, 183, 187, 205–7, 208

Gentiles, 70n37, 102–3, 118, 125–26, 136, 137, 139–40, 153, 164, 172, 178, 180
golden calf, 81, 85–87
good Samaritan, 22–24
grace, 13–14, 14n7, 21–22, 25n14, 27, 30, 31, 60, 61n25, 62, 63, 65, 68n32, 71n39, 81–83, 84–85, 88, 89–90, 91n15, 95, 97, 100–102, 109–10, 115, 146n7, 147, 149–51, 172, 177, 178, 185, 185n5, 192, 206–7
Grudem, Wayne, 28, 42n43

Hagar, 47–50, 53, 66, 70
Hawthorne, Gerald, 32, 33n27, 34–35

historicity of Adam, 165n12
hope, 22, 29, 31, 37, 42, 64, 66, 92, 93–94, 109, 111, 127, 136n4, 156, 159, 161, 162, 162n8, 168, 173–74, 177, 180, 183–86, 187, 189–90, 197, 197nn.14,15, 202, 210–11
Horton, Michael, 83n10, 190
House, Paul, 177n26
Huffman, D. S., 115n4
humility, 13, 14–15, 16–17, 20, 21, 23, 24, 32–35, 36, 42, 46, 53, 95, 107–8, 118, 127, 131, 133, 136, 139, 145, 148, 157, 163, 168, 178–79, 195, 208, 209, 210, 211

image and likeness, 21–22, 26, 37, 51–52, 53–55, 56n15, 57, 57n17, 104, 153, 200, 207
Immanuel, 116–17, 130
incarnation, 15, 16, 24, 26, 27, 29, 32, 33–35, 36–37, 38, 42, 42n43, 45–46, 70, 77n3, 114, 115, 127, 131, 161n5, 167, 185n5, 191, 207
Isaac, 50n6, 72, 75–76, 139
Ishmael, 49–50, 75

Jacob, 76–77, 78
Jerusalem, 44, 99–100, 162. *See also* New Jerusalem
Jonah, 84–85

Kaiser, Walter C., Jr., 116n6, 147n11
Keller, Tim, 52n9, 183
kingdom of God, 96, 96n5, 121, 134, 136, 137, 139–40, 141–44,

145–46, 148–49, 152–53,
156–57, 160–62, 163, 195, 199

law, 23–24, 41, 80, 109, 112, 123, 125,
129, 135, 136, 148, 175
Law and the Prophets, 23n8, 44,
163, 175
left behind (the righteous being),
62, 141–42, 145, 149, 192,
197–99, 200
Lot, 66, 67, 71, 91

Maalouf, Tony, 117n7
MacLeod, Donald, 129–30
McCullough, Donald, 150–51
McDermott, Gerald R., 209
McQuilkin, Robertson, 181–83
Melchizedek, 66–67
mercy, 14, 17, 21–22, 23–24, 59–60,
63, 65, 72, 73, 81–83, 84–85,
86–88, 90, 92, 95, 97, 100, 115,
137, 140, 146, 147n10, 167, 177,
187–88, 188n7, 207
Messiah, 67, 78n4, 92, 117, 117nn.6,8,
121–22, 125–27, 135n3, 143, 164,
195, 197, 199
metanarrative, 164, 199
millennium, 195n12, 197n14, 198,
198nn.16,17
Morris, Leon, 123
Mosaic Covenant, 80–82
Moses, 40–41, 42n41, 54, 67n31, 72,
78–83, 85–86, 87–88, 165, 207
Mother Teresa, 19–21, 22
Murray, John, 60n23
Musekura, Célestin, 12–13, 17

Naaman, 101–3
naming, 49–50, 52–53, 56,
56nn.15,16, 69, 76, 77n2,
116–17, 125n24,
New Covenant, 109–10
New Jerusalem, 59, 99, 199
Nickel Mines, 205–7
Noah, 61–63, 68n32, 91n15, 189

Oliphint, K. Scott, 170n17
Olivet Discourse, 161

pantheism, 169n16, 171
Passover, 90n13, 128
Pilate, 155
Plantinga, Cornelius, Jr., 9, 25n14,
35, 36, 211
Pope John Paul II, 20

Rahab, 89–90, 115
re-creation, 25, 25n14, 27, 56, 64, 68,
159–60, 164, 172, 183, 186, 187,
189–90, 199, 200
Red Sea, 79
regeneration, 15, 149, 190
Reymond, Robert, 77n2, 161n5
Ruth, 91–92, 115

Sabbath, 39
salt and light, 137–38
Scriptures, 13, 25, 28–29, 30, 34,
38, 38n36, 40–41, 41n40,
42–43, 44–45, 49–50, 57–58,
61, 64, 84, 111–12, 118,
135–36, 154, 163–64, 165–66,
172, 189, 191, 199

Serpent, 26, 57, 58, 59, 198, 202

Solomon, 98–100

tabernacle, 80, 85–86, 107

Tamar, 92, 115

Thomas (the apostle), 82

Thompson, Jennifer, 93–95

Tipton, Lane G., 167n15

Trinity, 27, 36, 45, 70n38, 203

truth, 30, 143, 163, 166, 170, 172, 176, 177, 184, 185n5

types of Christ, 78

virgin birth, 116–17, 120

Walvoord, John, 130

Westminster Confession, 30, 31

Wright, Christopher J. H., 89n12

Yancey, Philip, 113

ALSO AVAILABLE FROM P&R PUBLISHING

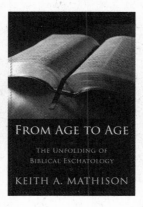

Readers will understand a book's final chapter only if they
have understood all that came before it. Likewise, "in order
to understand biblical eschatology," writes Keith Mathison,
"we must understand the entire Bible."

From Age to Age looks not only at the fulfillment of God's
purposes at the end of history, but also at the stages along
the way. The millennium and second coming of Christ are
eschatologically important—but Christ's *first* coming was the
beginning of the end. Deftly working through each book of
the Bible, Mathison traces God's preparations throughout
redemptive history, which have laid everything in place for
the last day.

"Meticulously comprehensive, this veritable compendium of
biblical theology from Genesis to Revelation examines every
possible nuance of eschatological insight."
   —DEREK W. H. THOMAS

ALSO AVAILABLE FROM P&R PUBLISHING

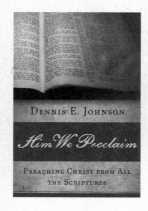

DENNIS E. JOHNSON

Him We Proclaim

PREACHING CHRIST FROM ALL
THE SCRIPTURES

Challenging modern preachers to expound the Bible like Peter and Paul, *Him We Proclaim* makes the hermeneutical and historical case for a return to apostolic preaching—preaching that is Christ-centered, redemptive-historical, missiologically communicated, and grounded in grace. But moving beyond theory, *Him We Proclaim* provides examples of how this method applies to all Old and New Testament genres, from history and law to psalm and prophecy to doctrine and exhortation.

"This book holds the promise of the recovery of biblical preaching for those who will give themselves to the demanding and glorious task of setting each text within the context of God's redemptive plan. This is a book that belongs on every preacher's bookshelf."
—R. ALBERT MOHLER JR.

"Apostolic hermeneutics? Dare we read the Scripture backward as well as forward? Dennis Johnson's answer is a marvelously informed and convincing 'yes!' *Him We Proclaim* is sure to be widely read and discussed both in the academy and by groups of serious-minded preachers of the Word."
—R. KENT HUGHES